Explaining American

The
poli
stre
bee
stud

pro
pret
trib
the
per
the
wea
ine:
poli

mir
stud
und
con

Rot
of :

Explaining American Politics

Issues and Interpretations

Edited by
Robert Williams

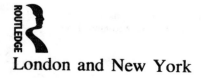

London and New York

Acknowledgement

The editor wishes to thank Manchester University Press for permitting Professor Joseph Hogan to draw upon materials incorporated in ' "Back to the 1970s": the context of the Reagan Presidency in *The Reagan Years: the Record in Presidential Leadership*, edited by Joseph Hogan (Manchester 1990) in writing his chapter on 'The "no-win Presidency" and contemporary presidential-congressional relationships'.

First published 1990
by Routledge
11 New Fetter Lane, London EC4P 4EE

Simultaneously published in the USA and Canada
by Routledge
a division of Routledge, Chapman and Hall, Inc.
29 West 35th Street, New York, NY 10001

© 1990 Chapters 1 and 6: Robert Williams, Chapter 2: Gillian Peele, Chapter 3: David McKay, Chapter 4: Joseph Hogan, Chapter 5: Michael Foley, Chapter 7: Richard Hodder-Williams, Chapter 8: Dean McSweeney, Chapter 9: John Zvesper

Phototypeset in 10pt Times by
Mews Photosetting, Beckenham, Kent
Printed and bound in Great Britain by
Biddles Ltd, Guildford and King's Lynn

British Library Cataloguing in Publication Data

Explaining American politics : issues and interpretations.
    1. United States. Politics
    I. Williams, Robert, *1946–*
320.973

0-415-01218-X
0-415-01219-8 (pbk)

Library of Congress Cataloging in Publication Data

Explaining American politics : issues and interpretations / edited by
    Robert Williams.
        p. cm.
    Includes bibliographical references.
    ISBN 0-415-01218-X. — ISBN 0-415-01219-8 (pbk.)
    1. United States—Politics and government. I. Williams, Robert,
1946 Sept. 10–
JK274.E96   1990
320.973–dc20   90-8285
                                                                    CIP

To R.H. Pear

Contents

Contents

Notes on contributors

ROBERT WILLIAMS is Senior Lecturer in Politics and Dean of the Faculty of Social Sciences at the University of Durham. He previously taught at York University and he has been a Visiting Professor at universities in the United States, Canada and Australia. He was Chairman of the American Politics Group of the Political Studies Association in 1984–5. His publications include numerous articles on American politics and he is a co-author of *Roosevelt to Reagan: The Development of the Modern Presidency*, M. Shaw (ed.), (London, Hurst, 1987).

GILLIAN PEELE is Fellow and Tutor in Politics at Lady Margaret Hall, Oxford. She is the author of a number of books on British and American politics, including *Revival and Reaction: The Right in Contemporary America* (Oxford, OUP 1984). Miss Peele is the present Chair of the American Politics Group.

DAVID MCKAY is Reader in Government at Essex University. He has held a number of visiting appointments and fellowships in the United States. He is a former Chairman of the American Politics Group and has published extensively on the United States. His most recent book is *Domestic Policy and Ideology: Presidents and the American State, 1964–1987*, (Cambridge, Cambridge University Press, 1989).

JOSEPH HOGAN is Professor of Politics at Birmingham Polytechnic. He taught previously at Robert Gordon's Institute, Aberdeen, and at SUNY Binghampton. His publications include a number of books and articles on American politics. He has most recently edited a book called *The Reagan Presidency*, (Manchester, Manchester University Press, forthcoming).

MICHAEL FOLEY is Lecturer in American Politics at the University of Wales, Aberystwyth. He is the author of the *New Senate: Liberal Influence on a Conservative Institution 1958–1972*, (New Haven, Yale

University press, 1980). His most recent book is *The Silence of Constitutions: An Essay in Constitutional Interpretation*, (London, Routledge, 1989)

RICHARD HODDER-WILLIAMS is Reader in Politics at the University of Bristol. He has held a Visiting Professorship at the University of California, Berkeley, and he served as Chairman of the American Politics Group from 1982–4. He has published extensively on the Supreme Court and among his publications are *The Politics of the US Supreme Court*, (London, Allen and Unwin, 1980).

DEAN MCSWEENEY is Senior Lecturer in Politics at Bristol Polytechnic. He is a former Chairman of the American Politics Group and he has published articles on parties and elections in the United States. His latest work (with John Zvesper) is a book entitled *Decline and Reform: The Changing American Party System*, (London, Routledge, forthcoming).

JOHN ZVESPER is Lecturer in Politics at the University of East Anglia. He has previously taught at Cambridge University and Claremont College, California. A former Chairman of the American Politics Group, he is the author of *Political Philosophy and Rhetoric: A Study of the Origins of American Party Politics*, (Cambridge, Cambridge University Press, 1977). His latest book (with Dean McSweeney) is *Decline and Reform: The Changing American Party System*, (London, Routledge, forthcoming).

Preface

I would like to thank my original editor at Routledge, Nancy Marten, for encouraging me to develop my idea for this book, and her successor, Sue Joshua, for seeing the project to a conclusion. I owe a great debt both to Mrs Jean Richardson who performed the role of editorial assistant as well as typist and to Mrs Dorothy Anson who gave valuable support at crucial stages.

I am, of course, particularly grateful to my contributors for the high quality of their contributions, their constructive responses to editorial criticism and for their tolerance toward the editor's own deficiencies.

Robert Williams
Durham

Chapter one

Introduction

Robert Williams

Textbooks on American politics generally come in two styles: there are the weighty, multi-authored volumes written to meet the needs of the Introduction to American Government courses found in almost all American universities and colleges. Then there is the British alternative which is a relatively slim, single-authored volume seemingly aimed at a wide student market ranging from 'A' level to advanced undergraduate work. What these differing approaches have in common is that their primary purpose is to impart to their readers essential information about the structures and workings of the American system of government. In both cases, their analytical aspirations are weighed down by the quantity of descriptive material they are required to include.

It is, of course, important for students to have some grasp of the organization and procedures of, for example, Congress, but it is difficult to make such necessary institutional descriptions very interesting or exciting. The American approach is to leaven the relentless recital of institutional 'facts' with photographs, cartoons and other visual aids. British textbooks largely eschew such devices in favour of making their books shorter in order to lighten the descriptive load. If the former approach tends to trivialize the subject, the latter risks serious omission through excessive selectivity. In essence, textbooks are concerned with imparting necessary information and, if they fail in this respect, they have not fulfilled their essential purpose.

Textbook writing confronts another academic problem, the competence of the author(s). The professional study of American politics displays the conventional vices and virtues of contemporary academic inquiry. Breadth is normally sacrificed for depth and specialization is the order of the day. In this respect, American scholars tend to be even more specialized than their British counterparts. Where a research reputation in a given area of American politics has been built over a number of years, scholars are often reluctant to explore new fields. When one profitable academic well represents twenty years of sunk costs, the attractions of drilling new wells in unfamiliar territory are not very compelling.

The academic division of labour is then becoming more and more refined and one important virtue is that, within specializations, there is an acute awareness and appreciation of research frontiers. But if the virtues of specialization are obvious in academic research, they frequently become vices when applied to teaching materials. If everyone is a specialist, textbook authors are bound to write on subjects where they have only a secondary knowledge.

Explaining American Politics constitutes one attempt to compensate for these almost unavoidable weaknesses of textbooks. It is designed to serve as a supplementary textbook, a resource to be used either in conjunction with a textbook or as a focus for a tutorial or seminar programme. It does not seek to provide comprehensive or even basic factual information about the structure and workings of American government because that task is admirably performed elsewhere. The focus of the book is on issues in American politics or, to be more precise, on interpretations of issues in American politics. It is analytical rather than descriptive in approach and it addresses a set of key questions or problems in explaining contemporary American politics. The principal aim of the book is to provide a catalyst of discussion by presenting clear and possibly provocative interpretations of some of the most important issues presented by the modern American system of government.

The earliest origins of the book are to be found in a number of conversations held at the annual conferences of the American Politics Group (APG) of the Political Studies Association. Some participants believe that most of the serious British discussion of American politics takes place at APG conferences and they certainly provide unique opportunities to gauge the value of research and publishing ideas. My original idea was to compile an up-to-date British version of the successful *New American Political System* (King 1978), but the present volume has somewhat different aims and objectives. Despite the reservations expressed earlier, I think some recent textbooks are more analytical than their predecessors (McKay 1987) and this weakens the case for the sort of institutional overviews provided by King's contributors. Longer chapters dealing with a number of themes may well serve as a good substitute for a textbook, but they also pose problems of coherence and clarity. My concerns here are that the contributors deal with one major problem in their particular field of expertise and they give their readers a clear sense of direction by developing distinctive interpretations of their chosen issue.

All the contributors to the book are senior members of the American Politics Group and all but two have chaired the organization in recent years. They are established authorities in their particular fields and their contributions focus on important and controversial issues. It is not difficult for students to become bemused by the complexities and uncertainties of American politics and this book is intended to demonstrate that there are ways of seeing the woods and the trees, ways of clarifying problems and placing them in an appropriate explanatory context.

Compiling any set of questions or issues produces problems of inclusion and omission. The purpose of this book is to guide students through the minefields of political analysis by helping them confront and comprehend major contemporary issues of interpretation and explanation in American politics. The book is not intended to be comprehensive, but twenty years' experience suggest there are important institutional issues that always puzzle students: for example, the inevitability of executive-legislative deadlock, the anachronistic and irresponsible nature of Congress, the activist political role of the Supreme Court and the lack of an effective national bureaucracy. But there are other obviously important issues such as presidential power and the rise of special interests, the prospects of electoral realignment, the alleged decline of party and the apparent revival of conservatism. All the above issues are authoritatively discussed in the chapters that follow. Other serious questions could have been posed, but it is surely beyond argument that the issues included in this volume are among the most significant and important.

Some chapters have an institutional focus, others are concerned with broader issues and the first contribution by Gillian Peele falls into the latter category. Even the less alert observers of American affairs can hardly have failed to notice the recent resurgence of conservatism as an ideology and political movement. To some this is evidence of a sea change in American political values and voting habits, but Gillian Peele's chapter acts as a powerful brake on accepting simplistic and cyclical interpretations of recent presidential election results. The successes of Ronald Reagan and the election of George Bush in 1988 might indicate a period of conservative hegemony, but the evidence is both contradictory and far from clear. Gillian Peele argues that to accept simplistic interpretations is both to ignore some major features of American political culture and to display insensitivity to the important differences between the various strands of conservatism and their potential political interaction.

Her chapter is concerned with addressing this central issue of how to interpret the ideological and political impact of the conservative movement during the 1980s. In the course of answering this important question she succinctly analyses the general role and significance of ideology in American politics, the effect of the conservative revival on party organization and campaigning, and the ways in which the economic climate has moved against liberal politicians.

David McKay is also concerned with alleged sea changes in American politics, but his chapter has a more institutional focus on what he terms the 'public-interest Presidency'. He asks why late modern Presidents have found it more difficult to create and sustain an image as defenders of the national or public interest than did early modern Presidents such as Roosevelt, Truman and Eisenhower. McKay analyses the changes in the domestic and international environment confronting late modern Presidents that have made their task so much harder and, in particular, he examines the constraints imposed by particularistic pressures from organized special interests.

He argues that a 'public-interest Presidency' is made possible if a number of specific political, social and governmental conditions are met. His central thesis is that since 1965 Presidents have been increasingly unable or unwilling to meet all or even some of the conditions. Just as Peele questions the contribution of the Reagan Presidency to the impact of conservatism, McKay examines critically the case for the alleged revival of the 'public-interest Presidency' under Ronald Reagan. Thus the chapter focuses on the issue of whether the Presidency is now perceived differently because of important changes in the political and economic environment of the United States in the past twenty-five years. McKay suggests that, whatever the political skills or lack of them of recent incumbents, the political world they confront is more hostile and divisive than ever before.

Although conceding that the political world has in some respects become more unfriendly and intractable for late modern Presidents, Joe Hogan's chapter challenges the 'no-win Presidency' thesis in relation to the problem of legislative leadership. No one pretends that it is anything but difficult for Presidents to exercise effective legislative leadership and Hogan carefully examines the sources and nature of the constraints on the 'no-win Presidency'. But he points out that, contrary to the assumptions of some American commentators and many foreign observers, the United States does not and never has had a system of presidential government. Those who lament the failures of particular Presidents are often, in effect, criticizing the fundamental principles of American government designed to prevent presidential dominance.

But to have a proper respect for the constitutional position of Presidents and to be sensitive to the very real constraints on their capacities to provide legislative leadership is not, in Hogan's view, ground for believing that the Presidency is enfeebled or paralysed. The staff resources available in the White House and in the departments are both considerable and underestimated. It should also be recognized that not all the changes in the political environment are negative ones where legislative leadership is concerned. Late modern Presidents face a Congress in which power is diffused and decentralized, but their predecessors confronted legislatures in which centralization made it difficult to outflank uncooperative committee chairmen. The new style

Congress not only presents new problems, but it also offers considerable opportunities to a President who is clear about his legislative priorities and professional in the way he goes about achieving them. Hogan's concise and authoritative account of the fluctuating fortunes of Reagan's legislative strategy make very clear the possibilities and limitations of presidential power in this crucial area.

If too many interpretations of American politics are President-centred, Michael Foley's chapter provides a different and vitally important perspective on the problems of policy-making in the American system of government. His concern is with the essential, underlying and enduring character of Congress rather than in accounting for short term resurgence or decline *vis-à-vis* the executive branch. He illustrates his interpretation of the real nature of Congress with examples drawn from the key area of foreign policy-making. To Foley, the centralization and discipline characteristic of many modern legislatures contributes to their emasculation. But because the organization of power in the House and Senate is elusive and transient, Congress has retained much of its autonomy.

Reformers who seek to tame Congress and make it more responsible and more disciplined have mistaken the nature of the beast. Independence from the executive branch and freedom of individual action are principles that unite legislators. It is, of course, precisely these qualities that contribute to policy incoherence both in foreign affairs and in domestic matters, but such incoherence is a price legislators are normally prepared to pay. The alternatives would be consistent deference to the White House or having to assume the major responsibility for policy-making. Congress is not organized to undertake the latter and it is unwilling to accept the subordinate status the former course of action implies. Foley's chapter contains a powerful and original interpretation of the sources of weakness and incoherence in American policy-making and my own contribution discusses the consequences of these systemic features as they relate to the work of the federal bureaucracy.

My chapter is concerned with exploring the reasons why the federal bureaucracy is unpopular, why it is perceived to be ineffective and why repeated efforts at major administrative reform have been less than entirely successful. Just as European observers sometimes see the American Congress as hopelessly disorganized and irresponsible, they also see the federal bureaucracy as incurably politicized and fragmented. The chapter describes the political forces that have shaped the structure and growth of the federal bureaucracy and relates the performance of the civil service to the organizational policy choices made by the bureaucracy's warring political masters.

While Foley demonstrates that Congress is largely indifferent to problems of policy incoherence, the chapter on bureaucracy shows that is it similarly unconcerned about the ineffective implementation of public policies. Centralization, co-ordination and discipline are largely executive branch concerns, but legislators prefer fragmentation, independence, and opportunities for individual intervention in the administrative process. If foreign affairs is an 'invitation to struggle' between the President and Congress, the federal bureaucracy is similarly squeezed between the White House rock and the hard places in Congress. The responsiveness of bureaucracy to the conflicting pressures and signals from the White House, Congress and interest groups makes inconsistent and ineffective implementation almost inescapable. Public administration reformers who want to take politics out of administration misunderstand the real nature of the bureaucratic animal. A political bureaucracy is not only the sort that Presidents want, but a fragmented and divided bureaucracy is the only sort that Congress will allow them to have.

The Supreme Court has long been a storm centre of American politics and Richard Hodder-Williams' chapter sets out to explain not only how and why the Supreme Court exercises political power, but what in practice this power means to the role of the Court and the working of the wider political system. Contrary to some opinions, Hodder-Williams maintains that the Supreme Court is not the most powerful branch of government and he points out that substantive involvement in many areas of policy is slight.

In assessing how the Court is drawn into policy disputes, Hodder-Williams focuses on the political consequences of the American propensity for litigation. He draws attention to important recent developments such as the growth of litigation as an interest-group strategy, to deep-rooted changes in the political culture reflecting an increased emphasis on the rights of individuals, and to changes in legal attitudes facilitating greater access to courts.

Hodder-Williams is concerned to dispel the myth that, because Supreme Court decisions have major political consequences, it is a political rather than a judicial body. He argues vigorously that those who describe judges as politicians in robes demonstrate an inadequate comprehension of the process of judging. His interpretation is that it is less a case of the Supreme Court choosing to be activist as the political process itself compelling the Court to assume a political role. Attacks on the Court's jurisprudence are often, in practice, complaints about the content of decisions rather than the process of legal reasoning which led to them. The challenge for the Supreme Court justices is that they are, in one sense, above politics, while simultaneously performing political roles in situations of intense political competition. Hodder-Williams convincingly demonstrates both that the forces which impel the Supreme Court into the political arena are extremely powerful and that the process of judging is so complex and difficult as to require judicial appointments of the highest calibre.

Dean McSweeney's chapter focuses on the much reported decline of parties in the American political system. It explores the evidence for decline, the causes of decline and outlines what he believes may be the consequences of decline. In considering the evidence for decline, he breaks it down into three categories, electoral, organizational and governmental. He points out that most studies of party decline in fact usually deal with only one category. He further points out that the weight and significance of the evidence varies greatly from category to category and, while there is an abundance of sophisticated data on electoral decline, there is a sparsity of compelling information on organizational and governmental decline.

If the fact of party decline is frequently demonstrated, there is, in McSweeny's judgement, less interest in explaining its causation. The problems of causation are such as to encourage many writers to compile lists of causes rather than seek to attach precise weights to particular arguments. Some see it as part of a long-term trend, others as a more recent phenomenon. Some see it in terms of macro changes in the nature of American society, while still others depict it in terms of specific new issues and changing cultural values. If societal pressures of many different kinds have contributed to party decline, there are some interpretations which focus more on internal, institutional reforms which have unintentionally weakened parties as organizations intended to nominate candidates and win elections.

The consequences of party decline have received less academic attention and, according to McSweeney, what analysis there is tends to depict them as harmful and damaging to the health of the body politic. But despite the apocalyptic tone of such analyses, McSweeney argues that a preoccupation with decline has underestimated the indications of strength and continuity. His interpretation suggests that change does not necessarily mean decline and he argues that reports of the death of the American political party are premature.

While McSweeney's concern is with the alleged decline of political parties, John Zvesper focuses on the important specific issue of party realignment. He notes that much academic attention has been given to understanding the critical elections and realignments of the past in the expectation that this will help shed light on present and future prospects. There is, of course, no compelling reason why the pattern of past realignments should repeat itself, but understanding why such changes are unlikely can alter our views of contemporary American politics.

Despite America's reputation for having a long-established, two-party system, Zvesper argues that the United States has effectively had a one-party system in the sense that since 1800 there have been long periods in which one party has dominated federal office holding. The dominant party in each period succeeded in redefining the policy agenda and

7

acquiring a sense of national legitimacy. In such circumstances, the opposing party was forced to adjust its rhetoric to echo that of the dominant party.

In determining what is or is not a critical election or realignment, Zvesper argues that realignments should be defined more in terms of the decisive issues presented by the party system rather than simply in terms of electoral consequences. In the contemporary period, he suggests that Reagan and Bush have been unable or unwilling to define a set of polarizing issues and command a mandate for change. Party realignment is still a possibility, but Zvesper has doubts both about the realignment potential of current issues and the seriousness of President Bush's realigning ambitions.

It was not my intention to impose a particular explanatory framework on the contributions to this book. The individual contributors have provided their own interpretations of important issues in American politics. There is therefore no formal conclusion because the contributions are independent and speak for themselves. Necessarily, all the contributors have come to terms with both the enduring and changing characteristics of the American political system. Multiple access points and fragmented state authority continue to ensure that electoral and policy victories are rarely decisive or permanent. But the United States has entered a post-industrial era in which her relative economic position has been eroded and the outcomes of the complex interactions of international and domestic forces, of institutional conflicts and partisan rivalries and of individual and group ambitions are difficult to predict.

One likely consequence of scarcer public resources is a still further intensification of political competition and this will undoubtedly impose fresh stresses and strains on the American political system and increase pressures for major institutional reform. But the concerns of this book are to explain current issues in American politics and interpretations of future upheavals will have to wait until a subsequent edition.

References

King, A (ed.) (1978) *The New American Political System*, Washington DC: American Enterprise Institute.

McKay, D. (1987) *Politics and Power in the USA*, Harmondsworth, Middlesex: Penguin.

Chapter two

Resurgence and reaction: the impact of the new right in American politics

Gillian Peele

The 1988 presidential election season found the United States at the end of a highly unusual experiment. The Reagan administration had come to power in 1981 at the head of a conservative coalition which was radical in purpose and ambitious in design. The degree of its ideological commitment would perhaps have marked it out from other administrations. But it was also significant because it appeared to signal the end of one of those cycles of American politics which have fascinated historians charting the movement between conservatism and reform and between progress and reaction (Schlesinger Jr 1986). Using the language of A.D. Hirschman, America seemed to be 'on the rebound' from Democratic liberalism and that Reagan's victory in 1980 could be represented as a fundamental shift from a public-sector orientation to a philosophy which celebrated the individual, the market and freedom from government restriction (Hirschman 1982).

Such a clear-cut interpretation has many attractions, including the extent to which it coincided with a resurgent conservatism in other countries (Cooper *et al.* (eds.) 1988; Girvin (ed.) 1988). The reality is, however, somewhat more complex and difficult to explain in the neat categories of progress and reaction, or conservatism and liberalism. And by 1988 matters had been further complicated by another apparent shift in the American mood. For, although George Bush defeated Michael Dukakis in a campaign which effectively depicted liberalism as an extremist position, the election was also one in which Republicans and Democrats acknowledged the need for greater government intervention to solve social problems. The 'kinder, gentler America' sought by Bush stood in contrast to the rugged individualism of his predecessor.

Even before the end of the Reagan Presidency, of course, the clarity and certainty of the administration's tone had faded somewhat. In foreign policy the transition from a rhetoric that spoke of the Soviet Union as an 'evil empire' to the negotiations with Mikhail Gorbachev was but the most obvious of the Reagan administration's accommodations with a changing world scene. Nor was there much evidence in electoral behaviour for a clear movement to the right, as analysts searching the entrails of opinion polls have frequently emphasised (Michler *et al.* in Cooper *et al.* 1988).

How then should we interpret the events of the Reagan years? Was the ideological impact of the conservative movement greatly exaggerated? Or were the politics of the 1980s significantly affected by new ideas, organizations and forces, even if their effect was less profound than their more vocal apologists claimed?

In order to answer these questions a number of preliminary points must be made. First, to make claims about the character of the Reagan administration or about the nature of the pressure groups which broadly supported it, is to say very little about electoral opinion as a whole or about why Reagan received more votes than Jimmy Carter in 1980 or than Walter Mondale in 1984. As we have seen with the Thatcher administration in Britain, a determined and radical government can be successful in getting its issues on the agenda without either convincing public opinion to shift its values on all questions or clearly achieving political realignment.

Second, to understand the extent of the conservative movement's impact on American politics it is necessary to examine the various strands of contemporary American conservatism because the movement was neither monolithic nor were its components of equal strength or significance. The extent to which it was able to cohere after 1981 was limited and the various elements of the movement have changed. Thus to assess its legacy and enduring contribution to American political debate it is important to unravel American conservatism.

Third, it is necessary to look a little more closely at some peculiar features of the American political system and in particular at the role which ideology plays in that system. Indeed it is probably essential to do that before investigating the phenomenon of conservative doctrine and new right activism because the political system and peculiar features of the American political culture have in a sense shaped the way in which American conservatism has developed.

Ideology and American politics

The first point to notice about the role of ideology in American politics is that it is, for the most part, a rather neglected one. Although Americans are comfortable talking about *values*, they are not at all comfortable talking about ideology, which remains associated with the foreign doctrines or infections of socialism and communism. The style of American political debate has always focused rather heavily on the practical and problem-solving aspects of policy rather than on the fundamental ideas behind programmes. The decline of party in the period after 1964 seemed to many to denude American political life still further of programmatic debate. The rise of the political consultants and single pressure groups decentralized and fragmented political discourse, while demands of the advertising media for shorter shots and more catchy advertisements reduced the intellectual content of candidates' appeals (Luntz 1988). This criticism was heard especially loudly in relation to the role of television in the 1988 presidential campaign.

However, some authors have seen the transformation of American campaigning as offering a new opportunity for a more ideological style of politics; and certainly some of the new techniques of winning elections were very happily married with extremely ideological appeals from the right in the 1970s (Peele 1984; Blumenthal 1986, 1983).

In reality, of course, ideology is as important in America as in other political systems. The confusing fact is that clashes of values are rarely expressed clearly through the system of party competition. Indeed the search for conflicting values in the United States is probably best conducted in the court system and especially at the level of the Supreme Court where different interpretations of constitutional morality are offered and where, although a Supreme Court decision does not necessarily stem argument, decisions have special claims to authority above the level of ordinary politics (O'Brien 1986). The American political agenda is shaped – positively and negatively – by appeal to such values as equality, democracy and freedom, although as any careful study of these ideas will reveal, the meaning of these values may vary from one generation to the next. Indeed one of the fascinating features of the period of alleged conservative resurgence has been not merely the extent to which America has seen explicit debate about the fundamentals of the public philosophy, but also the way in which the Reagan administration has sought to alter the language of public discourse. Thus in the field of civil rights the Reagan administration sought to transfer the public understanding of civil rights away from substantive conceptions of equality as measured, for example, by comparing the median incomes of blacks with those of whites. Instead the administration promoted a more formal and limited notion of civil rights which focused on the absence of deliberate discrimination (Peele 1989). And agencies such as the Civil Rights Commission were at the centre of conservative efforts to shift the focus of public attention away from blacks (the traditional object of federal government concern) towards a more varied selection of groups including the handicapped and the new-born.

The Reagan administrations's concern about the composition of the federal courts and the jurisprudence adhered to by the judiciary also reflected the importance which a conservative administration accorded to ensuring that conservative arguments prevailed in the judicial arena. Most Presidents have sought sympathetic judges to appoint to the

Supreme Court. Few Presidents have appreciated as much as Reagan did the extent to which the judiciary shapes the long-term political environment.

A second point to notice about the role of ideology in America is the extent to which that country's political culture has generally been seen as dominated by Lockean liberalism. The classic case has been put by Louis Hartz, who has suggested that in the absence of a feudal society there was no class on which to base reactionary conservatism and that in the absence of a united proletariat there was no class on which to base socialism (Hartz 1955). Hartz was writing in a period of consensus and he perhaps did not draw as sharp a distinction as he should have done between the existence of alternative intellectual traditions in the United States and their ability to make themselves heard in political argument. Equally, it has to be said that the Lockean liberalism Hartz identified as so clearly dominating the American political tradition is itself highly conservative. By comparison with the development of liberal ideas in Europe it appears frozen, devoid of the utilitarianism and collectivism which marks British liberalism, for example (Greenleaf 1988). Property rights and individualism, and laissez-faire attitudes to government and the economy are the celebrated values and assumptions in the American tradition, only occasionally punctured by appeals to the public interest.

A third point to note concerning the role of ideology in the American political system is the difficulty of translating coherent policy platforms into policy. The separation of powers in the United States, the diversity of interests and outlooks as well as the size of the country, have meant that the articulation of an idea in one part of the country, in one forum or in one policy arena is very likely to meet opposition elsewhere. The short time-span of presidential administrations (and the even shorter 'window of opportunity' for presidential initiative) – coupled with the fact that parties are not very effective carriers of policy proposals from one administration to the next – create discontinuities and reduce the likelihood of effective policy implementation. What looks in retrospect like a coherent set of policies reflecting a distinctive philosophical mood – the New Deal or the Great Society – in truth turns out to be rather more incremental in character and pragmatic in origin. Rare indeed in American political life is the administration inspired by a coherent philosophy, committed to a detailed set of policies and capable of implementing them systematically.

These points are made to emphasize the standards by which the Reagan administration must be judged. If the impact of ideology on its policies was not total, it was nevertheless a good deal more pronounced than in most administrations, while the degree of strategic consideration given to how to implement policy also made the administration distinctive.

The rise of the conservative movement – or movement conservatism –

in the 1970s was itself a significant development and one that had major implications for the conduct of American politics. The conservative movement occurred independently from and largely outside the Republican Party, although it had an impact on the party. It was self-consciously involved with promoting an intellectual debate about values and the way in which public policy was made. It was happy to use the word 'conservative', although what the adherents of the movement wanted was not the consolidation and preservation of a political order but the recreation of a purer, freer society than the bureaucratic state created by liberalism.

Yet, even with the remarkable resurgence of conservatism in the 1970s and its accession to power through the Reagan Presidency, one should not overestimate its strength. Internal contradictions existed in the movement even as Reagan was elected. With his departure it is not clear how effective the movement will be without a presidential-level champion. For while George Bush claimed to be the natural successor of Ronald Reagan the conservative movement in the 1988 election divided its preferences – at least in the nomination campaign – between Jack Kemp and Pat Robertson, the televangelist. In order to assess the likely future course of American conservatism it is therefore necessary to examine in more detail its component parts and to see how far its different strands have remained vibrant forces in contemporary American politics.

The components of American conservatism

Any broad movement can be endlessly divided and subdivided but the three most significant strands of the recent American conservative upsurge may be most conveniently discussed under three headings: the intellectual; the organizational; and the religious. Of course these headings overlap – intellectuals participated in organizational activities and religious groups contributed to the intellectual debate. But what was unusual about the late 1970s was the coming together into a broad political movement of a variety of individuals, organizations and causes and the establishment of a well-funded network or structure which could support right-of-centre activity on a number of different levels. In a sense, of course, the creation of this network had a double impact. In the first place it did provide a way for those with conservative ideas and attitudes to make common cause with others of the same outlook. No longer did the conservative expect to feel isolated or excluded from the mainstream of American life, much less without campus organizations and newspapers to read. The 'remnant' and the 'lonely persuasion' had been by the end of the 1970s transformed into 'conservative chic'. But secondly the very construction of journals and newspapers, institutes and think-tanks, legal foundations and pressure groups gathered a momentum of their own, both politically and financially.

The intellectual attack

Sidney Blumenthal, in a study of the rise of the conservative counter-establishment, noted that for some critics to speak of conservative intellectualism would have seemed 'oxymoronic' (Blumenthal 1986). Yet in fact there had been maintained a self-conscious conservative band of intellectuals and writers who, although by no means indentical in their views, had kept conservative values as they perceived them in the United States alive during the New Deal and immediate post-war period. When William Buckley founded the *National Review* in 1955 there was, moreover, a rallying point for the assorted and somewhat idiosyncratic individuals who delighted in the appellation 'conservative'. However, these conservatives were still very conscious of their minority position and were much better at offering scholarly critiques of current social trends rather than participating in the policy process or organizing to promote their ideas effectively.

The different groups who were drawn towards the right in American politics in the 1970s were not content to stay on the sidelines of policy and were much more able to integrate with other participants in American political discourse. The period was one of considerable intellectual vitality on the right, much of which rebounded to the benefit of Republican Party politics and the conservative movement. To call any of the tendencies or impulses of the right in the 1970s 'groups' is perhaps to suggest too great a degree of organization and coherence, but to the extent that there were shared agendas and assumptions, as well as common outlets for the discussion of their ideas, it is not an exaggeration to speak of a movement or tendency.

Three intellectual developments on the right should be distinguished at this point. The first was the emergence of a group of writers and academics who came to be known as 'neo-conservatives'. This group included Irving Kristol, Norman Podhoretz, Daniel Patrick Moynihan, Nathan Glazer and Daniel Bell. Many of them had been on the left of American politics until the 1960s but the events of that decade (and especially Vietnam, the Great Society programmes and the general revolution of cultural and moral values) caused them to criticize developments in America from a more conservative perspective.

The adherence of these new recruits to the conservative intellectual elite in the long run added substantive legitimacy to the cause of the right. The issues that concerned the neo-conservatives were important because they showed how the political agenda was changing and creating the potential for new alignments. The neo-conservatives were also important because they were able to bring major policy expertise, especially in foreign policy and social policy to the conservative movement and because they were highly visible polemicists appearing regularly both in their own 'in-house' journals such as *Commentary* and *The Public Interest* as well as in such newspapers as the *Wall Street Journal* and the *Washington Times*, which meant that their opinions reached a broad and influential audience.

Vietnam was significant because of the extent to which it separated a number of former liberals from the new left and its sympathizers and placed patriotism at the heart of political debate. Interestingly the Vietnam War was not merely crucial in moving liberals rightwards but it has been a topic which still figures prominently in the American conservative movement's activities. Thus the Olin Foundation, one of the many think-tanks and foundations with an interest in conservative issues, has, according to Blumenthal, given money to revise the interpretations of the war, suggesting that the new wealth of the right-wing entrepreneurs was in part at least to be devoted to fighting again the wars of the 1960s through the scholarship of the 1980s (Blumenthal 1986; Steinfels 1979).

Race was important because it prompted the formation of new alliances between those who had hitherto been liberal on the expansion of minority rights and those who had been sceptical about using governmental power to foster improved opportunities for blacks in particular. The change was brought about by the change of emphasis from campaigns designed to eradicate formal, legal discrimination to programmes aimed at producing greater equality of outcome through affirmative actions in such areas as university admissions and hiring policies and employment generally. Jewish scholars such as Nathan Glazer were especially critical of affirmative action programmes, which they dubbed 'affirmative discrimination' and the use of quotas became unpopular not merely amongst American Jews (who had reason to be sensitive about any quotas) but also amongst the general public. Not surprisingly, aspects of affirmative action came under judicial scrutiny throughout the 1970s and 1980s, and by the late 1980s a more conservative court had substantially restricted the use of race-conscious remedies.[1]

The role of the Great Society programmes in stimulating a revival of conservatism was equally important. For the perceived failures of those programmes produced a scepticism about the role of government in social life and, although many of the criticisms of the programme were unfair, conservatives criticized not merely the expenditure of vast sums of money on minority causes but also the assumptions underlying the programmes. The naive belief in the solution of the poverty problem was soon replaced by an equally stark denial that social ills could ever be cured, as well as a certain loss of confidence in the expertise of the social scientists who were the high priests of the Great Society projects.

15

The manner in which these events stimulated the formation of a new and more powerful intellectual community has been chronicled many times. Many of the most trenchant criticisms of developments came from former Democrats such as Daniel Moynihan, who at Harvard had argued that many of the problems of blacks were fundamentally cultural.

The neo-conservatives were, however, a very diverse group of individuals who often disagreed as much with each other as with writers outside their circle. While they undoubtedly contributed much to the self-confidence of the critics of liberalism in the 1970s, two other developments which gave the intellectual attack from the right its critical edge should be mentioned.

In addition to the largely sociological, foreign policy and cultural interests of the neo-conservatives, there were important developments within the discipline of economics which fuelled the growth of the American right. These developments were the rise of monetarism and supply-side economic theory – both important critiques of Keynesianism. And the revival of interest in the market economy was paralleled by philosophical developments which emphasized the values of freedom and autonomy as opposed to equality.

The development of supply-side and monetarist theories had the effect of giving the right in the late 1970s a credible alternative to the interventionist economic doctrines associated with Keynesianism. They fitted well with the more broadly based effort to reduce the role of the federal government in American society. However, these approaches were not entirely compatible and the supply-side remedy of a major tax cut (implemented in the first Reagan administration) when combined with the massive expansion in the defence budget helped to produce the deficit which has become a central concern in American politics since 1981.

Interest in libertarian philosophy had been heightened in 1974 by the publication of Robert Nozick's *Anarchy, State and Utopia*. As far as the broad conservative movement was concerned, however, many of the values of this group were incompatible with the social conservatism of the neo-conservatives who came increasingly to stress the importance of traditional morality and the family as keys to social stability. The libertarians, by contrast, were highly individualistic and concerned with rational choice rather than tradition. Indeed some of their ideas – such as the legalization of recreational drugs and the auctioning of unwanted children – would be totally unacceptable to most conservatives. Yet, extreme as some of the libertarian ideas were, conservatives could welcome their intellectual vitality as another sign of the right's resurgence.

The organizational conservative movement

Parallel to the intellectual blossoming of the conservative movement in the 1970s was the development of the new right's network of Political Action Committees (PACs), think-tanks, research institutes and direct mail entrepreneurs. The origins of much of this activity lay in the apparent decline of party in the late 1960s. Indeed, Blumenthal in *The Permanent Campaign* and *The Rise of the Counter-Establishment*, argued that there was an obvious link between the decentralization of political campaigns as a result of party erosion and the more ideological style of politics which emerged in the late 1970s. Certainly over the 1970s many observers noted the emergence of a network of single-issue groups and coalitions as well as organizations pressing for a more concerted form of right-wing political activity.

There was a sense in which much of this activity was shadow liberalism – a form of political activity modelled on earlier experiments by Democrats. Important organizations in the field were Howard Philips' Conservative Caucus, Terry Dolan's NCPAC and Paul Weyrich's Committee for the Survival of a Free Congress (which was very directly modelled on the liberal counterpart – the Committee for an Effective Congress). In the field of judicial politics, a range of legal institutes and foundations were formed to defend business groups and other right-wing causes in holy war against government regulation. And in a slightly different vein, the various enterprises sponsored by Richard Viguerie, the direct mail entrepreneur, offered technical help in fund-raising although the spread of the new direct mail methods could not long be confined to a single entrepreneur.

What made these organizations so significant was that they had a clear vision of what they wanted to achieve – a switch towards a more conservative set of policies especially on social and cultural issues. Second, they had the organizational tools to promote their causes and were in a sense first into the new style of electoral politics and fund-raising. Finally they had the stage to themselves at least initially in the sense that, although their activities were often modelled on liberal organizational efforts, the conservative new right groups had to be highly professional about organization and the use of new technology. The organizational efforts of these pressure groups and entrepreneurs met little resistance from the Republican Party, which for much of the early 1970s was traumatized by the experience of Watergate. Indeed during the period of Bill Brock's chairmanship of the Republican National Committee, the Republican Party was transformed organizationally and, although the party regulars had little liking for the newer political entrepreneurs like Weyrich and Viguerie, they were aware of the benefits to be gained from their methods and their activism.

17

The issues which the new right organizational network exploited were often those of the conservative intellectuals; but the need to raise money meant that the presentation of themes such as hostility towards the counter-culture and the changes wrought by the 1960s in sexual morality were often crude and simplistic. Anti-abortion and hostility to homosexuality were clear themes running through much of the new right's propaganda. Generally the social issues were seen as important fund-raising tools. Whereas the neo-conservatives, for example, framed their arguments in academic and intellectual circles, the new right PACs were more interested in converting large numbers of ordinary voters. The effective style of the new right 'on the ground' was thus populist and the strategy adopted was one which suggested that the instincts of ordinary Americans had been neglected by Washington politicians.

Sometimes the issues raised by new right activists were genuine reflections of concern about such problems as abortion. But sometimes they were either manufactured or exploited in a way which reflected a mixture of the right's own conspiracy mentality and a certain commercial shrewdness.

Religion and American conservatism

The identification of social issues as an important element on the right's agenda was greatly helped in the 1970s by the growth of religious sentiment in the United States. Indeed one of the distinctive features of American conservative organization in this period was the explicit attempt to link political and religious groups in the broad service of the right and the extent to which hitherto unmobilized groups of American society were seen as suitable for conversion to the conservative cause (Wuthnow 1988).

Religion has always played an important role in the American political culture and the themes of natural right and religion were used by the neo-conservatives particularly when they rebutted the arguments of the counter-culture and the anarchy and nihilism associated with the permissive society of the 1960s. Many of the leading neo-conservatives were Jewish, but there was also a strong Roman Catholic element in the movement. Irving Kristol himself was influenced by Leo Strauss's philosophy and many of the interns recruited for *The Public Interest* had come from the University of Chicago. Such associations were not, however, sufficient to ground a political movement. What made the difference was the perception by the entrepreneurs of the conservative movement that, if religious and political concerns could be properly integrated, there would be a huge electoral dividend.

One factor in alerting the new right to the potential significance of the religious groups and their agenda of concerns was the sheer size of the constituency. Whereas the mainline churches had been losing adherents in the post-war period, the more conservative Protestant churches had been gaining members. The area where many of the born-again Christians were concentrated (especially in the south) were seen as pivotal in any process of realignment. Party tacticians were also aware that conservative evangelicals could be a useful source of new votes because until the 1970s the traditional stance of many fundamentalist Christians had been to abjure politics altogether.

It was not only the Protestant religious groups who seemed possible recruits to the new right. Abortion had been given constitutional sanction by the Supreme Court in 1973 in a decision which had provoked fury throughout the Roman Catholic Church and generated a highly organized right-to-life movement.[2] Traditionally the Democrats – with their strong support among ethnic communities of Irish, Italians and other European immigrant groups – had been the Catholic party. New right strategists saw the abortion issues, as well as the decline of any sense of minority status amongst American Catholics, as offering an opportunity to separate Catholic voters from the Democratic Party.

Organizationally the mobilization of religion offered other advantages. The ideological message of the televangelists was very similar to that of the new right and there were cultivated political ties between them. Churches were good precinct organizations and local pastors excellent mobilizers of electoral effort.

But above all the churches in America were able to give a highly important religious sanction to the capitalist system, to Americanism and to the set of values cherished on the conservative right.

The formation of links between the right and the churches and the efforts of broad based pressure groups such as Moral Majority naturally generated criticism in the more liberal churches or even with the more liberal elements of the same church. But the study of the whole period in retrospect suggests two important points. First, the activity by the new right organizations and religious right underlined the extent to which there is an underlying culture of moral conservatism in the United States which is sharply at odds with the liberalism frequently displayed by its elites. Second, periods of activity such as that which occurred over the period 1976–82 can be important because they raise political awareness and the capacity to mobilize behind issues. This was the case in the United States; after 1980 all the churches were more involved in political issues than they had been before and at a number of different levels.

The Republican Party

It is important to emphasize the extent to which the strengthening of the conservative movement took place independently of the orthodox

Republican Party. Many of the new conservative intellectuals were ex-Democrats, and they only slowly made their decision to change partisan allegiance. Many of the new right entrepreneurs were contemptuous of the Republican Party, seeing it as elitist and consensual. In party terms, however, the Republican Party came to seem the only realistic vehicle for the promotion of the kind of ideas which the conservative ideologues held. Thus, although the leaders of the conservative movement were outside the regular party channels for part of the period before Reagan won the presidency, Republican leaders recognized the virtue of working in tandem with conservatives throughout this period. Brock's renewal of party organization was not in conflict with the movement's more varied activities, although there were personal disagreements and clashes.

It is of interest that some of the debates about Republican tactics in the period 1976–80, have been repeated in the Bush Presidency. Thus the conflict over whether House Republicans should adopt highly aggressive tactics in order to compensate for their minority position surfaced in the controversy over Speaker Jim Wright's problems with the Ethics Committee. Newt Gingrich, the Republican Whip, became closely identified with a hard style of politics which sought to capitalize on the personal vulnerabilities of opponents. Similarly Republican Party Chairman Lee Atwater became identified with a particularly mean style of campaigning and partisan promotion – a style which ultimately brought him into conflict with President Bush.

This points to one legacy of the new right and the broader conservative movement to the Republican Party in the 1980s. For the new breed of Republican, the older gentlemanly mores of legislative camaraderie were irrelevant. Politics was about winning, not about being a good loser.

The impact of power

It has already been seen that the conservative movement was composed of very varied elements. The intellectuals in the movement were inherently individualistic and although some took positions in the Reagan administration, others remained outside. The conservative network had the satisfaction of seeing its candidate in the White House, but the momentum behind the different aspects of the movement had to be maintained and the entrepreneurs therefore had to pursue their own agendas. The religious groups were sometimes divided by denomination and within the evangelical camp there were inevitable centrifugal tendencies as a result of the very individualistic role of pastors and congregations.

What had brought all these elements in the conservative coalition together in the 1970s was opposition to the broad enemy of liberal secular humanism. But once the White House was occupied by Ronald Reagan rather than Jimmy Carter, that enemy hardly seemed as threatening. It was therefore somewhat difficult for the new right to maintain its momentum.

However, it has to be said, although the conservative movement did experience some diffusion of effort and disappointment at the slowness of change especially on the key social issues, the conservative character of the Reagan administration was sustained beyond many people's expectations. This was in part because of the sustained thought that had been given to the appointments process, and the Reagan administration was able to bring into the departments and agencies a range of political appointees who had close links with such bodies as the Heritage Foundation and the American Enterprise Institute. Ironically it was former President Jimmy Carter who had made the politicization of the administration rather easier for his successor by the passage of the Civil Service Reform Act of 1978 and the creation of the Senior Executive Service.

Yet strains with the coalition did emerge. One of the first to erupt concerned economic policy as David Stockman revealed the extent to which the supply-side recipe rested on faith and more orthodox economists pointed to the dangers inherent in the spiralling deficit.

The handling of the social issues caused disillusionment at an early stage. Reagan's first nominee to the Supreme Court – Sandra Day O'Connor – was not seen as sufficiently ideological for the conservative movement and, despite efforts in the Senate to bring in amendments on school prayer and abortion, the Supreme Court resisted attempts to overturn its basic ruling on the abortion issue, although in 1989 there was a major change as the Court with a new conservative majority allowed the states to place extensive restrictions on abortion. Certainly throughout the Reagan Presidency there was evidence of a more politicized administration of the law and at the end of the Reagan presidency the lower federal courts reflected the determination of the Justice Department to appoint conservative judges. But their impact was not immediately apparent and they were by no means all conservatives of the same ideological stripe.

On foreign policy there was a major retreat from the assumptions of the conservative movement and of its true believers as compromises had to be made with Congress in Latin America and, later, as the administration was weakened by the Irangate scandal. The successful search for an arms control treaty with the Soviet Union automatically dampened the anti-communistic rhetoric, leaving the think-tanks and pressure groups of the right to deal with such details as verification.

The consequences of the Reagan administration

The experience of the conservative movement under Reagan was thus mixed. It had seen the notion of conservatism transformed from a rather idiosyncratic and isolated doctrine to a wealthy, self-confident and powerful movement with an alternative power structure to support the expression of conservative views in the media, in the universities and schools and in all aspects of public life. At the same time, and despite the real personal adulation that there was for Ronald Reagan, the ability of his administration to deliver major changes in the American social system (in relation to school prayer, abortion, etc.) was limited and in the field of foreign policy there was a major turn-around which added confusion to the right.

Certainly times were not easy either for the conservative entrepreneurs when the enemy was out of power. Viguerie, for example, experienced well-publicized financial difficulties and had to sell *Conservative Digest*. The Moral Majority's *raison d'être* seemed to have disappeared and in 1989 its crusade formally ceased. The empire of Jerry Falwell continued but its finances and political clout both seem substantially weakened by 1989.

The sensational stories surrounding some prominent televangelists (Jimmy Swaggert and Jim and Tammy Bakker) have cast some doubt on the credibility of the others. And Bush's success in the election of 1988 scored an important symbolic victory for those who do not want to see the Republican Party dominated by the right. Indeed Bush's style in office has been distinctly non-ideological emphasizing competence and compromise in government rather than ideas or principles.

Conclusions

In trying to assess how far the conservative movement has left its mark on American politics it is necessary to bear in mind not only how quickly events in the United States can change but also that the two keys to success in getting a message across are organization and money.

And here the conservative movement can celebrate very real achievements. The conservative movement may not have seen the implementation of its complete agenda but the range of well-funded think-tanks and research institutes is testament to an astonishing period of growth and to an ability to exploit the changed character of American campaigning. The conservative movement now has its own momentum and is unlikely to disappear.

Equally, the arguments and activities of the conservative movement – together with the eight years of the Reagan administration – have seen a shift in the agenda of American politics. For all the concern about the deficit, few of the candidates in the 1988 presidential election wished to be associated with the possibility of a tax raise, although Michael Dukakis asserted the need for raising additional revenue through indirect taxes. The bias against taxation reflected the extent to which the conservatives had moved the American political consensus in their direction and there was an even more pronounced bias against high-spending policies.

In one sense the direction in which the Reagan administration moved the country was towards the values of that part of the country – the Sunbelt – which was growing in population, in economic resources and in political power.

The conservative movement could claim another important victory also. Although neither Jack Kemp nor Pat Robertson ran well in the primaries, the mood of the Republican Party had been transformed during the period 1967–88. Although the self-conscious new right had become absorbed into the politics of Congress and of the GOP elsewhere, there was no real challenger to conservative values because the liberal wing of the party had declined substantially since 1976 (Rae 1989). And the more tough and hard-hitting style of politics promoted by the new right PACs such as NCPAC in the 1970s has become a feature of Republican politics generally.

All of these points leave open the question of whether American politics have become in any sense more ideological since the 1970s. Blumenthal's argument for suggesting that they have, rested on the decline of party. A party, of course, does act as a restraint on single-issue groups, individuals and factions since all of these have to aggregate their demands into a package which the party can present. If the party shell becomes less strong then these various causes and issues can circulate freely without any countervailing check. However, what seems to have happened in the two parties is not identical. The Democrats have become much more faction ridden and balkanized. After sometimes bitter clashes in the late 1970s, the Republicans have moved to pick up some of the new conservative ideas and techniques without the self-destruction sometimes seen in Democratic ranks.

Support for Blumenthal's argument about an increase in ideology can of course be gained by reference to the imperatives of political campaigning. Especially where fund-raising and indeed the media are concerned, the imperative need is for sharp images and often negative and frightening messages.

Above all the period since 1976 has highlighted those elements in the American political tradition which have reinforced the country's conservative bias – religion, family values, economic individualism and suspicion of governmental authority. The American political system has taken a sharp turn away from the use of federal government power to solve major social problems and indeed the deficit has placed an effective restriction on additional federal activity. A more conservative Republican Party is thus working with the grain of these underlying trends of American politics. Try as they might to revive support for liberalism, the Democrats are constrained by the legacies of the 1980s so that even if they control Congress they cannot implement liberal programmes. Although there may have been no detectable change in popular attitudes and no clear-cut political realignment, the logic of American politics at the end of the 1980s has surely been to make the country more hospitable for conservative values and less congenial for liberals.

Notes

1 See for example the cases decided in 1989, viz *City of Richmond v. Croson*; *Wards Cove Packing Co. v. Antonion*; *Martin v. Wilks* and *Patterson v. McLean Credit Union*.
2 See *Roe v. Wade* (1973) 93 S.Ct 705 410 US 113. In 1989 the Supreme Court reconsidered the principle of Roe in *Webster v. Reproductive Services of Missouri*.

References

Blumenthal, S. (1986) *The Rise of the Counter-Establishment: From Conservative Ideology to Political Power*, New York: Times Books.
—— (1983) *The Permanent Campaign*, New York: Touchstone Books.
Cooper, B., Korberg, A. and Mishler, W. (eds) (1988) *The Resurgence of Conservatism in Anglo-American Democracies*, Durham and London: Duke University Press.
Girvin, B. (ed) (1988) *The Transformation of Contemporary Conservatism*, London: Sage.
Greenleaf, W.H. (1988) *The British Political Tradition*, London: Routledge.
Hartz, L. (1955) *The Liberal Tradition in America*, New York: Harcourt Brace.
Hirschman, A.O. (1982) *Shifting Involvements*, Oxford: Martin Robertson.
Luntz, F.I. (1988) *Candidates, Consultants and Campaigns*, New York: Basil Blackwell.
Mishler, W., Hoskyn, M. and Fitzgerald, R.E. (1988) 'Hunting the Snark: Or Searching for Evidence of that Widely Touted but Highly Elusive Resurgence of Public Support for Conservative Parties in Britain, Canada and the United States', in Cooper, Kornberg and Mishler (eds) op. cit.
Nozick, R. (1974) *Anarchy, State and Utopia*, Oxford: Basil Blackwell.
O'Brien, D.M. (1986) *Storm Center: The Supreme Court in American Politics*, New York: Norton.
Peele, G. (1984) *Revival and Reaction: The Right in Contemporary America*, Oxford: Oxford University Press.
—— (1989) 'The Bush Administration and Civil Liberties', Paper delivered at the Political Studies Association Annual Conference.
Rae, N. (1989) *The Decline and Fall of the Liberal Republicans*, Oxford: Oxford University Press.
Roe v. Wade (1973) 93 S.Ct 705 410 US 113.
Schlesinger Jr, A.M. (1986) *The Cycles of American History*, Boston: Houghton Mifflin.
Steinfels, P. (1979) *The Neo-Conservatives: The Men Who Are Changing America*, New York: Simon & Schuster.
Wuthnow, R. (1988) *The Restructuring of American Religion*, Princeton: Princeton University Press.

Chapter three

The rise and fall of the public-interest Presidency

David McKay

Until the 1960s the traditional view of the Presidency was that alone among American political institutions it was capable of representing the public or national interest. The reasoning went something like this: only Presidents represent a national constituency. To get elected, Presidents have to appeal to the broad mass of the American people. No candidate can afford to neglect a major region, social group or class. Congress, in contrast, is highly particularistic. Individual members of Congress serve relatively small constituencies. Once in office, members put the particular interests of their constituents before those of the country as a whole. The same was true of state and local politics, which, if anything, were more prone to 'capture' by special interests.

This neat characterization appeared to have empirical application. Presidents Roosevelt, Truman, Eisenhower, Kennedy and (at least until 1965) Johnson all acquired reputations for putting the public interest before special interests. Since the late 1960s, however, Presidents have found it increasingly difficult to perform this function. In this context, the chapter has two main purposes. First to explain why it is that recent Presidents find it difficult to project themselves as champions of the public interest. Second to discover if in this new political environment, some Presidents may have found it necessary to serve particular interests over the general interest. Special attention will be paid to the experience of the Reagan administration when addressing this question.

Before embarking on this exercise, it is important to stress that no politician or institution – whether American or not – can represent the public interest in the purest sense. Politicians will always serve one constituency more than another. The point is, rather, that under certain conditions political leaders can effectively project themselves as champions of the national interest. They are more likely to be able to do this if the following apply:

1 They have been elected on the basis of a mandate from a broadly based political party.

2 Appeals for changes in public policy are based on distributing national resources in ways which benefit many citizens and penalize none or few.
3 Once in office, public support for policy reforms is at a high level.
4 The staffing of the government (executive and judicial branches) is mainly based on that party movement which has been responsible for nominating candidates to office.

While these conditions never apply in absolute terms there have been times in American history when they have been more relevant than at other times. Indeed between 1933 and 1965 incumbent Presidents conformed to most of these criteria. Since 1965, however, few Presidents have been either able or willing to meet these conditions. Let us look at these two periods in more detail.

Party mandates and the New Deal coalition

The realignment of voters towards the Democratic Party between 1928 and 1932 created an unusual degree of party solidarity in the United States. Support for the Democrats was based partly on social class in that Northern blue-collar workers became solidly Democratic during this period, partly on region (the South) and partly on ideology because intellectuals and media opinion shifted towards the Democrats (Chambers and Burnham 1975). Although the Democrats undoubtedly enjoyed a sectoral and class appeal, the new President, Franklin Roosevelt, was intent on projecting himself as the champion of all classes and regions. The economic depression was, indeed, deep enough to affect all economic interests. For example by 1933, 40 per cent of all existing mortgage debt was in default and in 1931 as many as 2,300 banks failed (Owens 1986). The national emergency had, in fact, begun in 1929, but the incumbent president, Herbert Hoover, was unable to project himself as the 'voice of the people' as Clinton Rossiter put it (Rossiter 1960). Not only was Hoover unable to free himself from what was seen increasingly as an inappropriate free-market ideology, he also lacked broadly based electoral support after 1930. For although he had won the 1928 contest with 58 per cent of the vote, the Republicans lost fifty-three seats in the House and eight in the Senate in the 1930 mid-term elections. By 1932 the Democratic share of the vote was almost precisely the same as the Republican share in 1928.

During the 1930s the Democratic hold on elections tightened at all levels of politics. As Table 3.1 shows, this came close to resembling a Democratic hegemony in Congress by the late 1930s. In this context, Franklin Roosevelt moved towards being able to fulfil the four conditions outlined earlier. The Democrats certainly projected themselves as

the party of the people while the Republicans were increasingly identified as the party of a special interest (big business). New Deal policies
were either re-distributive in nature (work relief, social security,
unemployment benefit, welfare) or were designed to protect both
producers and consumers from the vagaries of the market (banking
deposit insurance, home loan and farmers' loan insurance, regulation
of the stock market). Although Franklin Roosevelt was to experience
some electoral difficulties during the late 1930s, his popularity recovered
with the onset of war in Europe. In fact the Second World War proved
to be a major reinforcing influence on what might be called the 'public
interest Presidency'. It was widely perceived as a 'Good War', as Studs
Terkel has put it (Terkel 1985). Franklin Roosevelt was able, therefore,
to present himself as leader of a 'Free World' engaged in a Manichean
struggle with almost universally condemned enemies. No other major
war in which the United States has been involved this century has allowed
a President to achieve this status. Roosevelt became a President widely
perceived as above politics in international affairs.

Table 3.1 Party control of the House of Representatives and Senate 1929–41

House			Senate	
Year	Democratic % of all seats (number of seats in brackets)	Republican % of all seats	Democratic % of all seats	Republican % of all seats
1929	38 (167)	61 (267)	41 (39)	58 (56)
1931	51 (220)	49 (214)	49 (47)	50 (48)
1933	71 (310)	27 (117)	63 (60)	37 (25)
1935	73 (319)	24 (103)	72 (69)	26 (25)
1937	76 (331)	20 (89)	79 (76)	17 (16)
1939	60 (261)	38 (164)	72 (69)	24 (23)
1941	62 (268)	37 (162)	69 (66)	29 (28)

Source: US Congress, *Congressional Directory*, (various years)

Roosevelt was also the first President to staff his government using
cues drawn from a powerful social movement rather than relying solely
on state and local party machines. Until the 1930s federal posts were
very much in the gift of local party bosses whom Presidents rewarded
for their electoral support during the nomination process. While considerable elements of this system persisted through the 1930s and 1940s (and
beyond), the New Deal provided the President with new opportunities
for establishing much greater control over the patronage system. For
the first time, ideological factors played a major role. During the 1930s
there emerged a new breed of 'New Dealers' who were committed to

27

redistributive social policy and a strong national government. Many of these men and women were recruited to the Democratic cause in the early New Deal during Roosevelt's famous first 100 days (Schlesinger 1958). Although they were ideologically to the left of the President, Roosevelt had little choice but to enlist their support in order successfully to implement his New Deal programmes. His efforts to transform the bureaucracy – and especially the judiciary – with this end in mind are well documented (Leuchtenburg 1963). Crucially, these professional New Dealers were part of a wider social movement intent on nationalizing government and increasing the federal role in the American economy and society. Often they were able to take over state and local parties and turn them into organizations whose rationale was to extend the New Deal agenda. In this way the fourth condition was met in many parts of the country.

None of the above should be interpreted as evidence of a total revolution in party politics. It was a revolution, but a very incomplete one. The South, while solidly in the Democratic camp and supportive of some New Deal policies, remained hostile to the nationalization of politics. State and local party organizations persisted as conservative, corrupt and segregationist. The New Deal, with its agricultural support programmes and mortgage guarantees, was economically convenient, but no more. It was, indeed, Southern Democrats who insisted that many of the New Deal programmes should be implemented on a matching federal/state basis thus ensuring a high degree of interstate variation and local control. (McKay 1989).

Also, while Roosevelt projected himself as a public interest President, his programme clearly served some interests more than others. Big business was protected from national and international competition. Organized labour grew in size and strength throughout the 1930s, its greatest triumph being the enactment of the 1935 Wagner Act which gave workers the right to free collective bargaining and the union (closed) shop. The point is, however, not that certain interests benefited while those of others (for example, black Americans) were neglected. It is that as a *political institution* the Presidency became unambiguously associated with the national or public interest. By way of contrast, Congress and state and local governments became increasingly associated with special or particular interests.

Between 1945 and 1965 this pattern of political authority persisted – at least in its essentials. Important changes did occur, but none that seriously challenged the public interest presidency. Let us look at these in more detail.

The public interest Presidency 1945–65

The first major challenge to what might be called the political regime established by Roosevelt and the New Deal came with Harry Truman's second administration. Democratic hegemony appeared to break down with the Republicans capturing both houses of Congress. By 1952 the Truman administration came to be associated with what appeared to be the very antithesis of the public interest: corruption in Washington, an unpopular war abroad (Korea) and allegations of Communist infiltration into the federal government. While this is true, much of the New Deal regime remained intact, namely:

1 State and local Democratic parties remained dominant. Little in the way of renewed Republican organizational strength at these levels was evident.
2 Republicans offered little in the way of an ideologically coherent alternative to the New Deal regime. The Taft/Hartley Labor Relations Act did weaken the unions but in social policy the New Deal measures were if anything strengthened during the Truman years.
3 Criticism of the Truman presidency did not dwell on the institution itself, as much as on personalities. The twenty-second amendment which limited the presidency to two terms constituted a form of Republican revenge for the four-term Roosevelt Presidency. As such it was an attack on Roosevelt rather than on the Presidency *per se*.

Neither was Eisenhower's electoral victory in 1952 a fatal challenge to the New Deal regime. His success was highly personal in nature. Democrats remained firmly the majority party in terms of party identification – indeed they re-captured the House and Senate in 1954 and were to retain control of both until 1980. In social policy and economic regulation none of the major New Deal measures were challenged by the Eisenhower administrations. Ideologically it was a period of extraordinary consensus – so much so that Daniel Bell was inspired to write a book entitled *The End of Ideology: On the Exhaustion of Political Ideas in the Fifties* (Bell 1960).

As is well known, Eisenhower did much to advance the public interest Presidency. For although he was not supported by a broad social movement intent on a programme of social and economic change, he was always regarded as above politics. He was aided in this project not only by his own personality and proclivities but also by the international environment. The Manichean contest between the Axis powers and the Allies was replaced by another good versus evil contest between the Free World and Communism. President Eisenhower was widely regarded as the only Free World leader representing truly global interests. He and the United States were still seen as largely free from colonial or imperial ambitions – witness the US stand on Suez and the US led compromise on Indo-China in 1954. At the same time, Eisenhower was the guardian of freedom and democracy.

In domestic politics, the President's image as neutral arbiter was reinforced by his strategy of apparently letting subordinates take the difficult decisions (Greenstein 1982). On such delicate issues as civil rights and labour relations he was rarely regarded personally as partisan, even if his administration was. He was even able to criticize corporate decisions, as his famous comments on the dangers of the overweaning power of the 'military industrial complex' show.

President Kennedy's (admittedly narrow) victory in 1960 looked like a confirmation that the politics of the New Deal regime were still in place. Democrats dominated Congress, the Governors' mansions and remained the majority party in terms of voter identification. Kennedy took on the role as 'voice of the people and defender of freedom' with great zest and enthusiasm. Even the Bay of Pigs fiasco, when a group of CIA-sponsored Cuban exiles attempted to invade Cuba and oust Fidel Castro, did little to tarnish his image as world leader. He admitted the episode was a mistake (Schlesinger 1965) and shortly afterward his standing as world leader was re-confirmed by his handling of the Cuban missile crisis.

While Kennedy was less effective in domestic politics – his civil rights and education bills were to fare badly in Congress – no single domestic issue divided the nation along partisan lines. Indeed, civil rights, which were rapidly becoming a question of national concern, cut across party lines.

Lyndon Johnson's landslide defeat of Barry Goldwater in 1964 seemed yet further confirmation of the resilience of the New Deal regime. And until the autumn of 1965, when Johnson ordered the bombing of North Vietnam, the President was intent on grand policy initiatives, all of which were shrouded in the rhetoric of the public interest. The most famous of these was Johnson's Great Society – a package of policies designed to eradicate poverty, raise educational standards and improve the environment. These were truly public-interest issues. Who, after all, could be in favour of poverty, poor education or a polluted environment? They were, moreover, sold to the American people as low- or no-cost initiatives. Poverty would be removed not by massive injections of cash into new welfare programmes, but by encouraging the poor to participate in community action. This was to be a consciousness-raising not a public-spending exercise. Finally Johnson gave his full backing to the 1964 and 1965 civil rights bills. Both were passed – the former giving American blacks protection against discrimination in education, employment and public facilities, and the latter in voting. Outside the South, civil rights were firmly established as a non-partisan issue.

From late 1965, however, the Johnson Presidency came under siege. By 1968 it was fatally wounded. The specific reasons for this are well known. A backlash against civil rights enforcement and the Great Society programmes came not only from Southerners but also from many

Northern blue-collar Democrats. In addition, Johnson's escalation of the war in Vietnam deeply divided the Democratic Party. By the spring of 1968, when Johnson withdrew his candidacy for the forthcoming election, the institution of the Presidency was seriously damaged. Far from representing the public or national interest, Johnson was conducting the office in a way which seemed to divide rather than unite; to pander to particular interests – the military, corporate America – rather than serve the general interest.

In fact, the Johnson Presidency marked a turning point in the recent history of the institution. For since the mid-1960s the Presidency has failed to regain its status as that part of the government which is essentially above politics. Put another way, no President in the last twenty years has come close to fulfilling the four criteria set out in the introduction of this chapter. As important, no President has been widely *perceived* as fulfilling these criteria. This may, in fact, relate to the capacities and personalities of incumbents. But it is also related to important structural changes in the American political and world systems which have made it much more difficult for Presidents to convince the American people that they are indeed defenders of the nation's interests.

Regime fragmentation and the decline of the public-interest Presidency

Most students of the Presidency point to the personal failings of recent Presidents as the main explanation for the decline in the status of the office. At first sight this seems plausible. Lyndon Johnson clung tenaciously to his Vietnam policy in the face of fierce public opposition and a near-impossible military situation. Richard Nixon resigned in disgrace over the Watergate affair. Jimmy Carter was dubbed weak and indecisive. During his second term Ronald Reagan was widely accused of an excessive delegation of authority within the White House – a tendency which led to the Iran-Contra affair. While these personal responsibilities are clear, a number of structural changes have made it difficult for any President to avoid accusations of incompetence and/or errors in judgement. The major changes are:

The decline of the New Deal coalition

As earlier catalogued, Democratic Presidents from Roosevelt to Kennedy governed with the support of a broad coalition of social groups and regions intent on a general programme of social and economic change. This programme was not always clear and never wholly uncontroversial, but it involved an acceptance of re-distributive social policy for industrial workers, full-employment policies and the centralization of

31

power in the federal government in Washington. Even by the early 1960s the coalition was under threat from a South, which resented the addition of civil rights laws to the agenda. Later in the decade, Great Society urban and social policies became central to Democratic politics. Most of these policies were designed to help the urban poor, often poor blacks. Traditional Democratic voters found it hard to identify with such policies and many deserted to the Republicans or, in 1968, to George Wallace and his American Independent Party. Ever since, the Democrats have faced the same dilemma: they are the natural home for minorities and the disadvantaged, but adopting policies to help these groups alienates their traditional supporters.

Together with the effective loss of the Southern white vote to Republicans at the presidential-election level and the decline in the Democratic voting industrial working class, these changes have made it very difficult for Democrats to win presidential elections. Democratic Presidents and candidates find it hard to commit themselves on the 'old style' issues. When they do – witness Walter Mondale in 1984 – they lose. Crucially, however, no social movement for change has emerged to take the Democrats' place. In other words no genuine re-alignment has taken place. Instead, what might be called *regime fragmentation* has occurred. The issues and policies that bound the New Deal coalition together have fragmented, leaving a picture of atomized policy networks rather than coherent alignments. We will return to the point later in our discussion of the Reagan administration. Managing Congress is clearly likely to be more problematical during a period of regime fragmenta- tion. Ticket splitting will more likely produce a Congress controlled by the opposition party. As serious, rallying the faithful around the party programme cannot occur when there is no party programme to which at least a majority of members subscribe. Hence Jimmy Carter achieved few major successes in Congress even though he enjoyed Democratic majorities in both Houses. Ronald Reagan won a brief but significant series of victories in early 1981, but this was not in any sense the equivalent of Roosevelt's New Deal triumphs or of Johnson's success with the Great Society.

Declining American foreign and economic power

From the Vietnam War onwards, US power overseas has been circum- scribed. The Manichean struggles of the Second World War and the cold war have been replaced by much more complex foreign policy scenarios where it has often been difficult to know what is and what is not in America's national interest. As a result, the political consensus on foreign policy has largely broken down. Presidents have been held to be partisan, self interested or have even acted illegally. Such was the case with

Vietnam, the invasion of Cambodia, the Iranian hostage rescue, the invasion of Grenada and the bombing of Libya. At a more general level, profound disagreements exist over US policy in Central America and the Middle East. Even when a President strives hard to present his foreign policy as 'in the interests of all the American people', he often fails. Such was certainly the case with Jimmy Carter.

A parallel problem exists in many areas of economic policy. As Lester Thurow observed some years ago, modern industrial economies increasingly resemble zero-sum societies (Thurow 1981), where the trade-offs in the distribution of income and other resources are not so much between antagonistic social classes, but between social groups – blacks and whites, old and young, men and women. When one group gains (for example, women) the other (men) must lose. Such cross-cutting forces fragment traditional party alignments.

Since the late 1960s this has been the very stuff of politics in America. Declining relative US economic power has aggravated the problem by limiting the total pool of resources available for distribution. By the mid-1980s a combination of large budget and trade deficit made it almost impossible for Presidents to re-order priorities without some constituents being seriously damaged. Programmes designed to redistribute resources across groups, classes or regions such as the New Deal and Great Society are simply not on the agenda. Changes can be wrought, as the Reagan 1981 budget and tax cuts show. But these were achieved at a cost – no short-term losers, but many long-term victims of budget deficits and recession (Chubb and Peterson 1989). In some other examples, such as energy policy during the 1970s, there were no apparent winners at all, only losers. Clearly it is difficult for a President to project himself as defender of the national interest if he is closely associated with such policies.

Ronald Reagan and the failure of the public-interest Presidency

Following the failures and foibles of the 1970s' Presidents, Ronald Reagan's success in 1980 was hailed by many as a return to business as usual. Certainly Reagan took on the mantle of the public-interest Presidency. His rhetoric was extravagant in support of new right agenda with the disengagement of the federal government from economy and society as its central objective. Yet the Reagan Presidencies failed to meet the conditions required of the public-interest Presidency for the following reasons.

Reagan did not emerge on the wave of an ideologically charged social movement intent on a coherent programme of social and economic change

What is true is that he benefited from the deep disenchantment with the

33

pessimism and indecisiveness of the Carter administration. Reagan offered to re-build American confidence at home and abroad. He also possessed considerable personal charisma and was able to exploit the public doubts about big government – and especially the federal government – which had been growing throughout the 1970s. Surveys show that on a range of issues the public did move to the right during these years. But the move was small and a shift back towards identification with liberal issues occurred during the early 1980s. Polls have, indeed, consistently shown a low level of support for these reforms most associated with the new right agenda. A 1983 *Los Angeles Times* poll found that just 5 per cent considered regulations 'too strict', but 42 per cent thought they were 'not strong enough' (Ferguson and Rogers 1986: 15). A similar pattern exists with respect to most of the conscience issues – abortion, school prayers, equal rights and affirmative action (Ferguson and Rogers 1986: 16–18).

As earlier noted, the Reagan personal electoral triumphs were not to be extended to other electoral areas. The Republicans won the Senate in 1980, but were to lose it just six years later. Nor did the Republicans ever win majorities in the House of Representatives or of the Governors' mansions.

Reagan's policies favoured business interests and the wealthy and penalized the poor

While this is true of the 1981 tax cuts and associated cuts in federal programmes, Reagan administration reforms were always presented in public interest terms. Tax and spending cuts would stimulate the economy and in the longer run everyone would benefit. As indicated, however, the Reagan programmes were consistently *perceived* as favouring some interests over others. On the social issue, he was obliged to dissociate himself from some of the more extreme members of his own administration such as James Watt and Ann Gorsuch. All the evidence suggests strong support for Reagan personally, rather than for his domestic policies. The evidence on foreign policy questions is somewhat more ambivalent. Public support for the Reagan stand against the Soviet Union during his first term was high. However, on Central America, public opinion remained divided – a fact reflected by the reluctance of Congress to vote aid for the Contras. Over the invasion of Grenada and the bombing of Libya, the public were at first divided, but later rallied behind the president – almost certainly because both actions were perceived as successful.

Reagan staffed his government on the basis of ideology and personal preference, rather than by utilizing party cues

Reagan was more determined to transform the federal government and rebuild it in his own image than any President since Roosevelt. The crucial differences was, of course, that Roosevelt was obliged to rely on a revitalized Democratic Party in this endeavour. Many of his appointees were significantly more radical than he would have preferred. He had no choice but to recruit them, however, in order to sustain the New Deal.

Reagan's appointees were essentially *personal* choices. Little in the way of a social movement for change existed. It was the *President's* agenda, not the *party's* that dominated. As far as the executive branch was concerned, the President was aided by the 1978 Civil Service Act which created a new stratum of officials known as the Senior Executive Service, a small percentage of whom could be political appointees, and all of whom could be transferred to new positions and given merit pay awards. These new powers were used selectively by the Office of Personnel Management. Reagan loyalists were rewarded through promotions and merit awards. Detractors and agnostics were passed over. This pattern even applied to whole departments with 'favoured' departments (State, Defense, Justice, Treasury) being rewarded and 'unpopular' departments (Housing and Urban Development, Health and Human Services, Education) penalized (NAPA 1985). The biases inherent in the Reagan personnel policies were sufficiently blatant to force the resignation of OMP Director Donald Devine following hearings into his renomination (Senate Committee on Governmental Affairs 1985).

Generally, Reagan's personnel policies resulted in a lowering of morale in a number of agencies and departments (Goldenberg 1985; Lynn 1986). But in some cases these management techniques resulted in real changes in policy. As Lynn concludes: 'on balance, the Reagan Administration has succeeded in enhancing the role of the careerist as a passive extension of the presidency' (Lynn 1985: 402).

Finally, the Reagan administrations applied a similar strategy to the judicial branch. Several of Reagan's Supreme Court nominees did, of course, receive a very rough passage in the Senate, but almost as important was what was going on at the District and Appeals Court levels. As Goldman has shown, Reagan nominated few blacks or liberals to the District Courts (Goldman 1985). A similar analysis for the Appeals Courts shows that up to 1986 90.4 per cent of the Reagan nominees were categorized as conservative. None was considered liberal (McKay 1989, Table 7.2). Significantly, the Reagan judicial strategy was, in his first term at least, orchestrated directly from the White House. A special Committee on Federal Judicial Selection, chaired by Ed Meese, was created in the White House, effectively to take over the job of selection which had previously resided in the Deputy Attorney General's office (Goldman 1985).

Reagan employed a confrontational style when dealing with Congress and the bureaucracy

Prior to the Nixon years, Presidents rarely confronted Congress. Instead, bargaining and persuasion were the order of the day. Recourse to constitutional powers such as the veto were considered evidence of failure (Neustadt 1980). Congress was often at odds with Presidents, but state and local parties were too important in the nomination process and when providing cues for the distribution of presidential patronage, for Presidents to adopt an openly confrontational stance. Starting with Nixon and reaching a peak with Reagan, confrontation has gradually supplemented bargaining as a presidential strategy. Two weapons have been employed – the public and the veto.

As Kernell has observed: 'No president has enlisted public strategies to better advantage than has Ronald Reagan' (Kernell 1986: 4). This has involved frequent public addresses and appeals to the mass of the American population for support over such issues as the 1981 and 1982 budget cuts, the invasion of Grenada, the bombing of Libya, support for the Contras in Central America and Supreme Court nominations. At first, Reagan's appeals were interpreted as an attempt to maintain a climate of opinion rather than a way to confront political opponents. So Anthony King noted in 1983 that 'Reagan was not appealing to the people *against* Congress. Rather, he was trying to keep in existence that mood, that atmosphere, that climate of opinion which had won him the election' (King 1983: 211). In his later addresses, however, his style was much more confrontational and he was clearly using the public weapon as an alternative to bargaining. In both foreign and domestic policy the ideological content of his public appeals was high. Increasingly he encouraged an 'us versus them' environment where the forces of reason and morality (the administration) were pitched against the morally corrupt and misguided (the opposition). Such an approach is the very antithesis of bargaining with its implicit deals, compromises and trade offs. Interestingly, Reagan avoided those public confrontations – most notably press conferences – that do provide an opportunity for argument or the expression of opposing opinions.

Nothing better illustrated Reagan's confrontational style than his use of the veto. Even when the Republicans controlled the Senate (until 1986) he invoked the veto sanction on forty-nine occasions. This represents 8.2 vetoes per year in office, more than any recent President with the exception of the embattled Gerald Ford, who signed 24.4 vetoes per year in office (McKay 1989: Table 2). More significant, perhaps, is the eventual fate of the Reagan vetoes compared with those of his predecessors. Congress attempted to override ten Reagan vetoes and in no less than six cases the overrides were successful – the highest for any modern President (McKay 1989: Table 2). Revealingly, the average majority voting against Reagan in the Republican Senate was actually higher than the average majorities voting against Nixon and Ford, both of whom faced solidly Democratic Senates. (McKay 1989: Table 4). Moreover, Reagan has tended to veto more major bills than his predecessors and a number of these have involved appropriations and foreign policy-areas which almost never attracted the veto power prior to 1970 (McKay 1989: Table 5).

It should be emphasized that both the increased use of the veto and direct appeals to the public are trends in presidential power which have been in motion since at least 1968. The same is true of the tendency for modern Presidencies to downplay or undermine the influence of state and local parties and, in the case of Carter and Reagan at least, to strengthen national parties. In Reagan's case this took the form of an attempt to inject a high degree of ideological unity into the national Republican Party. Again, this is a long way from the sort of brokerage politics typical of presidential state/local party interaction in an earlier era. Then, the aim was to establish compromises between ideological and regional groupings. In Reagan's case the objective was to provide a united front against ideological opponents.

Richard Nixon was the first President to consider the federal bureaucracy as an 'enemy' staffed by liberals and 'do-gooders', but he was unable to transform bureaucratic values and practices (Nathan 1975). Ronald Reagan had more success in part because he had more time, but mainly because he was well organized and determined to imprint his ideological agenda on the federal administration. Use of the appointment power to further this objective has already been noted, but this was just part of a general centralization of managerial power in the White House.

Almost certainly the most dramatic example of the centralization of power involved the elevation of OMB to the position of rule-making gatekeeper for the whole of the executive branch. President Carter's wonderfully named Paperwork Reduction Act of 1980, which was designed to improve public access to government information, had created an Office of Information and Regulatory Affairs (OIRA) within OMB. One Senate committee concluded that OIRA had been used more as a means of restricting the dissemination of information than as a means to simplify public access to information (US Senate, Committee on Governmental Affairs 1986).

Related was the use of two executive orders, EO 12991 and EO

37

12498, to allow OMB to screen agency and departmental rules, including the framing of new legislation. Considerable evidence exists to suggest that these powers were used in a highly selective way. Those agencies responsible for implementing the Reagan agenda in social and economic policy were subject to a restrictive rule-making regime, while the Departments of Defense and Justice, whose officials were more loyal to the Reagan agenda, were given a freer reign. In many instances this was translated into a weaker enforcement of environmental, civil rights and occupational safety and health regulations (Senate Committee on Governmental Affairs, Subcommittee on Oversight and Investigations, Report and Hearings, 1985: OMB Watch 1986). OMB was used, therefore, not only to monitor and control public spending for all the departments and agencies, but also to control agency enforcement and rule-making powers.

The Reagan Presidency and the public interests: some conclusions

Ronald Reagan left public office on a high note. His public opinion ratings were favourable and, the budget deficit and Iran Contra affair notwithstanding, the general consensus was that his had been a successful Presidency. Reagan supporters would point to economic recovery and America's partially restored status in world affairs as evidence of a return to the public-interest Presidency. As earlier demonstrated, however, such a claim is hard to sustain. Reagan may have achieved a degree of personal popularity – he was dubbed 'the Great Communicator' with good cause. But the institution of the Presidency was not returned to its former status as a result of the Reagan experience. On the contrary, the American political system moved further away from meeting the criteria of the public interest Presidency. The new right did not constitute a national social movement equivalent to the New Deal. It failed to mobilize opinion through a dominant political party and relied instead on the charismatic appeal of a single national leader. Public support for much of the Reagan agenda was lukewarm at best. And the President's efforts to centralize power in the White House were more a reflection of personal ideological preferences than of anything resembling the implementation of an electoral mandate. Evidence in support of the view that the Reagan administration favoured special interests is substantial (McKay 1989). To repeat the point, the concept of the public interest is relative rather than absolute. All administrations favour some interests over others. But prior to the mid-1960s Democratic Presidents received mandates from the electorate for major societal changes. Such mandates are untenable in today's fragmented polity. As a result, modern chief executives have aptly been labelled *personal* Presidents, rather than party or public interest Presidents (Lowi 1985). Paradoxically they can be both popular and tendentious in their policy priorities in this role. This is particularly true if policy changes operate through the judiciary or via the administrative machinery of government. The public cannot easily relate the results directly to the person of the President. Put another way, Reagan's policies were often unpopular, but he was not. And when public approval of Reagan did decline, it was either because he *was* seen as personally culpable (the Iran-Contra affair) or because of economic recession (1981/82) which the public generally always blames on incumbent administrations.

Given the structural changes in the national and international environment – most notably the decline of political parties and of US world power – no new President whatever his ideological proclivities will find it easy to be seen as a champion of the public interest.

Presidents with a strong charismatic appeal facing weak opponents (Reagan) are likely to be able to make clear policy commitments without incurring electoral sanctions. Less appealing Presidents (Bush) will find it more difficult to order priorities for fear of the electoral consequences. Whatever the appeal of the incumbent, Presidents can always change some aspects of public policy if they want to. Their executive and command powers are sufficient for this. What they cannot do is return to the era of the public-interest Presidency when both nationally and internationally American chief executives were regarded as the embodiment of general rather than particular interests.

References

Barry, B. (1972) 'The use and abuse of the public interest', in Carl Friedrich (ed.) *Nomos V: The Public Interest*, New York: Atherton.

Bell, D. (1960) *The End of Ideology*, New York: Free Press.

Chambers, M.N., and Burnham D. (1975) *The American Party Systems: Shapes of Political Development*, New York: Oxford University Press.

Ferguson, T. and Rogers, J. (1986) *Right Turn: The Decline of the Democrats and the Future of American Politics*, New York: Hill and Warey.

Goldenberg, E.N. (1984) 'The permanent government in an era of retrenchment and redirection', in L.M. Salamon and M.S. Lund (eds) *The Reagan Presidency and the Governing of America*, Washington DC: Urban Institute.

Goldman, S. (1985) 'Reorganizing the Judiciary': the first team appointments', *Judicature* 68: 313–29.

Greenstein, F. (1982) *The Hidden Hand Presidency: Eisenhower as Leader*, New York: Basic Books.

Kernell, S. (1986) *Going Public: New Strategies of Presidential Leadership* Washington DC: Congressional Quarterly Press.

King, A. (1983) *Both Ends of the Avenue*, Washington DC: American Enterprise Institute.

Leuchtenburg, W.E. (1963) *FDR and the New Deal 1932-1940* New York: Harper Torchbooks.

Lowi, T. (1985) *The Personal Presidency: Power Invested, Promise Unfulfilled*, Ithaca and London: Cornell University Press.

Lynn, L.E. Jr. (1985) 'The Reagan Adminstration and the Renitent bureaucracy', in L.M. Salamon and M.S. Lund (eds) *The Reagan Presidency and the Governing of America*, Washington DC: Urban Institute.

McKay, D. (1989) 'Presidential strategy and the veto power', *Political Science Quarterly*, Fall.

—— (1989) *Domestic Policy and Ideology: Presidents and the American State 1964-1987* Cambridge: Cambridge University Press.

Nathan, R.P. (1975) *The Plot that Failed: Nixon and the Administrative Presidency*, New York: Wiley.

Neustadt, R.E. (1980) *Presidential Power: The Politics of Leadership from FDR to Carter*, New York: Wiley.

Owens, J.E. (1986) 'The regulation of financial institutions and services in the United States: from regulation to de-regulation', in Andrew Cox (ed.) *The State, Finance and Industry*, Brighton: Harvester.

National Academy of Public Administration (NAPA) (1985) *Final Report of the Presidential Appointee Project*, Washington DC: NAPA.

OMB Watch (1986) *Regulatory Review: OMB's New Public Disclosure Rules*, Washington DC: OMB Watch.

Peterson, P.E. and Chubb, J.E. (1989) *Can the Government Govern?*, Washington DC: Brookings.

Reichley, A.J. (1987) *Elections American Style*, Washington DC: Brookings.

Rossiter C. (1960) *The American Presidency*, New York: Harcourt, Brace.

Schlesinger, A.M. Jr. (1958) *The Age of Roosevelt Vol. II The Coming of the New Deal*, Boston: Houghton Mifflin.

—— (1965) *A Thousand Days: John F. Kennedy in the White House*, London: Deutsch.

Terkel, S. (1985) *The Good War*, London: Hamilton.

Thurow, L. (1981) *The Zero Sum Society*, Harmondsworth, Middlesex: Penguin.

US House of Representatives (1985 and 1986) 'Hearings before the Sub-Committee on Oversight and Investigation, Energy and Commerce Committee', *OMB Review of EPA Regulations*, Washington DC: US Government Printing Office.

US Senate (1986) 'Committee on Governmental Affairs', *Office of Management and Budget: Evolving Roles and Future Issues*, Washington: Government Printing Office: 185-256.

US Senate (1986) 'Sub comittee on Intergovernmental Affairs', *Testimony of James Miller*, Washington: Government Printing Office.

Chapter four

The 'no-win Presidency' and contemporary presidential-congressional relationships

Joseph Hogan

During the 1960s and the 1970s many politicians, political commentators and political scientists, as well as current and former White House aides and even Presidents joined ranks to argue that it had become increasingly difficult for the President and his men to bring effective legislative leadership to the American political system. Paralysis in government and rudderless government were feared by these critics of the contemporary American polity as following on from the President's inability to exercise leadership over Congress. The purpose of this chapter is to first define the sources and nature of the new constraints on what one political scientist has styled somewhat dramatically the 'no-win Presidency' (Light 1982). The second section will assess the 'no-win Presidency' thesis, which will also include an examination of what Presidents and their staffs might profitably do to bring leadership to the contemporary American polity. This section will entail an examination of the record of President Reagan's administrations to assess whether the contemporary Presidency can exercise legislative leadership.

The 'no-win Presidency' thesis

The 'modern Presidency' is dated from the inauguration of Franklin Delano Roosevelt in March 1933 and is distinguished from the so-called traditional Presidencies by an expectation amongst the electorate that because the President is the only politician elected by the entire nation he is the chief law-maker. This means that the President and his staff are expected to give the highest priority to developing an agenda of legislation for tackling what the occupant of the Oval Office regards as the key problems affecting the nation. The President and his men are further expected to impose this agenda upon the legislative calendar of Congress and pursue these proposals until they are enacted into laws. Thus, to be perceived as an effective leader, a modern President must be the driving force within the legislative system. Modern Presidents are consequently judged according to their success in persuading

Congress to enact their legislative agendas. Furthermore, this criterion is said to hold true for all Presidents, irrespective of their party and their political ideology. Individual presidents – and defeated candidates for the White House – in the post-Roosevelt era have deliberately encouraged and enlarged the public's expectations of presidential legislative leadership by claiming on the campaign trail that if only they were put in the Oval Office they would be able to pass laws to resolve the nation's problems (Greenstein 1978; Polsby 1983; Wayne 1978).

The critics of presidential governance readily agree that the institution of the Presidency itself and the structure of the federal policy process have remained fairly stable since the 1930s. They attribute the recent problems confronting presidential leadership to some fundamental developments during the 1960s and the 1970s in the President's immediate political environment. These major changes established constraints on presidential leadership which, as Eric Davis argues, 'would reduce any President's influence over Congress, whatever the circumstances of the moment' (Davis 1981: 104). The major changes identified include a reassertion by Congress of its powers that also involved the passage of statutes designed to curb the political and legal authority of the President in domestic and foreign policy-making, a series of internal reforms affecting the organization of power and decision making on Capitol Hill, and a range of developments in the larger political environment which concerned what Anthony King has described as America's 'extra-constitutional political institutions – the political parties, the electorate, and interest and issue groups' (King 1978: 374). It was argued that when taken together these new political developments had made it more difficult for what many in the late 1970s called an 'imperilled presidency' to bring coherent policy leadership and hence central direction to the federal government. Each of the above developments in the president's political environment will next be elaborated to indicate their respective contributions to the 'no-win Presidency' thesis.

The resurgence of Congress

With the advent in the 1930s of the modern Presidency the balance of power between the White House and Capitol Hill was tilted in favour of the chief executive. The following thirty years saw a steady if not continuous accumulation in the politicial authority of the Presidency, mainly in order to assist the President in undertaking his tasks as the chief law-maker. This accretion of power was supported enthusiastically by the American public, accepted by the federal courts – especially once Franklin Delano Roosevelt had abandoned his proposals to 'reform' (domesticate?) the Supreme Court – and was grudgingly admitted by Congress in order to bring central leadership to the modern American political system. Then a series of presidential misjudgements, most notably President Johnson's waging of undeclared war in Vietnam and President Nixon's involvement in the scandals of Watergate, led in the 1970s to pressures from the American public for Congress to reassert its authority. Large segments of the public and many members of Congress – especially Democrats in Nixon's Washington – moved to restore what they believed was the proper constitutional balance between the executive and the legislative branches of the federal government. These Congressmen felt that the Presidency had usurped legislative powers, and that the Congress had failed in its constitutional role as a check on the Presidency. Many members of the public and Congress wanted the legislature 'to become a more coequal branch of government, more assertive, more alert, more jealous of its own powers' (Cronin 1980: 190). This sentiment was reflected in a number of legislative initiatives taken by Congress to recover lost authority and discover new ways to participate more fully in national policy-making.

To redress the balance of power over war-making and foreign affairs, the legislature passed three main measures. Congress in 1973 passed the War Powers Resolution over the veto of President Nixon. This law declared that henceforth the President can only commit the armed forces of the United States pursuant to a declaration of war by Congress, or by specific statutory authorization, or in a national emergency created by an attack on the United States or its armed forces. After committing the armed forces under the third condition, the President is to report immediately to Congress; and within sixty days unless Congress has declared war, the troop commitment is to be terminated, with the proviso that the President is allowed another thirty days if he certifies there is unavoidable military necessity for such a delay. Ninety days having elapsed, the resolution permits Congress, by a procedure – both houses approving a concurrent resolution – that is not subject to presidential veto to disengage the troops. The measure is thus designed to prevent a sustained and unilateral engagement of the armed forces of the United States by the President. The National Emergencies Act of 1976 also terminated as of September 1978 the extensive powers and authorities possessed by the President as a result of the continuous state of emergency the nation had been in since the mid-1930s. It also established authority for the declaration of future emergencies in a manner that clearly define the powers of the President and provide for regular congressional review. The intent behind this statute is to prevent presidential reliance in non-crisis situations on powers intended for crisis situations. The Case Act on executive agreements of 1972, named after one of its major sponsors New Jersey Republican Clifford P. Case requires the Secretary of State to submit to the Senate within sixty days the final text of any international agreement made by executive agreement. The purpose behind this legislation is to restrict presidential dependence upon diplomacy by executive agreement.

In terms of domestic policy-making, Congress enacted in 1974 the Budget and Impoundment Control Act. This legislation sought to recapture the 'power of the purse' by establishing a new set of budget procedures to increase congressional participation in fiscal policy-making. The impoundment provisions of the legislation were designed to enforce congressional decisions to fund public policies upon the executive branch. In addition, Congress has increasingly utilized the so-called congressional veto as an instrument of policy making. The legislative veto is designed to ensure that the President and federal bureaucrats issue regulations (delegated legislation) that conform to laws passed by Congress. The veto gives Congress, depending upon the particular details written into a statute, the authority to disapprove a measure by vetoing it or to approve it by affirmative action within a specified period, normally sixty or ninety days. Such provisions have been incorporated into many laws including, for example, the Budget and Impoundment Control Act of 1974, and the Trade Act of 1974. At the same time, other steps were taken to increase the capacity of Congress to make public policy. This can readily be seen in the great growth of specialist information services on Capitol Hill, including the establishment of Congress' own 'think-tank' in the form of the Congressional Research Service and the Government Accounting Office. These specialist staff services enable Congress to better counter-analyse presidential policy proposals and develop alternative measures. The staffs of congressmen also doubled between the early 1960s and 1977, thereby giving individual members greater capacity both to analyse policies and to develop their own policy initiatives (Sundquist 1981).

The reform of Congress

Until the 1970s, Congress was governed by a series of formal and informal rules and sanctions which endorsed seniority as the basis for organizing and distributing legislative power. These rules allocated committee chairmanships to the most senior members, and protected them from removal by their colleagues. The chairmen enjoyed a near-monopoly over committee resources, especially staffing; the rules further provided chairmen with much influence on the floor of their chamber regarding matters within the jurisdiction of their committee. In effect, Congress over-rewarded seniority, making for government by oligarchs. Congressional elections between 1970 and 1974 brought into both houses newly elected members who were dissatisfied with the way that Congress was organized, especially the House of Representatives. These freshmen sought to reorganize the distribution of power within the House to diminish the power of seniority. They formed a group of over seventy-five members and worked through the House Democratic Caucus.

Between 1970 and 1975, seniority was toppled as the sole criterion for selecting committee chairmen because of changes made to the procedures of the House Democratic caucus for appointing chairmen. In effect, all caucus members now choose committee chairmen rather than a handful of oligarchs. The chairmen's power to structure their subcommittees, pick the members of their committees and nominate the chairman of their subcommittees was removed. Subcommittees were increasingly given independent status and authority, with their chairmen now being selected by all members of the House Democratic caucus. The caucus now limits subcommittee chairmenships to one per person, which reduced the authority of seniority and greatly dispersed power within the legislature; it is now the case that there are freshmen chairing a number of subcommittees. At the same time, subcommittee chairmen now control their own staffs. These changes – which have been styled as a 'subcommittee bill of rights' – have expanded reliance upon sub-committees in conducting the work of Congress. In turn, there has been a consequent expansion in the number of subcommittees from 130 in 1945 to 267 in 1977, which further indicates the dispersal of legislative authority (Mann and Ornstein 1981).

Prior to the 1970s, the work of Congress – which takes place mostly in its committees – was conducted largely behind closed doors. Committee markups on bills were conducted in secrecy. This enabled congressional oligarchs to control decisions through their authority over their committee's membership and resources. After 1973, nearly all committee markups were conducted in public. At the same time, the House moved via the Legislative Reorganization of 1970 to recorded teller votes on the floor of the House. This meant that a legislator's vote was public and thus known to his constituents. The move made members more accountable to outside interests, and further reduced the authority of seniority. Most of these reforms took place first in the House, but were quite quickly adopted by the Senate. In overall terms, the reforms changed the formal rules and the mores of Congress. The authority of oligarchs was greatly reduced, while junior members became more assertive and influential in the legislative process. This greater dispersal of power was also accompanied by measures that opened the deliberations of Congress to greater public scrutiny and participation in the legislative process, which made Congress a more porous as well as a more decentralized legislature (Dodd and Oppenheimer 1977).

The political environment

Relationships between the White House and Congress were much affected by some new developments and the acceleration of existing trends in the larger political environment. These changes especially influenced the behaviour of the political parties, the electorate and interest groups. During the 1960s and 1970s, America's political parties continued to atrophy as electoral organizations. Presidential candidates are now self-elected and self-financed rather than chosen by party machines and party bosses. This development represented little more than an acceleration of trends long since noted. What was new was that these same developments were now heavily affecting the roles parties played in congressional and state elections. The Vietnam and Watergate eras coincided with the rise of new types of political activists who were less tied than before to party organizations, leading in the 1970s to many congressional candidates who are also self-elected and self-financed. At the same time, party identification rates amongst the electorate continued to decline. Voters increasingly voted a split ticket, especially when choosing presidential and congressional candidates. More and more members of the public declined to vote, which further undermined both the roles of parties as electoral organizations and public confidence in American government (Ranney 1978).

An important development of the 1960s and 1970s concerned the growing convergence of interest groups on Washington. The anti-Vietnam movement fostered the growth in the 1960s and 1970s of interest groups that claimed to represent the public in the areas such as consumer protection, environmental regulation and general governmental reform. The social policy programmes established by the 'Great Society' initiatives further promoted the establishment in Washington of a seemingly ever-expanding number of groups advocating increased expenditure on welfare programmes. Other forms of interest group converged on Washington. As a result, whereas there were 365 lobbyists registered with Congress in 1961, a total of 23,011 were registered with the secretary of the Senate in mid-1987. Over the same period, the number of lawyers – who staff and direct most interest groups – increased from 12,564 members of the District of Columbia Bar Association to 46,000. America's corporations also discovered benefits lay in moving to the capital. Back in 1968 only 100 corporations had offices in Washington, whereas one business directory listed over 1,300 corporations in 1986. By the early 1980s, Washington had surpassed New York as the trade association capital of America and is now far ahead. By 1986, it had 3,500 trade associations' headquarters, more than triple the number in 1960 (Smith 1988).

The decentralization, democratization and staff growth in Congress also promoted the creation and growth of these and other interest groups. These groups were attracted to the capital because they benefit or seek to benefit from public policies and are concerned to protect and promote their policy and material interests. The convergence of interest groups on Washington has been styled as the 'new political mobilization' by Hugh Heclo because it represents a practice adopted by all sectors of American society (Heclo 1983: 36). These interest goups are increasingly professionalized, staffed and promoted by specialists; they often enjoy strong financial support and voting power, and have thus been able to participate on an increasingly influential basis in law making.

The proponents of the 'no-win Presidency' thesis claim that these separate political developments have combined to make it more difficult for the President to exert leadership over Congress. The dispersal of power within Congress means that the President can rely no more upon the support of a handful of party leaders to progess his agenda, but must now find time to court more but individually less influential members. As Anthony King has put it, 'The powerful few have become the considerably less powerful many' (King 1978: 374). The dispersion of power led to a more complex legislative process, one that makes it harder for the White House to steer legislation through Congress. The steps taken by Congress to become more autonomous of the President and more self-contained in domestic and foreign policy making means that the President must now compete for influence over the congressional calendar, and further limits his capacity to meet the demands of presidential leadership. The continued atrophy of party organizations is said to have deprived the President of one potential source of support in dealing with Congress. The convergence of interest groups on Washington has also impeded presidential leadership because they are so numerous and particularized that they serve as 'grand complicators' (Heclo 1983: 38) to the President's attempt to simplify complex policy issues in order to build support for his agenda.

These changes are said by Anthony King to have produced a 'new' American political system, one in which 'fewer and fewer cohesive blocks are to be found in the American polity'. Anthony King claims this has led to the 'atomization' of politics in that the 'materials out of which coalitions might be built simply do not exist. Building coalitions in the United States today is like trying to build coalitions out of sand. It simply cannot be done' (King 1978: 390–1). In broad agreement with this analysis, Hugh Heclo argues that these changes have led to an 'institutional estrangement' between the President and Congress, the bureaucracy and the courts. This estrangement is evident in a 'more impersonal atmosphere, more points for possible misunderstanding and frictions in relations among governmental institutions. They add up to a fragmentation of an already disjointed government community in Washington' (Heclo 1983: 42). It is said that these various developments have made it more difficult for the President both to build a coalition of support for his agenda and to exercise leadership over a more assertive Congress, hence the 'no-win Presidency' thesis.

Assessing the 'no-win Presidency' thesis

Like all interpretations of recent developments, the 'imperilled Presidency' thesis is subject to criticism. One key shortcoming is that the Constitution of the United States established a political system that is founded on a separation of executive, legislative and judicial powers and a related system of checks and balances in order to prevent a concentration of power in one branch of government. The political system that the Founding Fathers created is thus one of separated institutions sharing powers rather than one based upon presidential governance. Indeed, in terms of the formal distribution of powers, the Constitution specifically limits the President to two forms of legislative activity. These 'express' powers give the the President the right to recommend to Congress such measures 'as he shall judge necessary and expedient' and the power to veto a bill passed by Congress. The President further shares with the Senate the power to make treaties, which the Constitution states is part of 'the supreme law of the land'. Superimposed upon these express constitutional powers are other legislative powers either implied in the Constitution or developed by custom. These powers include grants of authority to make delegated legislation, regulations, proclamations and executive orders (Fisher 1987: 25). This listing indicates that the Constitution provides the President with legislative powers that are distinctly limited. As Richard Hodder-Williams notes:

> The President can raise no money; he can declare no war or edicts which are binding upon the people of the United States. These are the prerogatives of Congress. The Senate holds an absolute veto over the President's treaty-making and appointing powers, while the President's veto over congressional legislation can be overridden. (Hodder-Williams 1987: 11)

The framers of the Constitution deliberately devoted Article I to the legislature and relegated the executive to Article II to symbolize their belief that political authority, in fact the power to determine national policy, should be located primarily in the legislature. The framers of the Constitution did not regard the President as the chief legislator. This leads Larry Berman to observe that, 'Today's president must operate within the framework of an eighteenth-century document designed to *prevent* presidential primacy and success' (Berman 1987: 2).

The 'imperilled Presidency' thesis can further be criticized for overestimating the constraining force of Presidency-curbing legislation. In this regard, Thomas Cronin warned in 1980 that, 'It is one thing to enact new curbs, it is another to put them into practice and enforce them rigorously' (Cronin 1980: 196). Since the passage of the War Powers Resolution, Presidents have committed troops in situations where lives have been lost. President Ford responded to the Cambodian seizure of the United States container ship *Mayaguez* in 1975 by directing marines to rescue the ship and its crew, which led to the death of forty-one Americans. On 25 October 1983 President Reagan sent United States troops to attack a military force on the island of Grenada, leading to the death of eighteen soldiers. In both cases the President was not constrained by the reporting requirements of the War Powers Resolution, and the engagements were perceived as brave and successful actions, which increased the popularity of the President. The use of concurrent resolutions and other forms of legislative vetoes were ruled unconstitutional by the Supreme Court in *Immigration and Naturalization Service v. Chadha* in 1983, which thus makes inoperative the only action-forcing mechanism of the War Powers Resolution and other types of legislative veto (Hodder-Williams 1987).

Aside from these criticisms, the thesis aptly notes that the interplay of political forces has recently tilted the balance of political power away from the modern President. Changes within and outside Congress have led to a new equilibrium between the White House and Capitol Hill. These changes have stressed the separateness rather than the sharing of power between the President and Congress; divided government thus confronts and impedes the rather exaggerated expectations American citizens hold for their Presidents. This disparity has promoted many analysts and practitioners of American government to conclude that only significant constitutional reform can enable the President to meet the high demands of presidential governance. Proposed reforms include establishing a six-year presidential term and related measures to increase the President's control over the legislature and with it his capacity to provide central leadership to the separated institutions of American government (Sundquist 1986). However, as President Reagan's perennial and failed campaigns to obtain a line-item veto and to amend the Constitution to require a balanced budget indicates, there is little likelihood of achieving such reforms. Furthermore, the thrust of much of these proposals is to superimpose upon the federal government something like a parliamentary-style regime that fuses central executive and legislative authority; pursuing such radical change is tantamount to consciously steering into a dead-end street when searching for the open road.

Given the limited prospects for reforming the Constitution, what can the President and his men do to impart central legislative leadership to contemporary Washington? Despite recent political developments, it must be remembered that the President is not feeble. He possesses important resources in the political and policy staffs of the White House, supplemented by the work of his political appointees in the executive branch.

The public look to the President for leadership, which can also be harnessed as a support. To convert this potential into actual support the President and his men should concentrate on improving their statecraft. This requires adopting skilful leadership in managing relations with Capitol Hill, in seeking to persuade members to support the President's legislative initiatives (Bowles 1987). The White House should benefit from the experience of recent administrations and recognize that developments outside and within Congress provide new opportunities for presidential legislative leadership. As Hugh Heclo observes, in today's Washington 'there are considerable advantages for presidents and their staff to exploit. As policy agendas collide, as new groups mobilize, and as governmental institutions drift apart, there are new ways of pulling things together in the executive branch' (Heclo 1983: 142). In the past, Presidents complained that, 'the *centralization* of power in Congress made it impossible to get bills past uncooperative committee heads:' (Fisher 1987: 61). The White House should therefore take advantage of the permeability of the reformed, open Congress to progress its agenda. In sum, contemporary Washington offers new opportunities for presidential leadership, which requires new sensitivities and creative leadership allied to traditional political skills.

Studies of the Ford and Carter Presidencies concur that to capitalize upon these new opportunities the White House should develop a comprehensive and co-ordinated legislative strategy (Cronin 1981; Davis 1981; Heinemann and Hessler 1980; Light 1982). This should include adopting a strategic approach to determining and managing the President's legislative agenda; only a few legislative initiatives should be adopted, which means that they must be tightly prioritized. Second, the President should adopt a professional approach to legislative liaison, appointing persons who are experienced 'insiders', wise in the ways of contemporary Washington, to his White House unit for courting Congress. Finally, these priorities should be subjected to centralized management by the White House; administrative coherence and centralism should be pursued to counter fragmentation in the political environment and on Capitol Hill. Each component will next be elaborated. The success and failures of President Reagan's administrations on each count will also be established. The record demonstrates that the President enjoyed much more success during his first than in his second term. The overall experience of the Reagan administration in liaising with Congress further suggests certain lessons for future administrations in liaising with Capitol Hill.

Strategic agenda management

In planning during the transition period their approach to conducting relations with Congress, Ronald Reagan's advisers were much influenced by Jimmy Carter's failure to exploit the favourable opportunities that exist for presidential legislative leadership during the first few months of a new administration. During these early months in office the President enjoys a 'political honeymoon' with Capitol Hill because the legislature has yet to set its own agenda and priorities and is therefore receptive to presidential leadership. An empirical study conducted by Paul Light of the fortunes of the presidential agendas of Presidents Kennedy through to Carter found that, in overall terms, they obtained passage of 72 per cent of agenda requests sent to Congress between January and March of their first year in office; the success rates for items introduced in April and June drops to 39 per cent and falls to 25 per cent for items introduced in the second half of the first year (Light 1982, 45). The Carter administration failed to set its agenda early and thus exploit the opportunities available in the honeymoon period. The administration further failed to prioritize its agenda, and then sent too many initiatives to Capitol Hill, which overloaded Congress and destined the President's initial agenda to failure. Jimmy Carter thus gained a reputation as an ineffective leader at the start of his Presidency which, despite subsequent successes, endured in the minds of American voters (Cronin 1980).

The first Reagan administration resolved to move boldly in its early days to capitalize upon its honeymoon period and other opportunities for presidential leadership. In the 1980 elections, Ronald Reagan had obtained a solid 9.7 per cent margin over Jimmy Carter in the presidential election, and the congressional races had given the Republicans control of the Senate for the first time since 1954 and had narrowed the Democrats' 'Watergate Majority' in the House to only fifty-one seats. Polling analyses reveal that these favourable results did not represent either powerful presidential coattails at work or an embrace of 'Reaganism'. But there was quite a widespread perception of a presidential landslide and an ideological sea change in America, and Reagan's advisers sought to build upon this sense of impending change by moving quickly and boldly (Pfiffner 1983).

To avoid 'Carterism' and to make the most use of favourable political opportunities, Reagan's advisers adopted a strategic approach to liaising with Capitol Hill. They resolved to send Congress a few, highly prioritized legislative proposals as quickly as possible. It was decided early during the transition period to limit this agenda exclusively to economic proposals, which comprised a radical economic proposal to cut federal taxes, slash domestic spending and accelerate defence spending. The narrow focus was consistent with candidate Reagan's campaign charges that the federal government was, because of its 'excessive' taxes and domestic expenditures, responsible for the country's economic problems, and his claim that America's defences were vulnerable. Other campaign issues were put aside to avoid distracting attention from Reagan's bold economic initiatives. Working at double-quick pace, the new administration delivered its economic agenda to Congress within only forty-nine days of taking office, which permitted the administration to take full advantage of its opportunity to set the early legislative agenda of the ninety-seventh Congress. The President's initial legislative agenda was folded into his first budget submission, which thus enabled the administration to utilize the action-forcing process in the federal government to pursue hundreds of across-the-board economic policy changes. As a result, Reagan's narrow agenda was one that was also far-reaching in its scope. The administration's simplified agenda also made Reagan's priorities easily comprehensible to the public and thus much facilitated the building of support outside and within Congress.

The administration decided to make strategic use of a split Congress to put the President's economic agenda on a 'fast track'. This entailed using Republican control of the Senate speedily to pass the President's legislative initiatives. Gaining control of the Senate enabled the adminis-tration to place its legislative agenda at the top of the congressional calendar. It also enabled the administration to concentrate its resources upon lobbying the Democratic-controlled House of Representatives. The administration also evolved a strategy for lobbying the House. Reagan's advisers knew that they only had to maintain unity among the House Republicans and attract support from just twenty-six Democrats to gain control of the House. The President's strategists targeted the forty-seven members of the Conservative Democratic Forum as the most promising source of support; in effect, the administration sought to resurrect the conservative coalition in the House. Showing good strategy, they further decided to put this coalition sparingly to the test.

The administration's game-plan divided the President's legislative agenda into three legislative components that were carefully spaced apart both to sustain control of the congressional calendar and buy time to lobby the House. The first component was moved forward when the Senate in early April passed a first congressional budget resolution – which sets the spending and taxing priorities for the federal budget – that endorsed Reagan's economic policies. The President's first legislative victory came on 7 May 1981, when the House approved a budget resolution that had Reagan's backing. The House Democrats had proposed a resolution which departed significantly from Reagan's economic blueprint. The administra-tion took the bold decision to challenge the resolution on the floor by presenting a substitute resolution – known as Gramm-Latta I – which had been worked out with the leaders of the House Republicans and the Con-servative Democratic Forum. The substitute measure was supported by a 'blitz lobby' of Capitol Hill that involved an orchestrated and dramatic courting of Congress. This lobby persuaded sixty Democrats to join ranks with 190 Republicans and thus gain control of the House.

The second victory came in mid-summer when the House voted to implement a package of spending cuts that had the support of the White House. The plan to retrench domestic spending involved rewriting hundreds of past laws to mandate lower spending levels. This beckoned predictable opposition from the committees which had advocated the initial spending levels and their client interest groups. To circumvent this opposition the White House utilized the reconciliation process of the still-evolving congressional budget process. This enabled the administration to package all the spending cuts into one omnibus bill. Reagan's strategists reasoned that they then only had to sustain the bill with one successful vote to reorder federal spending priorities. Once more, the Senate led the way, again providing motor-force to the administration's agenda. The House Democrats again revised Reagan's spending policies, but this time they sought to protect their handiwork by bringing it to the floor on a rule that required the bill to be voted in six sections, which meant putting the conservative coalition under great pressure. The strategy failed because the administration successfully challenged the Democrats for control of the House. The administration managed by 217 to 210 votes to overturn the Democrats' rule and substitute their own bill – Gramm-Latta II – which was to be voted on in its entirety in one vote; it was then voted on and passed, thereby enacting hundreds of changes in federal spending.

The third victory came in late July when the House approved a bill to cut federal taxes that Reagan supported. The administration had sensibly reasoned that the tax cuts – Reagan proposed, for example, to cut federal taxes on individuals by 30 per cent over three years – would be popular with the public and congressmen, and had decided to reserve the measure to third place as an inducement to members to vote for – in terms of political pain – the more demanding proposal to retrench domestic spending. Again the Senate led the way. Once more there was a struggle between the Democrats and the administration in the House. This time the administration won because it offered more concessions to waverers, thereby obtaining the support of forty-eight Democrats, who voted with 190 Republicans to enact the Economic Recovery Tax Act.

The administration's carefully planned legislative strategy produced a string of victories that provoked favourable comparisons with the impressive achievements of Lyndon Johnson's early Presidency, and helped to restore public confidence in the capacity and efficacy of presidential government. The strategy had been supported by impressive unity amongst the ranks of the Republicans in both houses of Congress. This solidity demonstrated that the alleged decline in party cohesion had certainly been exaggerated in the case of the Republicans. Evidently party ties can be a valuable support when the President offers policy proposals that are considered to be attractive to voters, which is definitely the case with the proposal to reduce personal income taxes by 25 per cent. The President also succeeded in effecting a major increase in defence spending – projected to grow at a full 9 per cent above the rate of inflation throughout the fiscal 1982-5 period – to counter what many voters believed to be a military imbalance with the Soviet Union, and was an achievement which helped to restore national self-confidence after the Tehran hostage crisis and the Soviet invasion of Afghanistan (Bowles 1987; Hogan 1988; Leloup 1982; Ornstein 1982). The administration's legislative strategy led to the passage in 1981 of a series of significant and, given the 'imperilled Presidency' thesis, unexpected changes in public policies and therefore ensured that President Reagan obtained a most favourable reputation as a leader at the very start of his first term.

The successes of 1981 had been, however, bought at a most costly price. The administration had accepted lesser reductions in domestic spending than it had sought, and bigger reductions in federal taxes than it proposed. While the administration sought cuts of $40 billion in domestic spending for fiscal 1982, the actual reductions enacted amounted to only $12-15 billion; the administration failed in similar ways to obtain its proposed reductions in domestic spending over the 1983-6 fiscal period. In order to obtain enough support to enact the Economic Recovery Tax Act legislation, the administration agreed to index the tax structure for individuals after 1985 and granted much more generous reductions to business. The consequence was to reduce revenues much more than planned. Indeed, it has been estimated by the office of Management and Budget that the legislation reduced federal revenues by $963 billion over the fiscal 1981-7 period, whereas the Congressional Budget Office projected the loss over the same period as $1,041 billion. Along with a steep increase in defence spending, this combination of economic decisions pushed the federal budget into a deficit of unprecedented and massive proportions (Hulton and O'Neill 1982; Schick 1982).

The administration feared this change in economic conditions would lead to congressional proposals to move the spending and revenue parts of the federal budget more closely together and thus jeopardize the implementation of the President's tax cuts, and thereby affect significantly Reagan's prospects for being re-elected in 1984. The White House consequently decided to submit a second budget, which kept faith with his initial tax policies. The strategy challenged Congress to take the lead in determining a budget, which would enable the administration to decide whether it could buy on to what was on offer. Congress did reject the second budget, but no congressional consensus developed regarding an alternative model. The impasse led to negotiations between the administration and leaders of both chambers of Congress in April of 1982. The talks failed, but were regarded as a public relations victory for the President because of his willingness to 'go the extra mile' and meet with

Speaker O'Neill on Capitol Hill to work out a compromise budget. The talks also enabled the administration to signal to Capitol Hill what measures it would and would not support in reducing the deficit. Republican moderates in the Senate then developed an alternative plan, which protected the tax cuts for individuals, but raised $97 billion in new taxes over a period of three years and also revised federal spending policies to lower the deficit. The President quickly supported the proposal. But this time he had to work with a coalition of 123 Democrats and 103 Republicans to enact a measure that he described as a necessary 'mid-course correction'. The action was depicted by the White House as indicating the President was flexible and prepared to make necessary compromises with Congress, which helped the Republicans to retain control of the Senate in the November congressional elections of 1982.

In 1983 the White House pushed economic policy issues down its agenda and placed military spending and nuclear arms reductions at the top of Reagan's agenda. The President adopted a flexible strategy in pursuit of his new agenda, bending to compromise solutions that suited his interests and using the Senate as a legislative gatekeeper to block proposals from the House that he opposed. For example, when faced with opposition to his MX missile programme the President supported a suggestion made by the late Senator Henry Jackson to appoint a bipartisan national Commission on Strategic Forces to resolve the matter. The panel recommended that the MX missile be deployed, but in smaller numbers than the President had requested and in conjunction with the smaller and less vulnerable Midgetman missile. The President supported the proposal as it enabled him to keep his MX missile programme alive despite strong opposition. The Senate was used as the administration's legislative gatekeeper when, for example, it tabled a nuclear freeze resolution passed by the House. A protracted stalemate over reducing the deficit further had the positive advantage for the President in that it retained intact his taxing and defence spending policies (Hogan 1988). The adoption of a flexible approach to legislative strategy thus enabled the President both to protect his legislative achievements from significant reversal and to present himself to the voters in 1983 as an effective national leader, which contributed greatly to his re-election.

Professional legislative liaison

President Carter got off to a particularly bad start with Congress because neither he nor the head of his congressional relations unit appreciated the demands involved in liaising with the new, reformed Congress. During his campaign Jimmy Carter presented himself as an anti-Washington 'Mr Clean', a political outsider whose career had not been tarnished by the experience of Watergate, which meant that he would be more critically judged by Congress. But Carter compounded his problems by adopting an aloof approach to Congress. He did not involve – and thus implicate – congressional leaders in the development of his legislative agenda. Rather, he bypassed Congress and appealed directly to the public for support, anticipating the public would exert sufficient pressure on Congress to have his agenda enacted. The bypass strategy amounted to government by surprise to Congress, and Carter's initiatives regularly failed to gain a place on the congressional calendar. Carter's often turgid and technical explanations of his policies further failed to win public support. In sum, Carter's bypass strategy and leadership style was ill-suited to winning with Congress (Jones 1985).

Ronald Reagan and his advisers learned from Carter's mistakes. Ronald Reagan gave a high priority to establishing good working relations with Capitol Hill. He visited the Hill frequently during the 1980 campaign and the transition period to open two-way lines of communication. The Reagan team worked closely with congressional Republicans to determine conjointly the new administration's legislative strategy. The Democrats in the House were also carefully courted. This quickly paid dividends when the Democratic leaders also agreed to put the President's agenda on a 'fast track' in the House rather than obstruct and delay consideration of the President's legislative proposals. When it came to lobbying the Hill, the President enlisted enthusiastically as the 'chief salesman' for his agenda. He met frequently in the White House and on Capitol Hill with party leaders and committee chairmen from both sides of the aisle to build support. Wavering members were given personal audiences in the Oval Office, which enabled Reagan to put his apparently powerful persuasion skills to work. These individual meetings were supported by carefully timed television appeals by Reagan that led to a deluge of calls from the public in support of the President's agenda to congressional offices, which included one 'blitz lobby' by the public of Capitol Hill that overwhelmed and led to the closure of the telephone exchange for Congress. President Reagan thus actively and carefully persuaded both Congress and the public to support his agenda (Hogan 1988).

To organize his one-on-one meetings the President needed a legislative liaison team that knew its way around the reformed Congress, knew which members needed 'stroking' and in what ways. During the transition period Reagan's advisers recruited a strong congressional liaison team. Its members were required to have substantive experience as presidential or departmental liaison officers in previous Republican administrations and experience working on Capitol Hill for Republican congressmen. In contrast to the Carter administration, the President's liaison team were accommodated in the prestigious West Wing of the White House, with the overflow located in the East Wing. This decision demonstrated that the liaison aides had status and should thus be regarded as influential go-betweens in the conduct of presidential-congressional relations. The political intelligence gathered by these aides was quickly disseminated in the White House. As a matter of routine, the head of the unit participated in the daily meeting at 8.00 am of senior White House aides and, when legislative matters were to be discussed, the daily meeting of James Baker, the Chief of Staff, and Edwin Meese, the Counselor to the President, at 8.30 am with President Reagan in the Oval Office. These meetings thus enabled the administration speedily to assess, respond and thus adapt to political developments affecting the President's agenda.

To dovetail with the administration's strategy of building support from both outside and within Congress, the activities of the liaison unit were made part of a broader team effort that was organized to win support for the President's agenda. The liaison team were supported by a series of political outreach units located in the White House and the Executive Office of the President whose job was to solicit support from political institutions and interest groups representing different sectors of the American polity. These outreach units consisted of an office of Inter-governmental Affairs, to liaise with state and local governments; an Office of Public Liaison, to gather support from business, industrial, and commercial companies and organizations; an Office of Political Affairs to liaise with various organs of the Republican Party, and an Office of Communications to conduct relations with media organizations. These individual units stroked their individual clienteles by organizing briefing sessions with the President, Cabinet Secretaries and executive aides in the White House. The aim of these meetings was to generate an outpouring of support for the President's legislative proposals just before key votes in Congress, thus supplementing the work on Capitol Hill of the liaison unit (Hogan 1988).

Centralized agenda management

Divisions within the Carter White House adversely affected his legislative proposals. The Carter administration spent too much time on infighting and did not present a united front in support of the President's legislative agenda, which accordingly suffered on Capitol Hill. To impart coherence to its proposals, to marshall the entire administration behind its legislative strategy, and to adapt its policy proposals to changing political circums-tances in the national political environment and on Capitol Hill the Reagan White House established in the early days of the new administration a 'Legislative Strategy Group' (LSG). The group became the dominant coalition in the administration and maintained its ascendancy over the President's agenda throughout the first term.

The group's meetings were chaired by James Baker, who was the person responsible for leading the administration's legislative strategy and tactics. The individual members of the LSG consisted of the heads of the main policy and political units in the Reagan White House. Its meetings were called to assess developments affecting the President's agenda. These meetings were held as events dictated; the group did not function as a bureaucratic unit. Instead it behaved more like a 'political SWAT team', meeting to decide how to respond to 'hot' issues. Because the groups' members controlled the levers of power in the White House they could rapidly implement their decisions. As one member stated, 'The beauty of this group, is that if people around the table agree, they represent what's necessary to get things done' (Kirschten 1981: 1242). Centralized management of the President's legislative strategy by an informal 'committee of the Presidency' imparted an unusually high degree of coherence to the administration's dealings with Congress, especially in the area of domestic policies. It enabled the Reagan White House to blend policy and political considerations, and to adopt a fluid operating style that was especially well-suited in 1981 and other years in the first term to conducting relations with a decentralized legislature and in organizing relations with the extraconstitutional political institutions of the 'new American political system' (Hogan 1988).

President Reagan was the first President since Lyndon Johnson to obtain his initial legislative priorities. This achievement ran contrary to the claims of the conventional wisdom that contemporary Presidents are unable to provide central leadership and that America is thus ungovernable. The administration's positive legislative achievements led to Reagan being perceived by the public as an effective leader, which facilitated his re-election with the support of forty-nine states in 1984. The second term, however, was marked by a poorer legislative record. This represents to a large extent the growing impact of the Twenty-second amendment to the US Constitution upon the political authority of the Presidency. Because the amendment limited presidents to only two terms in office, it is unhappily the case for Presidents that their capacity to exercise legislative leadership wanes as their second term progresses to its conclusion. There are several limiting factors on presidential legislative leadership in the second term. To begin with, Presidents have normally promoted their favourite and most innovative policies in the earliest days of their first term. By contrast, Presidents attempt to protect their initial accomplishments from attempts to undercut them in the second term. Secondly, public expectations about presidential leadership tend to diminish, especially after the mid-term congressional elections. As the administration ages, political appointees tend increasingly to depart for new appointments, often in business and academic institutions. In line with this, a kind of political fatigue sets in, with the level of energy and emotion that marked the early days declining. There is normally a decrease in the President's popular standing and approval rating. To a large extent, the President – and, it must be noted, his aides – have already spent his political capital and strike increasingly less fear in his critics and opponents (Bonafede 1988).

In stark contrast to the first term, the Reagan administration offered few fresh legislative proposals in the second term. Tax reform was about the only new initiative. This proposal was pressed as the President's major domestic policy initiative of the second term and led to the Tax Reform Act of 1986. This legislation sharply reduced the rate of taxation for upper and middle incomes, and also took many low income individuals off the tax rolls altogether. The rest of the Reagan agenda largely remained unchanged; there was no attempt at a second 'Reagan revolution'. In effect, this meant that the administration oriented its legislative agenda to protecting the domestic policy accomplishments of the first term. The Reagan administration therefore continued to present Congress with budgets that opposed adopting some combination of tax increases and reductions in defence spending to lower the deficit. The administration's proposals were rejected in 1985, which the administration anticipated: in refusing to offer fresh proposals to lower the deficit the White House expected that a Congress still split between a Democratic-controlled House of Representatives and a Republican-controlled Senate would be unable to develop a popular alternative, which would mean political deadlock and thus enable the president to protect his domestic policies from significant reversal.

President Reagan's intransigence much worried Republican Senators, especially those who – unlike the President – had to face the voters again. They were concerned that they would incur the wrath of the voters for failing to take new steps to tackle America's major domestic policy problem. Consequently, a group of conservative Republicans in the Senate developed a proposal – the so-called Gramm-Rudman-Hollings plan, which was named after its leading architects – that set maximum allowable annual federal deficits for fiscal 1986 to 1991 in order to lower the deficit each year by tranches of $36 billion until it was thereby eliminated in fiscal 1991. Failure of Congress and the administration to agree voluntarily a package of deficit reductions in any year would trigger automatic reductions of $36 billion, drawn in roughly equal amounts from defence and domestic spending. The measure thus promised a way forward from fiscal deadlock and consequently spread like a prairie fire in Congress. The measure clearly was a desperate attempt to force the administration to negotiate a politically viable package of deficit reductions, and thus give Republicans a chance to retain control of the upper chamber in the 1986 elections. Even one of the plan's leading authors described it 'as a bad idea whose time has come'. The plan was readily accepted in principle by the White House without really analysing that one of its intended consequences would be to penalize President Reagan for continuing to refuse to come to the negotiating table by cutting the Pentagon budget. The administration continued to refuse to compromise on reducing the federal deficit, and this led in 1986, 1987 and 1988 to cuts in defence spending which marked the end of Reagan's military buildup.

The limited legislative record of the administration, and the related decline in presidential popularity contributed significantly to the Republicans losing eight Senate seats in the 1986 congressional elections. The losses, despite aggressive campaigning by President Reagan, led to the loss of Republican control of the Senate. This much hurt the Reagan administration as it had used its control of the Senate to promote and – especially in the second term – then protect the President's agenda. Democratic control of the Senate also coincided with a change in leadership of the House of Representatives when 'Tip' O'Neill retired from politics and was succeeded as Speaker by James Wright. The new Speaker sought to reduce the deficit by methods that sought to change President Reagan's tax and defence policies. This threat encouraged the administration to accept a plan determined by congressional Democrats in late 1987 to lower the budget deficit over a two-year period by $76 billion. The Balanced Budget Reaffirmation Act of 1987 raises $32.1 billion in new taxes, which represented a significant reversal for the president. At the same time, the administration and Congress agreed to the appointment of a National Economic Commission that would enquire and report in the spring of 1989 on ways to reduce the budget deficit. The establishment of a blue-ribbon inquiry effectively removed, along with the two-year agreement on budget reductions, domestic policy issues from the legislative agenda until President George Bush took office, clearly demonstrating that the Reagan administration had run its course in domestic policy initiatives (Cohen 1987a; Hogan 1989).

This sharp diminution in partisan political leadership of Congress by President Reagan adversely affected relations with congressional Republicans. Abdicating presidential legislative leadership meant that congressional Republicans played a largely defensive game in the second term, with their attention increasingly directed to preparing a new set of issues and political talking points for President Reagan's successor. This led to significant policy differences surfacing between Republicans at each end of Pennsylvania Avenue. This was clearly shown in 1987 when Congress overrode Reagan's vetoes of clean water and highway construction bills. A much publicized trip by President Reagan to the Capitol failed to persuade a single Senate Republican to uphold his veto of the highway measure. The consequences of sustained neglect of Capitol Hill could not be reversed in a single visit. Congressional Republicans frequently complained that the administration was ignoring them. Representative Mickey Edwards, a member of the House Republican leadership, lamented that the administration had not,

> tried to develop a partnership. We find out on the radio their position on contra aid or reflagging [of Kuwait ships] in the Persian Gulf. I constantly complain about this to the liaisons, but they shrug their shoulders. It's a problem from top to bottom in the Administration.
>
> (Cohen 1987b)

These differences continued through the last year of the second term, and led on 22 March to a congressional override of President Reagan's veto of civil rights legislation and to final defeat of his proposals to fund the Nicaraguan Contras, demonstrating that the administration confronted significant difficulties when it needed congressional support for its policies.

The administration's relationships with Congress undoubtedly suffered heavily because of the decision in 1985 to replace James Baker with Donald Regan as head of the White House staff. This meant that legislative strategy in the second term was led by a person who had spent his career on Wall Street before joining Reagan's administration, and was thus an amateur in liaising with Congress. Donald Regan pursued a confrontational approach to Congress, which was poor human relations. The Regan White House failed to consult with Republican leaders on the Hill in preparing its legislative strategy and tactics, which led to the administration's proposals languishing on Capitol Hill. Regan compounded his problems in liaising with Congress by embracing the bypass strategy. Especially after the mid-term elections, the President relied increasingly upon televised and well-controlled news management, and interviews with selected journalists to convey his views rather than deal direct with Capitol Hill. Reagan's speeches charging Congress with responsibility for the deficit might have gone down well with the party faithful in the hinterland, but they failed to build support within Washington. Eventually this dismal performance led to Regan being replaced with Howard Baker in early 1987, whose knowledge of Capitol Hill – gained as the Majority Leader of the Senate over 1981–6 – was instrumental in negotiating the agreement with Congress to take fiscal policy issues off the legislative agenda until Reagan's successor took office (Kirschten 1987).

Whereas James Baker had given a high premium to presenting a united front to Congress, the Regan White House was noted for internal divisions and policy conflicts. These rivalries were most manifest in the area of foreign policy and national security issues. The Iran-Contra arms scandal symbolized these divisions. The scandal surfaced in November 1986 and led to a dramatic decline in the President's popularity ratings and weakened severely his standing with Congress. The administration's Legislative Strategy Group also fell in importance in the Regan White House. As a result the administration regularly lacked adroitness in dealing with Congress. In sum, the Regan White House failed to match the standards set in the first term for strategic agenda management, centralized agenda management and for conducting liaison with Congress.

These shortcomings must not, however, be taken as indicating that President Reagan was a 'lame duck'. This term suggests that the President was something like a 'bankrupt politician' because he was serving out the remainder of his fixed term in office. In practice, President Reagan enjoyed significant political influence, albeit mainly directed in the areas of foreign policy and national security. The President exercised his power as commander-in-chief of the armed forces by dispatching US military forces to the Persian Gulf and Honduras. Most dramatically, the President asserted his prerogatives in foreign policy by pursuing a major strategic arms reduction treaty with the Soviet leader, Mikhail Gorbachev, via a series of international summit meetings in Reykjavik, Geneva, Washington and Moscow that dominated the international and national media for over two years. This key achievement, along with successfully exerting pressure on the Soviet Union to negotiate a withdrawal of its troops from Afghanistan, helped propel a great revival in the popularity of President Reagan in mid-1988, which he then sought to use to obtain a 'third term' in the form of campaigning hard for the election of George Bush. The traditional perception of a lame duck President is evidently outdated in the nuclear age. The President continues to be the focal point during any international crisis, which bolsters his power. The President's relatively greater freedom to manoeuvre in foreign than in domestic policy affairs normally enables him to surmount the limitations involved in seeking partisan support from Congress during the latter end of his second term, all of which encourages Presidents to seek accomplishments in the field of foreign affairs.

In conclusion, the overall record of President Reagan's first term indicates that a contemporary President can bring central leadership to the American polity if he and his advisers are skilful in their statecraft. Setting early and tightly prioritizing the administration's legislative agenda, utilizing Washington insiders to set and manage the President's legislative strategy, and centralizing the political and policy operations of the administration under the control of a dominant coalition in the White House can pay great dividends. In support of this co-ordinated approach to legislative strategy the President must be prepared to involve himself deeply in the arts of persuading individual members as well as subcommittee chairmen and party leaders in Congress to support his agenda; interest groups can be mobilized to support the president, especially when the President's policy proposals are designed to appeal to their self-interest which was particularly the case with Reagan's programme of tax cuts; the President's party colleagues – in the hinterland and on Capital Hill – can further be harnessed to provide valuable supports. But the second term demonstrates that the President progressively encounters obstacles in the area of liaising with Congress because he has largely accomplished what he can achieve in the area of domestic policy initiatives. The Reagan administration sought to deal with this limitation by taking domestic policy issues off the legislative agenda and concentrating on foreign policy initiatives, which did mean that domestic policy leadership somewhat disappeared into a political vacuum. The overall record of liaising with Congress in the Reagan administration indicates that the President can provide central leadership, the American polity is governable but also suggests that presidential legislative leadership can not be provided on a sustained, continuous basis.

References

Berman, L. (1987) *The New American Presidency*, Boston: Little Brown.

Bonafede, D. (1988) 'Fighting Off Lameness', *National Journal* 20, 19: 1188–91.

Bowles, N. (1987) *The White House and Capitol Hill: The Politics of Presidential Persuasion*, Oxford: Oxford University Press.

Cohen, R. (1987a) 'Quick-Starting Speaker', *National Journal* 19, 22: 1409–14.

—— (1987b) 'Living with a Lame Duck', *National Journal* 19, 31: 1956–60.

Cronin, T. (1980) *The State of the Presidency*, Boston: Little Brown.

Davis, E. (1981) 'The President and Congress, in Arnold J. Meltsner (ed.) *Politics and the Oval Office: Towards Presidential Governance*, San Francisco: Transaction Books

Dodd, L. and Bruce Oppenheimer (eds) (1977) *Congress Reconsidered*, New York: Praeger.

Fisher, L. (1987) *The Politics of Shared Power: Congress and the Executive*, Washington, D.C.: Congressional Quarterly Press, second edition.

Greenstein, F.(1978) 'Change and Continuity in the Modern Presidency', in A. King (ed.) *The New American Political System*, Washington D.C.: American Enterprise Institute: 45–85.

Heclo, H. (1983) One Executive Branch or Many?', in A. King (ed) *Both Ends of the Avenue*, Washington D.C.: American Enterprise Institute: 26–58.

Hodder-Williams, R. (1987) 'The President and the Constitution', in M. Shaw (ed.) *Roosevelt to Reagan*, London: C. Hurst & Co: 11–45.

Hogan, J.(1988) 'Legislative Liaison in the Reagan Administration', in J. Leeds and M. Turner (eds) *Reagan's First Four Years: A New*

Beginning? Manchester: Manchester University Press: 69–94.

Hogan, J. (1989) 'Reagonomics and US Economic Policy', in Dilys Hill and Phil Williams (eds), *The Reagan Presidency*, London: Macmillan.

Hulton, J. and O'Neil, J. (1982) 'Tax Policy ' in J. Palmer and I. Sawbrill, (eds) *The Reagan Experiment*, Washington D.C.: The Urban Institute Press: 97–128.

Jones, C. (1985) 'Carter and Congress: From the Outside In', *British Journal of Political Science* 15: 269–98.

King, A. (1978) 'The American Polity in the Late 1970s: Building Coalitions in the Sand', in Anthony King (ed.) *The New American Political System*, Washington D.C.: American Enterprise Institute: 371–95.

Kirschten, R. (1981) 'Reagan's Cabinet Councils May Have Less Influence Than Meets The Eye', *National Journal*: 1242–47

—— (1987) 'The President's Counselor', *National Journal* 19, 21: 1332–37.

Leloup, L. (1982) 'After the Blitz: Reagan and the US Congressional Budget Process', *Legislative Studies Quarterly* VII: 321–39.

Light, P. (1982) *The President's Agenda*, Baltimore: Johns Hopkins University Press.

Mann, T. and Ornstein, N. (eds.) (1981) *The New Congress*, Washington D.C.: American Enterprise Institute, second printing.

Ornstein, N. (ed.) (1982) *President and Congress: Assessing Reagan's First Year*, Washington, D.C.: American Enterprise Institute.

Pfiffner, J. (1983) 'The Carter-Reagan Transition: Hitting the Ground Running', *Presidential Studies Quarterly* XIII: 623–45.

Polsby, N. (1978) 'Some Landmarks in Modern Presidential-Congressional Relationships', in A. King (ed.) *Both Ends of the Avenue*, Washington D.C.: American Enterprise Institute: 1–25.

Ranney, A. (1978) 'The Political Parties: Reform and Decline', in Anthony King (ed.) *The New American Political System*, Washington D.C.: American Enterprise Institute: 213–48.

Schick, A. (1982) 'How the Budget Was Won and Lost', in N. Ornstein (ed.) *President and Congress: Assessing Reagan's First Year*, Washington D.C.: American Enterprise Institute: 14–43.

Smith, H. (1988) *The Power Game*, London: Collins.

Sundquist, J. (1981) *The Decline and Resurgence of Congress*, Washington D.C.: Brookings Institution.

—— (1986) *Constitutional Reform and Effective Government*, Washington D.C.: Brookings Institution.

Wayne, S. (1978) *The Legislative Presidency*, New York: Harper and Row.

Chapter five

Congress and policy-making: can it cope with foreign affairs?

Michael Foley

The emergence of the United States as an established world power generated as many changes inside the country as it did outside in the international arena. In particular, the transition appeared to lead to a basic recognition that America's unique set of governing arrangements has been fundamentally altered through the sheer force of international circumstances. By the 1950s, the dangers and disciplines of the cold war were thought to have ushered in a system of foreign policy-making geared to the demands of America's situation, rather than to the traditional structure of its constitutional dynamics. Foreign policy had not only become central to American government, it was in turn centralizing the government in accordance with its special requirements. The chief beneficiary of this process was the Presidency, which appeared to have developed a symbiotic relationship with the conduct of American foreign policy. By the same token, the chief victim was widely regarded to be the Congress. In spite of the formal powers in foreign policy afforded to the Congress by the Constitution, America's experience after the Second World War seemed finally to have sealed Congress's fate and to have dispatched the institution – in this most important of all governing responsibilities – to a peripheral and largely irrelevant position. The Constitution had once been described as an invitation to both Congress and the Presidency 'to struggle for the privilege of directing American foreign policy' (Corwin 1940: 200). In the atmosphere of a cold war, that struggle looked to be at an end (Carroll 1965: 150–70; Corwin 1948: 207–74; Rossiter 1960: 20–28; Schlesinger 1974: 127–76; Sundquist 1981: 103–22).

This essay refracts Congress through the testing prism of foreign policy-making. First, it examines Congress's decline as exemplified by its apparently irreversible withdrawal from foreign policy in favour of presidential pre-eminence. Second, it appraises that reputation in the light of Congress's sudden resurgence into foreign policy-making during the 1970s and 1980s. And finally, it employs foreign policy to arrive at a number of conclusions concerning not so much Congress's decline or revival, as its basic underlying nature as an institution.

Foreign policy as a sign of Congress's decline

The special affinity of the Presidency with the field of international affairs was seen to be based upon three closely connected factors. The first was the office's functional and organizational capacity to react to pressing needs with the appropriate speed, expertise, secrecy and unity of purpose. The immediacy of the executive's access to the available resources of the state represented not merely an inherent functional property, but also a social responsibility. The obligations of executive prerogative, even within a system based upon consent, had been apparent as early as the seventeenth century, when John Locke had referred to the executive serving the public good 'without the prescription of the law, and sometimes even against it' (1960: 393). The extent to which such prerogative responsibilities had been implicitly implanted into the Constitution had always remained a subject of conjecture. With the rise of the United States as an international power, however, the weight of argument shifted in favour of executive responsibility as more demands made upon government originated from overseas sources. By the end of the 1930s, the gravity of the times determined that the pace and responsiveness of the outcomes were more critical than the procedures by which they were arrived at (*US v. Curtiss-Wright Export Corp.*). As a result, the responsibility for foreign policy developed progressively upon the only agency in government with the capacity for such measured action. Just as the inherent nature of foreign affairs seemed to require executive 'decision, activity, secrecy, and dispatch' (Hamilton 1961: 424), so it also appeared that the executive's inherent attributes drew the Presidency ineluctably to the demands of foreign policy. It is true that Congress had its functions and its constitutional powers, but they were increasingly regarded as not being cognate with the government's function of last resort – namely the political, diplomatic and physical means of national security.

The second factor in the Presidency's pre-eminence in foreign policy was the accumulation of historical precedents and customs which sanctioned executive prerogative through a process of continuous default by the other agencies of government. When challenged, modern Presidents would allude to their predecessors' actions and claim them as legitimizing standards of behaviour. Whether it was President Jefferson's dispatch of a naval force to the Barbary states (1801) without congressional consent, or President Lincoln's unauthorized blockade of Southern ports (1861), or President McKinley's initiative in sending troops to China during the Boxer rebellion (1900), or President Theodore Roosevelt's secret 'executive agreements' with Japan (1905) and Britain (1906), the pattern of congressional and public acquiescence was set in favour of the presidentially inspired deployment of executive power (Javits 1973: 36–209). As a result, every President felt obliged to preserve and to cultivate what his predecessors had bequeathed to him in the way of convention in that area most susceptible to the force of accustomed usage. It was this consolidation of precedent, combined with a steady inventiveness in constitutional construction, which allowed for the progressive growth of an executive-centred foreign affairs establishment geared to presidentially enunciated 'doctrines' of American foreign policy.

These functional and historical elements of presidential power in international relations were fused together by the catalytic experience of the cold war. This provided the third factor in the modern Presidency's apparently unassailable connection with foreign policy. When it became clear that the United States could not revert to 'Fortress America', it plunged, with characteristic totality, into an overseas peacetime engagement of wartime dimensions. Americans became convinced of the Soviet Union's conspiratorial assault upon the 'Free World', and of the requisite need for the United States to establish a string of coalitional alliances and to develop an operational military capability abroad. These convictions led to a policy of 'containment' in order to 'confront the Russians with unalterable counterforce at every point where they showed signs of encroaching upon the interest of a peaceful and stable world' (X 1947: 581). The subsequent confrontations (e.g. the Berlin crisis of 1948–49, the Korean War 1950–53) set against a background of insecurity, espionage and the 'big fear' of communist subversion, propelled the United States into an emphatic rejection not only of isolationism, but of that brand of congressional government with which the discredited doctrine had been so closely associated.

The ratchet of tension turned even further in the 1950s when the Soviet Union broke America's nuclear monopoly. Each confrontation, thereby, became a potential crisis endangering the security and even the very survival of the United States. This led to a permanent condition of barely suppressed emergency, in which presidential power flourished. Functional and historical arguments for executive authority abounded and, under the pressure of events, were rapidly transmuted into a simplified imperative for enhanced presidential prerogative. There was neither the time, nor even the inclination, to quibble with the new reality of presidential pre-eminence. The bipartisan consensus on foreign policy was extended to the executive-dominated means that were believed to be necessary to its conduct. Presidents for their part gravitated towards the severe responsibilities of international affairs and towards the executive prerogative and political licence that were implicit in such a critical field of policy.

As the cold war froze into its characteristically static assumptions,

67

the central role of the Presidency became almost indistinguishable from the properties and objectives of American foreign policy. American foreign policy appeared to be nothing less than the projection of American national interests through the medium of presidential government. In this context, Congress became the embodiment of a lost age of American isolation from the world; an age in which national autonomy had been a viable concept and when the integrity of America's governing principles had been preserved beyond their natural life in the asylum of the new world. Even though the century that had been 'hard on legislatures' (Truman 1959: 1) arrived late in America, its effect was the same as it had been elsewhere. The executive character of the age had insinuated itself into the United States not only by way of foreign policy requirements, but in the guise of such requirements.

The perceived attachment of foreign policy to the Presidency at the time should not be underestimated. It was not merely a matter of opinion that 'the executive called the tune' (Hilsman 1967: 557) and that presidential authority had become the *sine qua non* of an effective and coherent foreign policy. It was seen as a fundamental political development. In these circumstances, the Presidency's functional characteristics and historical precedents were integrated into a unified conception of the office's meaning and development. Relying heavily upon biological terms of reference, the Presidency's past was converted into an evolutionary process which had culminated in the modern office's organizational ability to respond to the nation's most urgent problems and challenges. Placed in a wider context, the modern Presidency's development assumed the greater significance of representing the political system's evolutionary response to the anarchic and executive-dominated conditions of the international environment. Writing in 1966, Aaron Wildavsky declared that the world had become 'a highly intractable place with a whirl of forces we cannot or do not know how to alter . . . Compared with domestic affairs, Presidents engaged in world politics are immensely more concerned with meeting problems on their own terms' (1968: 101). This was seen to have had its effect and the office came to represent the organic embodiment of both history and environment. In these circumstances, any challenge to the organizational basis of America's adaptive reaction to the world seemed quite futile, even though it ran counter to, or at best transcended, the constitutional mechanics of checks and balances. In retrospect, 'the growth of Presidential authority in this area seemed to have been almost inevitable' taking into account as it did the 'practice of other nations and the logic of history' (Rossiter 1960: 24). Consequently, Americans were not disposed to contest the Presidency's commanding position in foreign policy for in their view 'executive dominance . . . was a fact of life' (Lehman 1976: 15).

The dominance of the modern Presidency in conjunction with the associated importance of foreign policy had profound implications for the US Congress. Capitol Hill became strongly identified with the mistakes of the 1930s and with an irrepressible inclination to perpetuate those mistakes into the present. 'Congressional government' smacked of the late and unlamented age of isolationism – of myopic neutrality, of the misplaced zeal of 'America First', and of appeasement. Congress was not just saddled with having foisted the wrong foreign policy upon pre-war America. It was also accused of having rejected the very notion of a foreign policy *per se*. After the war, the United States entered a new age of global responsibility and international commitment with the glistening modernity of a Presidency fully equipped and trained for the world. The old isolationist America had been abandoned but much doubt and anxiety remained over the question of whether Congress itself would be similarly abandoned, or whether its formal co-equality would generate a disruptive influence within the dangerous subtlety of the post-war world. Observers fretted over Congress's disorderly organization, its legendary parochialism, its lack of collective leadership, its populist irresponsibility, its strident amateurism, its dilatory procedures and its suspected inability to assimilate even the concept of sustained international involvement. (Burns 1949; Dexter 1963: 305–24; Fulbright 1961: 1–13; Galloway 1946; Huntington 1965: 5–31). Congress began to look like an anarchronism from the horse and buggy era. It was the risk that it would start trotting onto the international stage which threatened to make the institution a *dangerous* anachronism.

In the event, there was little cause for concern. Congress rose to the occasion by falling back on its own deficiencies. The dominant foreign policy posture in Congress became one of 'self-restraint on the part of the leadership' based on the principle 'that the President knew better than they and that the nation must speak with only one voice' (Hargrove 1974: 164). Senator Arthur Vandenberg, chairman of the illustrious Senate Foreign Relations Committee set the tone in 1947 when he conceded that the Congress did not 'enjoy original jurisdiction in foreign relations' because that was 'the prerogative of the Chief Executive' (Leigh 1976: 168). Such an abnegation of legislative authority would have been unthinkable in the 1930s, but in the post-war era it was seen to be a measure of the need for Congress to limit its drives to the internal sphere of policy, where its organizational configuration seemed better matched to the landscape of domestic dispute and fragmentation. When Congress did occasionally venture into the foreign policy field, it appeared to confirm all of the worst suspicions concerning its inappropriateness for the job. Whether it was the McCarthyite purges, or the annual butchery of the foreign aid legislation, or the obsessive fixation over Taiwan, Congress revealed itself to be still the old Congress – an institution suffused with special interests, pork barrel politics, vote-trading and log-rolling from a membership split into a profusion of enclaves of obstruction and negativism. Analysts and even distinguished Senators continued to warn against leaving 'vast and vital decision-making powers in the hands of a decentralised, independent minded, and largely parochial minded body of legislators' (Fulbright 1961: 7).

Despite patches of colourful resistance, however, the general underlying pattern was characterized by a bipartisan consensus expressed by an instinctive legitimation of an executive-directed foreign policy. Furthermore, all indications pointed to an increasing level of congressional compliance. After reviewing the 1955–66 period, Holbert Carroll concluded that since the mid-1950s the Presidency had 'gained additional initiative, discretion and authority in foreign affairs relative to the Congress' (1966: 351). Aaron Wildavsky dismissed members of Congress as serious competitors with the President because they followed 'a self-denying ordinance' in that 'they did not think it was their job to determine the nation's defence policies' (1968: 96). This attitude was reflected in their relationship with an agency like the CIA, in which congressional 'supervision' was characterized by a deep reluctance even to acquire information about the agency's activities (Marchetti and Marks 1974: 371–9). The same outlook was prevalent in the defence budget. According to Samuel P. Huntington, 'throughout the dozen years after World War II . . . Congress never vetoed directly a major strategic programme, a force level recommendation, or a major strategic weapon system proposed by the administration in power' (1961: 124). Far from the legislature disrupting foreign policy therefore, the net effect of the post-war period was an exponential growth of presidential power in which 'perhaps the most remarkable fact . . . was how seldom it was challenged by Congress' (Crabb and Holt 1980: 190).

The pattern of congressional derogation seemed self-evident and firmly set as an immutable condition of Pax Americana. Commentators could assert in conclusive terms that in foreign affairs 'committees demur, parties are muted; Congress looks to the President for leadership and accepts a very limited policy-making role' (Hinckley 1978: 167). It was felt that Congress simply could not match the executive's sources of information, its techniques of appraisal and its prodigious ability to 'set the framework in which policies were discussed' (Hilsman 1967: 557). Moreover, the Congress was a legislative institution and, as such, it was always going to be confined to legal prescriptions and to abstract enactments, while the President would always be in a position to redefine the reality of external conditions and even, on occasions, to alter the very diplomatic or military circumstances on which congressional formulae may have been based.

Observational generalizations concerning Congress's functional incapacities and attitudinal predilections were further supported by an array of scholarly studies. Under the influence of much of this research, Congress was perceived to be an irredeemably insular and fragmented organization consisting of a membership congenitally geared to the acquisition of personal political capital through the indiscriminate promotion of constituency interests, through the attainment of particularized benefits for localities, and through the ruthless reduction of legislative responsibilities to individual re-election strategies (Mayhew 1974). This utilitarian attitude towards congressional politics was seen to lead first to such an excessive interest in the distributional characteristics of the defence budget that specialist panels such as the Armed Services Committees could be dismissed as only being concerned with the 'real estate' aspects of defence policy (Dexter 1963: 310–12). It led second to a judiciously subservient dependence upon the Presidency for the high risk 'calculation of where the public interest lay . . . on matters of foreign policy' (Miller and Stokes 1968: 228), especially on those matters of conspicuous importance during periods of international tension. In both instances, Congress's contribution to the substance, strategy and objectives of American foreign policy was seen as negligible.

The acknowledged decline of Congress in the field of international affairs was significant because it provided a continual affirmation of the centrality of executive prerogative. Congressional weakness became a structural and functional analogue to presidential pre-eminence. Congress not only provided the measure of the President's need to prevail, but also the extent of that prevalence. As a result, it was foreign policy that mercilessly exposed Congress's 'adaptation crisis' (Huntington 1965: 7) as an institution in contemporary American politics. In an age of America's global involvement when the identities of both the Presidency and the nation were becoming fused together into a solid unity, Congress increasingly appeared as an ingrown and recidivist body 'oriented to the "conscience" of its constituents rather than to the "conscience of mankind"' (Kendall 1960: 320). Post-war concern that Congress should not insinuate its regressive characteristics into the nation's foreign policy processes turned firstly into relief that Congress had not encroached into the area, and secondly into a widespread belief that the institution could not, and therefore never would, apply itself to the responsibilities of foreign policy. Congressional passivity in the area was even rationalized by Aaron Wildavsky's popular concept of two 'Presidencies' (1968: 93–102) which was nothing less than an attempt to establish a new axis in American government based on the territorial criteria of international and domestic policy. Life was different abroad and, therefore, foreign policy demanded different institutional arrangements. Such arrangements had grown up and had been assimilated and legitimated by custom, precedent and, even on occasion, by explicit constitutional sanction. The balance of power was assumed to have swung decisively and permanently to the Presidency as a superior product of political evolution.

Foreign policy as a sign of Congress's revival

Just when this basic relationship within the foreign policy-making process appeared to be most established, the world was turned upside down in the 1970s as a suddenly truculent Congress encroached into the previously sacrosanct area of presidential prerogative. Defying the hitherto accepted logic and compulsive necessity of executive hegemony in foreign affairs, Congress embraced the heresy of changing its status from that of a sleeping partner to one of a senior consultant in the determination of foreign policy. Legislative pretensions to power graduated from the early guerrilla warfare against President Nixon's management of the Vietnam war (e.g. 'end the war' amendments, fund cut-offs); on to generalized investigations and critical appraisals of America's foreign policy and national security arrangements (e.g. the composition of the defence budget; the costings, performance and strategic needs of individual weapon systems; the conduct of the CIA); and through to the establishment of long-term statutory procedures enabling Congress to acquire information and to sustain its rights of consultation and participation in the formulation of foreign policy (e.g. the War Powers Resolution 1973, the Hughes-Ryan Amendment to the Foreign Assistance Act 1974, and the Nelson-Bingham Amendment to the Foreign Aid Authorization Act 1974). This was no longer the subservient Congress of 'low policy and real estate' pre-occupations, but an apparently transformed institution moving both into the development of high strategic policy and also into the very implementation of policy itself (Bergner 1987; Crabb and Holt 1980; Destler 1985; Franck and Weisband 1979; Haas 1979; Hodgson 1979; Leyton-Brown 1982; Muskie *et al* 1986; Purvis and Baker 1984; Spanier and Nogee 1981; Sundquist 1981: 238–314).

The deregulation of foreign policy meant that members of Congress became almost a part of the diplomatic corps. A congressional delegation went to Moscow to conduct Congress's own discussions on the SALT 2 treaty with the Soviet leadership. A similar delegation travelled to Panama so that Senators and Congressmen could survey at first hand the problems associated with the defence of the Panama Canal. It was also allowed to engage in direct negotiations with the Panamanian government in readiness for the Senate's consideration of the two treaties between the United States and Panama that had already been agreed to by the Carter administration. This intrusiveness on the part of Congress became part of a pattern of legislative self-assertion that projected itself into the world's headlines. Whether it was the suspension of military assistance to Turkey – a fellow NATO ally – following that country's invasion of Cyprus in 1974; or the Jackson-Vanik amendment which, by formally incorporating the pre-condition of liberalized Jewish emigration into the 1974 trade bill with the Soviet Union, effectively wrecked one of the keystones of Henry Kissinger's detente policy; or the technical specifications of what avionics should be fitted to the AWACS and F--15 planes being sold to Saudi Arabia in 1981, it was clear that after the original post-Vietnam impulse to prevent any repetition of the abuse of executive power, the Congress was sprawling over any area of foreign policy that took its interest.

This form of congressional behaviour seemed tantamount to a direct and concerted challenge to executive authority. It was felt, and felt with profound discomfort, by those in a position to sense the disturbance. Presidents Nixon, Ford and Carter all protested against congressionally imposed restraints upon what they took to be their constitutional and historical prerogative to conduct foreign policy. President Ford's cry of anguish about there being no longer an 'imperial Presidency but an imperilled Presidency' was typical (Cronin 1980: 137–51). It is indicative of the change in mood and of the change in conditions that the remark was not taken to be an exaggeration. Observers and analysts were rewriting their scripts in the sort of purple prose befitting a traumatic and epic development. The 1970s were reputed to have witnessed developments 'reversing at least three-quarters of a century in which the Presidency had become a steadily stronger and eventually a very powerful centre' (Davis 1984: 103). By the end of the decade it seemed that

> an increasingly embittered Congress (had) set out to reverse the flow of power to the Presidency under the guise of putting controls on the President at a time when the American people were hostile to him, Congress in truth was set on its own power grab.
>
> (Evans and Novak 1981: 18)

To many observers, that assault had been successful. It was not just that the 'trend toward Presidential power had been significantly reversed' (Nogee 1981: 189). It was that with the 'development of detente and the ending of the United States role in Vietnam, the dialectic (i.e. between the Presidency and the Congress) once again asserted itself' with the result of a 'resurgence of Congressional dominance' (Lehman 1976: 23). Such dominance in such an area was to Thomas Franck and Edward Weisband nothing less than a 'revolution' in which 'an entire system of power had been overturned' (1979: 3). Moreover, there was evidence to suggest that the renewed 'Congressional ascendance was not just a swing of the pendulum' but a 'revolution that would not be unmade' (1979: 6).

If a revolution had occurred, it was not limited to the content and constituent procedures of American foreign policy. Logically, there had to have been something akin to a revolution within Congress as well, in order for it to have incorporated itself within the foreign policy-making structure. For a generation, Congress had been processed out of foreign policy by constitutional theory and political custom. Congress's functional deficiencies, its structural inadequacies and introverted attitudes were thrown into high relief by the demands of foreign policy. So much so that the very field of international affairs and national security had not only represented the *leitmotif* of Congress's decline as an institution, but had raised the 'profound question of Congress's contemporary utility as an instrument of democratic rule' (Kolodziej 1970: 94). After the events of the 1970s, however, the question had been changed to the nature of the 'impact of the new Congress on American foreign policy-making' (Destler 1981: 329). Clear inferences of a changed Congress were being drawn and are still being drawn today. The implication is that of a newly assertive Congress reactivating its powers and prerogatives in the international environment, which, by its nature, only admits participants on its own adaptive terms. Bearing in mind its past, Congress must presumably have undergone a profound metamorphosis in which its old habits have been replaced by a mature broadening of perspective, by an enlarged scope of responsibility and even by an ennobling obligation to monitor American interests and ideals around the world. The conduct of American foreign policy, therefore, has sharpened contemporary interest in Congress and succeeded in generating considerable controversy over the true extent to which Congress's adventurous incursions into foreign policy actually represent a transformation of the old institution.

The general tone of much of the current literature gives the impression of radical change. Certainly, the *prima facia* evidence for innovative development is strong. In support of the contention, it is possible to cite the large increases in staff, investigative facilities, information resources and overall expertise that Congress has introduced to improve its position in foreign policy-making. Also deployed as evidence of deep change, is 'the intensity of Congressional interest in most foreign policy issues' and the general desire amongst members of Congress 'to be in on the action' (Purvis 1984: 10). This has extended to the House of Representatives demanding to join the Senate in the forefront of foreign policy participation. It has also led to a breakdown in the old monopolies of the Foreign Relations and Armed Services Committees, which had traditionally laid claim to being the Congress's exclusive tribunes in their respective areas. The taboos and proprietary rights previously attached to such sensitive fields as foreign policy and national security have been broken to reveal an apparent meritocracy of highly knowledgeable foreign policy 'entrepreneurs' surveying complex international issues and mobilizing support for innovative measures both within Congress and, significantly, amongst the general public.

Despite these celebrated allusions to congressional change, it will here be contended that the weight of evidence lies in favour of an underlying continuity of legislative characteristics and attitudes. In arguing this position, the intention is not to rely upon the common device of making derogatory references to the motivations and activities of members of Congress and of extrapolating such idiosyncracies to a collective portrait of the institution. Clearly there are individual 'horror stories' in the foreign policy field as there are in any area of congressional activity. It is common to draw attention to the 'Koreagate' scandal (1977-8) in which a lobbyist for the South Korean government spent between a half and one million dollars per annum creating a 'favourable legislative climate' for his country's interests. In subsequent indictments, twenty-five members of Congress were cited as having received gifts, contributions and entertainment from the South Korean government. In the Abscam scandal of 1980, FBI agents, masquerading as Arab investors, implicated seven members of Congress for bribery and conspiracy. Six were convicted. One Congressman (Rep. Michael Myers, D-Pa) and one Senator (Sen. Harrison Williams, D-N.J.) were expelled from their respective chambers. Other stories revolve less around mercenary proclivities than around Congressmen's legendary ignorance and superficiality in relation to the grave depths of foreign policy. In the Greece-Turkey dispute over Cyprus in 1974, for example, the energetic Greek-American lobby strongly supported congressional moves to suspend US military assistance to Turkey. The plan was bitterly opposed by the Ford administration, as Turkey was regarded as the more valuable NATO partner. Nevertheless, there was no Turkish-American lobby capable of offering resistance within Congress. As one Congressman put it, 'there are more Greek restaurants in my district than there are Turkish baths' (Hodgson 1979: 11).

Such stories do not in themselves prove anything. Their notoriety may be derived from their conspicuous unrepresentativeness. For every headline-grabbing knave, there may well be two unsung statesmen. If, on the other hand, the 'horror stories' are entirely representative of normal congressional conduct, even that in itself does not constitute proof of an ineffectual Congress in foreign affairs. Craven and capricious behaviour can be indicative of a craven and capricious institution and, as such, of an increasingly redundant agency of government. But such behaviour can just as easily lead to the 'continuous renovation of American public policy through the hidden hand of the self-promotion of its members' (Polsby 1971: 8). It is a mistake, therefore, to allow accounts of individual myopia to be the sole and conclusive basis for evaluating Congress's performance in foreign policy and for assessing its constituent properties as an institution. The real nature of Congress can only be determined by reference to its systemic qualities and it is the contention of this chapter that such qualities are not only best revealed by foreign policy issues, but that they possess a depth, subtlety and durability which have persisted throughout the 'Congressional revolution' in foreign policy.

One basic characteristic of Congress that prevails above all the others is its fragmented structure. Congress's disaggregation into a multiplicity of committee enclaves generates a specialized cellular basis to legislative power and status, whilst simultaneously undermining collective party allegiance and discipline to the point where party solidarity becomes only a notional term of putative attachment. It can be argued that Congress is inherently and irretrievably pre-disposed towards decentralization. Certainly, all the efforts to reverse the disarray of its committee system and to encourage Congress to develop a structured framework of central direction have fallen, either sooner or later, by the wayside. It is this congenital condition that was one of the major reasons for Congress being regarded as a wholly unsuitable institution for the 'intrinsic authoritarian necessities of foreign policy' (Spanier and Uslaner 1982: 3) in the post-war era. This being so, it might be thought that Congress's recent incursion into foreign policy would have been accompanied by evidence of a new corporate identity capable of applying the institution's resources into an effective co-ordinated exertion of power. Nothing could have been further from the truth.

Far from legislative foreign policy-making coinciding with an increase in party solidarity or with a reduction in committee decentralization, the 1970s witnessed a further turn in the spiral of congressional devolution. The rate of party voting continued to decline, and the committee system became yet more diffuse and undisciplined. The decade was characterized by a stream of rule changes geared towards satisfying the ambitions of the newer and more impatient junior members of Congress. The old oases of disciplined and assured power dried out in the scorching heat of competitive political individualism. Not only were the baronial prerogatives of the committee chairmen (e.g. the selection of subcommittee jurisdictions and chairmen, the control of staff, budgets and agendas) withdrawn or at least greatly circumscribed, but the solidarity of the committees themselves was undermined by reforms that allowed for the proliferation of strong subcommittees with fixed jurisdictions and protected facilities (Deering and Smith 1985: 189–210). Coinciding with this renewed atomization in congressional structures were further reforms that increased the levels of the membership's personal staffs and opened up committee and sub-committee work to a much greater degree of public visibility. As a result, both the opportunities and the incentives for conspicuously personal participation grew markedly. 'Everyone seemed to be getting in on the policy-making act' (Davidson 1981: 119) and to such an extent that the President appeared to be 'faced by 535 secretaries of state, each of whom felt competent to take the initiative in foreign affairs' (Steiner 1987: 14).

It is a testament to the depth of Congress's recent 'democratizing' impulses that the previously sacrosanct fields of foreign policy and national security were affected to the same extent as any other area of responsibility. The prestigious exclusivity of the foreign relations committees, or the ingrown *esprit de corps* of the armed services committees have been broken by a greater willingness on the part of the members to treat defence and international issues with the same eye to critical licence, policy challenge, individual assertion and self advance as their colleagues in other committees. Senator Sam Nunn (D-Ga), for example, first rose to prominence in the Senate, and consequently in the country at large, through his position as chairman of the Subcommittee on Manpower and Personnel of the Senate Armed Services Committee. During the mid-1970s, Nunn was able to use this base to conduct broadscale investigations into the state of the US Army. In doing so, he not only helped to influence public opinion on America's military posture and strategic policy, but established himself as a highly respected military analyst who by the mid-1980s was being widely cited as a future presidential candidate (Woll 1985: 114–22: Muravchik 1980: 48–52).

The old mystique of foreign policy's functional impregnability to Congress's dissolute politics has been dispelled to the extent of non-specialist members outside the relevant committees adopting foreign policy issues on their own initiative. Such members have sought to arouse a type of in-house congressional populism, in order either to force issues on to the specialist committees, or to circumvent them altogether in an effort to direct foreign policy from the floor of the House or Senate. The congressional move to suspend military assistance to Turkey in response to its invasion of Cyprus in 1974, for example, did not originate in any of the committees pertaining to foreign policy. It began with four young Congressmen – John Brademas (D-Ind), Paul Sarbanes (D-Md), Gus Yatron (D-Pa), L.A. Bafalis (D-Fla) – who were not international specialists but who generated enough support from the floor to begin the momentum towards a formal cut off of aid. Similar non-specialists, and junior non-specialists at that – Senators John Tunney (D-Ca), Thomas Eagleton (D-Mo) – led the way in the Senate. 'Not only the State Department but the frustrated Senate leadership recoiled in pain at the effrontery of the junior Senator from Missouri who was not even on the Senate Foreign Relations Committee' (Franck and Weisband 1979: 39). Nevertheless, Eagleton managed his own floor amendment to victory by fifty-seven votes to twenty.

The level of vociferous political licence in areas primarily given over to silent compliance was so great that it extended to single individuals steadfastly obstructing the congressional process until they had received some measure of satisfaction. One of the most celebrated cases of such intransigence came during the Senate's consideration of the Panama Canal Treaties of 1978. After ten years of negotiation, the two countries had finally reached an agreement ceding US jurisdiction of the Canal in the year 2000, whilst safeguarding American rights to ensure the Canal's neutrality. In an increasingly acrimonious atmosphere, President Carter had been forced by several Senators to seek further 'clarification' from the Panamanian government of America's remaining rights of intervention – even though this request risked jeopardizing the treaties. The Carter administration required a two-thirds majority. Therefore, it had to accommodate as many Senatorial doubts and objections as possible, whilst at the same time preventing General Omar Torrijos's leadership position in Panama from being compromised by Senate attempts to redefine the treaties to the advantage of American interests. Just when all the verbal formulae and 'statements of understanding' appeared to have been levered into place, the treaties once again became hostages to fortune with an objection by the Democratic freshman Senator from Arizona. The price of Dennis DeConcini's vote became the administration's endorsement of an American right to military intervention, in order to keep the Canal open and operating even in the event of an *internal* crisis in Panama (e.g. a national strike). This reservation was quite unacceptable to the Carter administration, but the Senate nevertheless voted to incorporate it into the treaties. As a result, administration officials met with DeConcini to impress upon him the need to change the reservation. DeConcini was unrepentent. He 'refused to budge, suggesting that the Panamanians were bluffing, and later told newsmen that Panamanian dissatisfaction was a problem for President Carter and the State Department' (Opperman 1984: 93). In the end, this particular piece of blackmail was settled in a flurry of diplomatic negotiation and verbal invention. The DeConcini amendment revealed the extent to which individual members could and would exploit with impunity Congress's decentralized structure and its licentious atmosphere to drive foreign policy changes through to their conclusion.

Such is the degree of fragmentation that members of Congress will now translate foreign incentives and sanctions into domestic policy objectives and *vice versa*. It used to be part of the normative framework of foreign policy-making that domestic policy considerations were expected to be confined to internal American politics and to home based issues. While this distinction was always overdrawn, it nevertheless reflected a sense of discipline that no longer exists. The custom of assigning foreign and domestic policy to separate compartments has fallen into disuse. In other words, the old exclusivity and protective privileges afforded to foreign policy in Congress has been abandoned and, as a result, foreign policy-making has entered the legislative mainstream of bargains and bluff, sticks and carrots and the whole gamut of tactics involved in building coalitions in a disparate environment of groups, smaller groups and individuals. (Drischler 1985) This attitudinal decentralization has led to foreign policy being used to serve purely domestic purposes. For example, at the end of the Senate's consideration of the Panama Canal treaties, Senator James Abourezk (D-S.Dak) sought to extract concessions on legislation to re-regulate the natural gas industry, which was also reaching the final stages of congressional consideration during the same period. Abourezk made it quite clear that his concern for natural gas was the price of his vote for a treaty with another country on a matter involving America's national security. The reverse of drawing upon domestic measures for ulterior foreign policy objectives is just as common. The addition of non-germane amendments ('riders') to imperative legislation is one particularly popular device. For example, Senator Edward Kennedy's (D-Mass) 1983 and 1984 campaigns for a nuclear freeze as an objective in the United States-Soviet Union arms talks assumed the legislative form of amendments to the regular, but always urgent, domestic housekeeping measure of raising the ceiling on the national debt.

The deliberate intermingling of political capital in foreign and domestic issue areas typifies what has been termed the 'balkanization of American politics' (Phillips 1983), in which ever increasing numbers of ever more narrowly based interest groups strive for section advantages and preferments with no sense of inhibition or responsibility. As a representative and already highly atomized institution, Congress has not only been unable to withstand the fissiparous forces outside its doors, but has further stimulated the fractured intensity of such forces by fragmenting itself further into a labyrinth of seductive committees, access points and veto barriers. To Cecil Crabb and Pat Holt 'Congress appears to be more decentralised, fragmented and resistant to unifying influences than in any previous period of American history' (1980: 215). Far from foreign policy evoking a rationalization of congressional structures, the institution's new international obligations have merely succeeded in providing a lot more grist for the old mill of decentralization.

Another traditional characteristic of Congress that was once thought to disqualify it from any substantive role in foreign policy-making, has been its reputedly provincial and sectional orientation. It is customary to view Congress as being so dominated by local pre-occupations, and members of Congress as being so exclusively motivated by the need to accommodate constituency interests in order to secure re-election, that the Congress as a whole is assumed to be incapable of providing an expression of national representation or an embodiment of the national interest (Clark 1964; Burns 1963; Huntington 1965; Davidson *et al.* 1966). It was on this assumption of legislative parochialism that critics argued for, and rationalized, the Presidency's supremacy in determining foreign policy. It was also on this basis that members of Congress themselves deferred to the President on foreign policy issues, while aggressively retaining their freedom of action in domestic affairs. The folklore surrounding Congress remains a persistent one of craven submission to constituency pressures and of considering one's district first when voting. The view of Rep. Ken Hechler (D-W. Va), who once declared that he was going to stand upon his 'hind legs and roar until West Virginia got the fair treatment she deserved' (Lens 1970: 45) in the defence budget, is seen as typifying the adopted role and driving force of Congress's membership.

With the folklore, however, has come a profusion of empirical research subjecting the traditional picture to factual scrutiny. The conceptual and operational problems engendered have been immense and have prompted even more elaborate methodologies for examining the subject. The results have been mixed and often at cross purposes to one another. What can be said is that the position is a lot more complicated than was first thought. It has been discovered that members possess sets of different adopted roles rather than just one; that there exist separate and distinct political constituencies within unitary geographical constituencies; that voting cues come from a variety of sources; that ideology is an underrated but highly significant component in voting behaviour – to mention only a few of the findings (Bernstein and Anthony 1974; Clausen 1973; Fenno 1978; Miller and Stokes 1968; Kingdon 1981). But in spite of all these provisos and qualifications, pressures from local sources and especially the need for members to cultivate their local power bases to ensure their re-election, remain an elemental force in congressional politics that cannot be discounted.

The comparison of motivations and behaviour across time frames is even more problematical than comparing legislative structures. Nevertheless, there is every indication that here too Congress's emergence into foreign policy has not been marked by any concomitant reformation of behaviour, through which its drives have been rationalized into a far fewer number of far more statesman-like channels. On the contrary, Congress gives the appearance of having sloughed off the strictures and sanctions of the cold war and of having the confidence to deploy its own disparate network of independent resources and alternative categories of appraisal to the task of ascertaining the merits of contemporary foreign policy for itself.

The intense publicity surrounding Congress's renewed interest in foreign affairs has had two important effects. Firstly, it has prompted

Congress to remove the lid on what before had remained knowledge discreetly concealed within its midst (e.g. the CIA's intelligence activities, the Defense Department's arrangements for weapon system procurement, American troop movements). Such information has been duly exposed to the politicizing attention of the general membership and, thereby, to a wider variety of interests and purposes. For example, in the early 1970s following the debacle of the Vietnam war and several scandals involving huge cost overruns for individual weapon projects, the defence budget received damaging criticism from liberal non-defence specialists outside Congress's military establishment of the Armed Services Committees and the Defense Subcommittees of the Appropriations Committees. Liberal members wished to rearrange national priorities towards social reform programmes and to those liberal constituencies served by them. A period of congressional reductions in the defence budget was succeeded by one in which Congress sought to persuade President Carter to increase defence spending.

The change in Congress's posture could be attributed to a shift in national mood, but that shift was not unassisted by the Pentagon's centrality to many local economies, nor inhibited by its practice of either concentrating contracts into a limited number of favoured states, or by spreading contracts around to affect as many Congressional constituencies as possible. Over 95 per cent of the prime contracts for the Strategic Defence Initiative, for example, have gone to only five states – California, Washington, Texas, Alabama and Massachusetts. In the case of the F–18 Hornet aircraft, on the other hand, contracts have been signed with over 20,000 companies located in forty-four states. Both strategies can be extremely effective in generating an economic, and subsequently a political, constituency in support of selected military programmes. It is true that research on congressional voting behaviour in this area has tended to support the proposition that members cast their votes on the basis of personal ideology, rather than in response to constituency interests (Bernstein and Anthony 1974). Apart from the difficulty of satisfactorily untangling ideological from constituency concerns, close observers of Congress are swift to point out that 'representatives from militarily dependent areas have a long history of banding together to vote in favour of programmes that will benefit their states, from F–18 fighters to B–1 bombers to A–10 attack planes' (Harting 1986: 23). In the case of Reagan's SDI, it is noteworthy that over three-quarters of the prime contracts have been awarded to those states and constituencies served by members of Congress's four military committees. Even in research findings on ideological voting in Congress, it is conceded that anti-defence spending liberals from areas experiencing a very high level of benefit from the Pentagon do 'not really have a choice but to vote with the economic interest' (Fleisher 1985: 209). Therefore, whether it is a crusade against the defence budget by liberal gadflies, or whether it is the traditional nexus of Congressmen from pro-military areas gravitating towards pro-military committees, the forces of group interest and parochial allegiance remain as evident as ever.

The second effect of Congress's incursion into foreign policy has been to bring international and defence issues directly into the bright lights of the electoral arena and, in particular, into the personal re-election strategies of individual Congressmen. The new profusion of new foreign and defence policy interest groups, for example, have not only brought the world to the congressional parish, but have primed the parish pump with vast numbers of campaign contributions. Whether these political action committees (PACs) represent the corporate interests of Pentagon contractors (e.g. Grumman Political Action Committee, General Dynamics Corporation Voluntary Political Contributions), or the concerns of a particular ethnic group or foreign government (e.g. America Israel Public Affairs Committee), or the objectives of an ideological grouping (e.g. National Conservative Political Action Committee), the magnitude of their financial resources has led to members of Congress becoming increasingly dependent upon both their contributions and their good will in the costly struggle for re-election.

Another facet of foreign policy encroaching into the bread and butter of electioneering has been the growing influence of the Presidency's public popularity as an instrument of congressional persuasion. The office's resources are particularly evident at election time when Presidents can sometimes break down congressional obstruction in foreign policy by projecting an issue directly onto the electoral landscape. In 1984, for example, President Reagan intensified his drive for aid to El Salvador by publicizing the issue through a televised presidential address. Congressional attention began to turn to the difficulties of justifying opposition to the President in a contentious foreign policy area at election time. Speaker Thomas O'Neill (D-Mass) felt that his attempts to impose stringent conditions upon the aid package were hampered by members wondering 'what kind of mess would I be in, in my district, if El Salvador were to fall to the communists?' (Oberdorfer et al., 1984).

Occasionally, the electoral need for public prominence is so intense that it can lead to individual members suddenly launching legislative measures in the most conspicuous of policy areas. Senator Thomas Eagleton's (D-Mo) controversial campaign for the military aid cut-off to Turkey in 1974 happened to coincide with his re-election drive in Missouri. But perhaps the most overt example of foreign policy being used for local electoral purposes came in December 1975, when Senator John Tunney (D-Calif) faced the prospect of a difficult Democratic primary election, in which his chief challenger would be the veteran anti-war activist Tom Hayden supported by his wife Jane Fonda. Having been a largely anonymous member of the Senate for five years, 'Tunney was in urgent need of instant visibility and an enhanced dove image. Angola came along like the serendipitous answer to an underdog's prayer' (Franck and Weiband 1979: 52). Tunney's staff worked to introduce an amendment to the Defense Appropriations Bill which would cut off all Defense Department funds for the CIA's involvement in the emerging civil war in Angola. Tunney was not a foreign policy specialist. He sat on no committee involved with the issue and he had previously taken little or no interest in African affairs. Nevertheless, his staff had selected this issue to cast the Senator in a favourable light. Senator Dick Clark (D-Iowa), who was an African specialist and who had his own more graduated prohibitory amendment, was persuaded to yield to Tunney's more flamboyant measure on the political grounds that Tunney 'needed' his amendment more than Clark needed his. Tunney's amendment secured passage in the corrosive atmosphere of post-Vietnam Washington and so 'in a sense the Angola War was lost in the Californian primary' (Franck and Weisband 1979: 53).

In recent years, the penetration of electoral priorities into foreign policy issues has received a further twist with the rise of the Senate as an incubator for presidential aspirants. With the Senate's special prerogatives in international affairs at their disposal and with foreign policy leadership as the critical requirement for the modern Presidency, aspiring Senators have sought to use foreign and defence issues to increase their prominence and to establish their credentials for the White House. For example, Senator Howard Baker (R-Tenn), the Senate Minority Leader and presidential aspirant, was told by Senator Robert Dole (R-Kans) that his support for the Panama Canal treaties would ruin his chances of securing his party's presidential nomination in 1980. Senator Dole, who was also in line for the party's ticket, duly announced his opposition to the treaties in accord with the objections of the Republican Party's influential right wing movement. Baker supported the treaties, but was stung by the critical assault directed at him by right-wing political action committees and by critics within his own party. This reaction was thought to be not unrelated to Baker's opposition to the SALT 2 treaty in 1979. With the presidential election only a year away, Baker had little choice, in the conspicuous position he held, other than to reconcile himself to the Republican conservatives. The infection of presidential ambition has even spread to the House of Representatives, where included in the hopefuls for future elevation was Rep. Jim Wright (D-Texas). Wright was the Speaker of the House, and in November 1987 was prepared to use his position to engage directly in promoting a diplomatic reconciliation between the Sandinista government of Nicaragua and the Contra rebels. President Reagan and the Secretary of State, George Shultz, were both appalled by Wright's intervention, but in Hugh Sidey's words 'there was nothing wrong with House Speaker Jim Wright that being President of the United States would not cure' (1987).

Foreign policy as a sign of Congress's nature

The response to the issue of Congress and foreign policy, therefore, is a mixed one. It is true that Congress has established a sizeable stake for itself in the structure of foreign policy-making. Nevertheless, it is also true that the contrast between the period of Congress's reputed 'quiescence' in the 1950s and 1960s, and the period of Congress's reputed 'insurrection' in the 1970s and 1980s has been overdrawn to the point of caricature. It needs to be recalled first that Congress was not quite the deaf-mute that it has so often been depicted as being during the height of the cold war. Congressional opinions and positions had to be anticipated and carefully taken into account by the decision-making centres around the White House (Rourke 1983; Nelson 1987). The second caveat is that where Congress concurred with the administration, it was almost invariably on the basis of genuine conviction and political expectation, rather than simply the results of neglectful disengagement. It was an artful and premeditated indolence in the cause of a policy that required executive characteristics for its global effect. Congress was an integral, but also an active, part of the silence that surrounded the cold war consensus. It lent its weight to those political and moral strictures of the era that placed a premium upon solidarity for the national interest in the face of a common and ubiquitous danger. Members of Congress used their support of presidential foreign policy to help forge what became a self-reinforcing linkage between the notion of executive unity, the property of policy coherence and the existence of critical world conditions needing a highly centralized structure of policy-making. Congress's complicity in the development of this almost impregnable syndrome of political mobilization – in which the single executive and the singular foreign policy became synonymous with one another even to the point of affording physical form and force to each other – represented the legislature's chief contribution to the consensus that shrouded America after the Second World War.

When that consensus began to weaken, Congress accordingly began to increase its activity in the foreign policy field. In many instances Congress shifted from a position of compulsive consent towards a basic and indiscriminate posture into a position of criticism and even dissent within an emerging context of creative and discriminatory policy-making. Prior to this period, Congress had been separated from the detailed substance of foreign policy through the dynamics of 'cost push' (i.e. the political costs likely to be incurred by legislative interference) and 'demand pull' (i.e. the public's expectations of presidential prerogative).

These dynamics now reversed themselves sufficiently to bring Congress into direct contact with foreign policy.

The following represent just a few of the most commonly cited factors in the crumbling of America's cold war solidarity. A greater access to, and an improved understanding of, the theories underlying national defence and nuclear strategy; a higher level of scepticism shown towards the skill and judgement of the political and military leadership in the wake of the Vietnam debacle; a relaxation in superpower relations and a subsequent lowering of the critical nature of world events; and a sharp increase in the interdependency of the American economy upon world resources and markets leading to the erosion of the old distinction between foreign and defence policy and to the emergence of high profile, but non-military, 'intermestic issues' (e.g. trade, currency, energy resources) that have simultaneously both foreign and domestic implications. These developments have all had their effect in changing the political system of an international power in relative decline. Since the Presidency's role and status have always been closely connected to the international position of the United States, it was only to be expected that the office would suffer from America's perceived weaknesses. Congress fell into this partial vacuum and immediately aroused a storm of protest from the many who now hailed the past as a 'golden age' of American certainty and security. Mistaking the symptom for the disease and, as a result, confusing the old structure of foreign policy-making with the solution to America's problems and with a return of the past glories of United States foreign policy, Presidents and their acolytes have condemned Congressional behaviour as heretical and dangerous meddling in the international arena (Kissinger 1977; Kissinger 1982; 246, 593, 1000-2, 1192). Congress, on the other hand, has also appreciated the linkage between means and ends. It now acted on the assumption that if the ends were no longer so clear, then the means could be diversified accordingly to allow for an element of congressional participation. To the 'President's party', this was by definition 'a recipe for disaster' (Spanier 1981; viii) and final proof tht American foreign policy was in a state of dissolution.

What has been significant about this continuing debate is that while it has been predicated upon a belief in the breakdown of the foreign policy consensus surrounding the Presidency, the manner and conduct of Congress's insurgency has revealed, ironically, that most of the original infrastructure of that consensus has remained intact and in operational use. Articles and books proclaim a 'farewell to the President knows best' (Yankelovich 1979) in favour of an 'unchained' (Gregorian 1984: 92) and 'ascendant' (Rourke 1983: 255) Congress that has perpetrated a revolution in foreign policy. And yet, the actual record reveals a Congress more aware than ever of its own limitations and of its continued dependence upon the Presidency for assuming the basic responsibility for foreign policy direction and international action. Congress is portrayed as revolutionary because it has deviated from the norm of the 1950s and 1960s. Nevertheless, it is a sign of the durability of that very norm that what has in effect been only a marginal departure from it has been presented as an extraordinary radical break with the past.

The custom of cold war discipline and of necessary policy emanating noiselessly from the White House is still evident from the character of the many studies made of the issue of Congress and foreign policy. The tenor of these studies is normally one of reporting congressional activities as if something daringly illicit had been divulged. This is because such behaviour is still implicitly set against the background of past rules and prescriptions. Legislative encounters with foreign policy, therefore, remain depicted as being self-evidently controversial because they are still seen to be challenging an accepted structure of authority and an established code of conduct. The irony is that it is precisely because such a format of authority and practice remains largely intact – not least among members of Congress themselves – that makes any form of legislative participation look akin to the drama of a mutiny or even that of a revolutionary movement. It is a measure of the absolutist traditions of presidential dominance in foreign affairs, therefore, that not only cast congressional actions in the false light of insurrection, but, in the very process of such an over-reaction, reveal the continued salience of the old established practices and conceptions of foreign policy-making. As a result, legislative challenges in this field are far more a commentary upon congressional dependence rather than upon the institution's independence.

Congress remains an institution that thrives upon the spirit of heroic insurgency and studied resistance to executive power. The objective is not to be triumphant but to engage in the American clamour of populist protest and amateur opposition to government. Any notion that Congress intends to take over responsibility for foreign policy, or that it has already done so, is completely to misunderstand congressional motivations. Congress relies as much as it has ever done upon the Presidency and the executive branch to assume the huge and complex burden of running the country's foreign policy on a day to day basis and for assuming responsibility for America's conduct and interests around the world. Congress is also fully cognizant of the fact that it is completely and utterly incapable of ever relieving the Presidency of even a fraction of the foreign policy burden. It may be expedient to attack the White House, but members of Congress know that their own institution is very far from being above reproach. Indeed, it is just as politically judicious for representatives to criticize their own institution as it is for them to criticize the Presidency (Fenno 1978: 168). Congressmen and Senators are conscious of the fact that their local orientations, their electoral constraints and most of all the openly fragmented nature of their institution renders Congress a wholly inappropriate body to direct foreign policy. Congress's endemic localism and its chronic lack of co-ordination, however, are the very keys to its institutional power.

Legislative disorganization, incoherence and even irresponsibility are the sources of Congress's mercurial nature. It has been the very elusiveness of organized power in Congress that has allowed the institution to sustain its autonomy in a century notorious for centralized, disciplined and thoroughly emasculated assemblies. In response to charges of policy incoherence, therefore, most members of Congress would acknowledge the condition, but be unwilling to forego any of their independence to remedy it and would dispute whether it was a problem to anyone other than the President. Marching under the banner of the separation of powers, members of Congress condone and even celebrate their own fragmentation as the ramshackle defence against the streamlined presumption of executive force. They would be loath ever to jeopardize their freedom of manouevre by assembling together and being co-opted by the executive foreign policy-making establishment in one deathly embrace. Amongst the membership, congressional decentralization is recognized as a vice where overall policy is concerned, but it is also an acknowledged virtue in the more valued areas of specific policy and legislative independence. It is by 'splintering its own authority and turning its members loose' that Congress has devised and insists upon retaining 'an ingenious, formidable and undependable array of methods for giving the agencies a run for their money' (Mansfield 1975: 19).

Thus the overriding strategy for Congress is to challenge but not to succeed to the point of having to assume responsibility for policy measures. The latter is ultimately reserved for the Presidency, and Congress will resort to the most elaborate and subtle devices by which it can appear to suborn presidential authority and policies, while at the same time leaving the principle of presidential responsibility largely undisturbed. When there has been dramatic legislation such as the War Powers Resolution (1973), for example, it is noticeable that what was billed as a revolutionary restriction upon presidential power has proved in reality to be a symbolic vehicle for defusing, rather than resolving, the constitutional issue of war powers. It has left the President with arguably more discretionary powers than ever before, given that he now has a ninety-day period to commit armed forces into combat *without* a congressional declaration of war. Furthermore, no President has ever accepted the constitutionality of the legislation, and Congress has never really forced the issue to a point where that disputed constitutionality has been tested. As a result, the War Powers Resolution has never been properly invoked since its inception. The only time its provisions were partially engaged was in 1983, when President Reagan agreed to sign a formal congressional extension to the initial ninety-day commitment of the US marine force in Lebanon. As part of the agreement, however, Congress gave an extraordinary extension of eighteen months (i.e. 540 days) and allowed the President to declare, in signing the provision of the War Powers Resolution, that he did not recognize its constitutionality – a fact made quite evident soon afterwards when he launched an unannounced invasion of Grenada. The Grenada action was successful and popular and, therefore, congressional criticism of the administration in connection with the War Powers Resolution was muted to say the least. Much the same pattern of congressional quiescence was repeated with President Reagan's popular decision to launch a bombing assault upon Libya in 1986.

It is often in Congress's interests to rock the executive boat in line with the waves of public sentiment over foreign policy. But it is most definitely not in Congress's interests to capsize the craft. Congress has to tread a narrow line between pressing for its constitutional rights of co-equality with the President and omitting to exercise such rights in deference to the exigencies of changing international situations. The more Congress exerts itself in the name of the co-determination of foreign policy, the more it places itself in jeopardy firstly of having to assume real responsibility for it; secondly of bringing down upon itself the public opprobrium associated with just that disarray in America's world position which afforded Congress a role in foreign policy in the first place; and lastly of accepting the humiliating need to make the ultimate admission that co-equality in foreign policy is a practical impossibility. These are penalties that have to be avoided and, as a result, congressional incursions into foreign policy are normally only carefully impulsive and cautiously disruptive in nature.

Time and time again what passes outside Washington as audacious congressional actions are behind the scenes and in the small print really examples of Congress's genius for measured agitation and for securing positions of disengaged influence in foreign policy. The War Powers Resolution's accommodation of presidential prerogative is only one example among many. In its most concerted effort to control the activities of the country's intelligence agencies and, in particular, the covert operations of the Central Intelligence Agency, Congress passed the Intelligence Oversight Act in 1980. In the measure, Congress established by law that the President had to notify Congress's two intelligence committees of any covert operations *before* they were carried out. Having set out the principle, however, Congress thereupon proceeded to compromise it first by allowing the President the right to restrict notification to a handful of party leaders and ranking intelligence committee members; second by making arrangements for the President to inform the committees 'in a timely fashion' of those covert operations where he had not provided prior notice; third by explicitly stating that the two intelligence committees had no statutory right of veto over any covert operation; and lastly by stating in the preamble to the act that the reporting requirements were to be followed 'to the extent consistent with all applicable authorities and duties, including those conferred by the constitution' (McCormick and Smith 1987: 31).

The long history of Congress's intermittent funding of the Contra rebel forces in Nicaragua provides another example of the legislature's ingenuity for acquiring a double indemnity in foreign policy. First, it implicated itself in the formal, legal and financial basis of American policy in Central America. In this way, Congress could be seen to be discharging its constitutional responsibilities and to be fulfilling its representational role. Second, it laid a trail of complicated, ambiguous and inconsistent legal markers. By these means Congress provided enough imprecision in its lines of guidance to allow executive discretion to prevent such guidance from ever acquiring the status of total control. It also secured for itself a treasury of legal reference points that could be selectively drawn upon to suit future political contingencies.

Two cases of congressional indirection were particularly conspicuous in the Contra funding episode. In 1982, Congress passed the Boland Amendment, which barred the Pentagon or the CIA from using defence appropriations to provide military aid 'for the purpose of overthrowing the government of Nicaragua.' This was a landmark declaration, which provided the central basis to Congress's approach to American involvement in the war between the Contra rebels and the Sandinista regime. The question is whether the measure really amounted to a significant limitation, or whether it was ever intended to be the decisive restraint it was given credit for at the time. Since the Reagan administration supported the Boland Amendment and since Congress established an accompanying legislative history through the defeat of the Harkin Amendment – which would have barred *any* assistance to groups carrying out military activities in or against Nicaragua – the Boland measure in effect vindicated the Contras effort but only so long as they were not too successful. The determination of how funds were to be used to pressure the Nicaraguan government into changing its ways, but not to the point of being changed into another government, was left to the licence of executive discretion.

The other case of Congress's propensity for tactical equivocation came in 1984 when it appeared to ban the CIA, the Pentagon or 'any other agency or entity of the United States involved in intelligence activities' from using their appropriated funds to aid the Nicaraguan resistance movement. Although Congress went to the length of listing which agencies it was referring to, it nevertheless made no mention of either the President or the National Security Council. It also omitted the customary blanket phrase prohibiting the use of *any* government funds authorized for other purposes being used for the proscribed activity (Crovitz 1987: 25). The effect was to provide a signal to President Reagan to leave the National Security Council to its own devices in generating private covert aid for the Contra forces (Smith 1988: 620, 630; *Time* 1987). It was the alacrity with which Colonel Oliver North, in particular, exploited the legal loophole that later led to the channelling of Iranian funds into the Nicaraguan resistance movement in 1986 and, subsequently in 1987, the Congress's outraged declamations that its laws had been broken.

Congressional integrity can also be impugned by the way that its land-mark legislative controls have been used. The Arms Export Control Act which provided a legislative veto over major US arms sales was hailed at the time as a considerable restriction upon the Presidency's use of military equipment as a tool of foreign policy. And yet before its veto provisions were struck down by the Supreme Court in 1983, (*INS v. Chandha* 1983), the ultimate sanction had never been successfully invoked. In 1985 Congress did finally block an arms sale. Using the ordinary legislative technique of passing a bill, it rejected President Reagan's proposed $2 billion sale of advanced aircraft and missiles to Jordan. Even in this case, however, the details revealed that all was not what it seemed. The rejection was only a conditional rebuff for a period of time during which it could be determined whether or not Israel and Jordan were engaging in 'direct and meaningful negotiations' (*Congressional Quarterly* 1986a).

The lack of assiduous follow-up was not just confined to arms sales to non-Arab countries. During Congress's renewed insurgency, it had passed measures such as the Harkin amendment prohibiting aid to any country that consistently violated human rights. There were other similar measures requiring the executive branch to give regular reports on a whole range of matters like intelligence information, nuclear non-proliferation, military sales and arms control. But after having set up the infrastructure of control, Congress has been notorious for not using it in any consistent manner. Such neglect raises several pertinent questions.

> Did Congress really want all those reports it requested? . . . Were these statutes serious efforts to improve Congressional information, or the brain children of ambitious staffers, or consolation prizes for Congressmen unable to legislate actual changes but wanting something to claim credit for? If they were serious – and they took hundreds of man-hours for executive officials to complete – why did Congress usually ignore them?
>
> (Destler *et al.* 1984: 144–5)

Critics point out that the problem lay not with Congress passing regulatory measures, or with it wishing to share in defining the purposes of American foreign policy. The real problem is that Congress has opted out of making the laws work in a way which engages the legislature in a steady and constructive manner (Johnson 1987). As a result, Congress is commonly indicted for avoiding the real choice of 'either sharing responsibility for the President's policy or imposing a coherent alternative' (Destler *et al.* 1984: 143).

These changes are wholly justified but, in making them, the critics miss the point of what Congress's purposes are in this field. Coping with foreign policy in this context lies not in settling foreign policy issues, or in providing foreign policy leadership. It lies in retaining its proprietorial rights to be a *de jure* partner in foreign policy-making, and in maintaining a practical capability to participate in international affairs whenever it is politically prudent or profitable to do so. Congress relies wholly upon the President to be 'to a greater or lesser degree, a constant and insistent force in all foreign policy areas' (Woll 1985: 436). What Congress is intent upon is preserving its licence to intervene in the guise of a loyal opposition addressing itself to the nation's mistakes and offering attractive solutions, but never to the length of assuming responsibility for the delicate network of interdependent diplomatic understandings and military arrangements which characterize the nature of foreign policy. This form of self-denial is, of course, synonymous with self-indulgence. Just as Congress claims the right to intervene, it likewise assumes the equal right to withdraw at a moment's notice leaving the Presidency to resume control.

In this way, congressional participation in American foreign policy is not dissimilar to taking a bus ride. Congress gets on and off at its pleasure. The members take no personal responsibility for the organization of the drivers, maintenance crews, traffic managers, fares, routes, manning, etc., but they expect the bus to arrive and to stop in order for them to board it. During the journey, the members look to any pedestrian out in the rain to be part of the bus. The Congressmen and Senators may enjoy the view and the sense of motion, but they are not directly in control of the route or of the speed. Given the choice of assuming the driver's position or of leaving the bus altogether, any normal member of Congress would choose the latter and resume his role of complaining about the bus company from the safety of the pavement. Coping with foreign policy in this congressional context, therefore, is knowing how, when and where to get on and off the bus. Legislative eclecticism of sudden surges of zealous interest in a particular issue followed by an equally sudden rush of disinterest and indifference is an integral part of this implicit strategy for tackling foreign policy problems (Nathan and Oliver 1987: 106–90; Bailey 1987). Congress's management of the American politics of international affairs is not simply about the content or even the effect of

91

adopting positions upon foreign policy. It is also about ensuring that the occasions and devices for participating in foreign policy, in a manner that commands some attention and authority, are made available on demand. In other words, the bus-stops are just as important to Congress as any of the journeys made between them. They provide the optional access to foreign policy that Congress values so much and which provides Congress with the means to regulate the state of tension in legislative-executive relations at any one time.

By accident or design, Congress may make a substantial and even at times a wholly positive and beneficial contribution to foreign policy-making, but that is not Congress's chief collective criterion of success. That criterion is to achieve a sustainable fusion of presidential support and opposition; of congressional dependence and independence; of national unity and pluralistic disunity; and of both insider and outsider status within the foreign policy-making establishment. The irony here is that while the field of foreign policy can no longer be used to establish Congress as a derelict institution in an international age, it also shows in revealing clarity that Congress is still the same old Congress. Its motivations and sensibilities have simply been applied in an active rather than a passive sense to the previously exclusive field of international affairs. Congressional activism has been conditioned by the institution's traditional subtlety in concealing its inherent weaknesses and in calibrating its activities to the changing profile of public expectations and presidential support. Implicit within the congressional 'revolution' in foreign affairs, therefore, is an understanding that the Presidency will always be relied upon not only to make the world safe for democracy, but to make it safe for congressional politics as well.

References

Bailey, C.J. (1987) 'President Reagan, the U.S. Senate, and American foreign policy, 1981–1986', *Journal of American Studies* 21, 2: 167–81.
Bergner, J.T. (1987) 'Organizing the Congress for national security', *Comparative Strategy* 6, 3: 281–304.
Bernstein, R.A. and Anthony, W.W. (1974) 'The ABM issue in the Senate, 1968–1970: The importance of ideology', *American Political Science Review* 68 (3): 1199–1203.
Burns, J.M. (1949) *Congress on Trial*, New York: Harper and Brothers.
—— (1963) *Deadlock of Democracy: Four Party Politics in America*, Englewood Cliffs: Prentice Hall.
Carroll, H.N. (1965) 'The Congress and National Security Policy', in D.B. Truman (ed.) *The Congress and America's Future*, Englewood Cliffs: Prentice Hall.
—— (1966) *The House of Representatives and Foreign Affairs*, rev. edn., Boston: Little Brown.

Clark, J.S. (1964) *Congress: The Sapless Branch*, New York: Harper and Row.

Clausen, A.G. (1973) *How Congressmen Decide: A Policy Focus*, New York: St. Martin's.

Congressional Quarterly (1986a) 'Jordan arms sale: Senate deals blow to Reagan, Hussein on arms', *Congressional Quarterly Guide to Current American Government* Spring 1986: 83–8.

Corwin, E.S. (1940) *The President: Office and Powers*, New York: New York University Press.

Crabb, C.V. and Holt, P.M. (1980) *Invitation to Struggle: Congress, the President and Foreign Policy*, Washigton D.C.: Congressional Quarterly.

Cronin, T.E. (1980) 'An imperiled Presidency?', in V. Davis (ed.) *The Post-Imperial Presidency*, New Brunswick: Transaction.

Crovitz, L.G. (1987) 'Crime, the Constitution, and the Iran-Contra Affair', *Commentary*, October.

Davidson, R.H., Kovenock, D.M. and O'Leary, M.K. (1966) *Congress in Crisis: Politics and Congressional Reform*, New York: Wadsworth.

Davidson, R.H. (1981) 'Subcommittee government: New channels for policy making', in T.E. Mann and N. Ornstein (eds) *The New Congress*, Washington D.C.: American Enterprise Institute.

Davis, V. (1984) 'Presidential politics and the policy process: The President's key players', in S.C. Sarkesian (ed.) *Presidential Leadership and National Security: Style, Institutions, and Politics*, Boulder: Westview.

Deering, C.J. and Smith, S.S. (1985) 'Subcommittees in Congress', in L.C. Dodd and B.I. Oppenheimer (eds) *Congress Reconsidered*, 3rd edn., Washington D.C.: Congressional Quarterly.

Destler, I.M. (1981) 'Trade consensus, SALT stalemate: Congress and foreign policy in the 1970s', in T.E. Mann and N. Ornstein (eds) *The New Congress*, Washington D.C.: American Enterprise Institute.

Destler, I.M., Gelb, L.H. and Lake, A. (1984) *Our Own Worst Enemy: The Unmaking of American Foreign Policy*, New York: Simon and Schuster.

Destler, I.M. (1985) 'Executive-Congressional conflict in foreign policy: Explaining it, coping with it', in L.C. Dodd and B.I. Oppenheimer (eds) *Congress Reconsidered*, 3rd edn., Washington D.C.: Congressional Quarterly.

Dexter, L.A. (1963) 'Congressmen and the making of military policy', in R.L. Peabody and N.W. Polsby (eds) *New Perspectives on the House of Representatives*, Chicago: Rand McNally.

Drischler, A.P. (1985) 'Foreign Policy Making on the Hill', *The Washington Quarterly* 8: 165–75.

Evans, R. and Novak, R. (1981) *The Reagan Revolution*, New York: Dutton.

Fenno, R.F. (1978) *Home Style: House Members in their Districts*, Boston: Little Brown.

Fleisher, R. (1985) 'Economic benefit, ideology, and Senate voting on the B–1 Bomber', *American Politics Quarterly* 13, 2: 200–11.

Franck, T.M. and Weisband, E. (1979) *Foreign Policy by Congress*, New York: Oxford University Press.

Fulbright, J.W. (1961) 'American foreign policy in the twentieth century under an eighteenth century constitution', *Cornell Law Quarterly* 47, 3.

Galloway, G.B. (1946) *Congress at the Crossroads*, New York, Crowell.

Gregorian, H. (1984) 'Assessing Congressional involvement in foreign policy: Lessons of the post-Vietnam period', *Review of Politics* 46, 1: 91-112.

Haas, R. (1979) 'Congressional power: Implications for American security policy', *Adelphi Papers* 153: 1-39.

Hamilton, A. (1961) 'Federalist Paper Number 70', in A. Hamilton, J. Madison and J. Jay *The Federalist Papers*, New York: Mentor.

Hargrove, E.C. (1974) *The Power of the Modern Presidency*, New York: Knopf.

Harting, W. (1986) 'Star Wars pork barrel', *Bulletin of the Atomic Scientists* 42, 1: 20-24.

Hilsman, R. (1967) *To Move a Nation: The Politics of Foreign Policy in the Administration of John F. Kennedy*, New York: Doubleday.

Hinckley, B. (1978) *Stability and Change in Congress*, 2nd ed., New York: Harper and Row.

Hodgson, G. (1979) *Congress and American Foreign Policy*, London: Royal Institute of International Affairs.

Huntington, S.P. (1961) *The Common Defence*, New York: Columbia University Press.

Huntington, S.P. (1965) 'Congressional responses to the twentieth century', in D.B. Truman (ed.) *The Congress and America's Future*, Englewood Cliffs: Prentice Hall.

Immigration and Naturalization Service v. Chadha 462 US 919 (1983).

Javits, J.K. with D. Kellerman (1973) *Who Makes War: The President versus Congress*, New York: William Morrow.

Johnson, L.K. (1987) *A Season of Inquiry*, Lexington, The University Press of Kentucky.

Kendall, W. (1960) 'The Two Majorities', *Midwest Journal of Political Science* 4, 4: 317-45.

Kingdon, J.W. (1981) *Congressmen's Voting Decisions*, 2nd edn. New York: Harper and Row.

Kissinger, H. (1977) 'Kissinger on Kissinger', *The Observer* 12 June.

Kissinger, H. (1982) *Years of Upheaval*, London: Weidenfeld and Nicholson and Michael Joseph.

Kolodziej, E.A. (1970) 'Congress and foreign policy: Through the looking glass', in W.R. Nelson (ed.) *American Government and Political Change: A Contemporary Reader*, New York: Oxford University Press.

Leigh, M. (1976) *Mobilizing Consent: Public Opinion and American Foreign Policy, 1937-1947*, Westport: Greenwood.

Lehman, J. (1976) *The Executive, Congress and Foreign Policy: Studies of the Nixon Administration*, New York: Praeger.

Lens, S. (1970) *The Military-Industrial Complex*, London: Kahn and Averill.

Leyton-Brown, D. (1982–83) 'The role of Congress in the making of foreign policy', *International Journal* 38, 1: 59–76.

Locke, J. (1960) *Two Treatises of Government*, intro. P.J. Laslett, Cambridge: Cambridge University Press.

Mansfield, H.C. (1975) 'The dispersion of authority in Congress', in H.C. Mansfield (ed.) *Congress Against the President*, Montpelier: Academy of Political Science.

Marchetti, V. and Marks, J.D. (1976) *The CIA and the Cult of Intelligence*, London: Coronet.

Mayhew, D. (1974) *Congress: The Electoral Connection*, New Haven: Yale University Press.

McCormick, J.M. and Smith, S.S. (1987) 'The Iran arms sales and the intelligence oversight act of 1980', *PS* 20, 1: 29–37.

Miller, W.E. and Stokes, D.E. (1968) 'Constituency influence in Congress', in S.C. Patterson (ed.) *American Legislative Behavior: A Reader*, Princeton: D. Van Nostrand.

Muravchik, J. (1980) *The Senate and National Security: A New Mood*, Beverly Hills: Sage.

Muskie, E.S., Rush, K. and Thompson, K.W. (1986) *The President the Congress and Foreign Policy*, Lanham, University Press of America.

Nathan, J.A. and Oliver, J.K. (1987) *Foreign Policy Making and the American Political System*, 2nd edn., Boston: Little, Brown.

Nelson, A.K. (1987) 'John Foster Dulles and the bipartisan Congress', *Political Science Quarterly* 102, 1: 43–64.

Nogee, J.L. (1981) 'Congress and the Presidency: The dilemmas of policy-making in a democracy' in J. Spanier and J.L. Nogee (eds) *Congress, the Presidency and American Foreign Policy*, New York: Pergamon.

Oberdorfer, D., Omang, J., Drozdiak, W. and McCartney, R.J. (1984) 'Congressmen, wary of voter reaction, give Reagan the money', *Guardian Weekly*, 20 June.

Opperman, J. (1984) 'The Panama canal treaties: Legislative strategy for advice and consent', in H. Purvis and S.J. Baker (eds) *Legislating Foreign Policy*, Boulder: Westview.

Phillips, K. (1983) 'The balkanization of America', in W.H. Chafe and H. Sitkoff (eds) *A History of Our time: Readings on Postwar America*, New York: Oxford University Press.

Polsby, N.W. (1971) 'Strengthening Congress in national policymaking', in N.W. Polsby (ed.) *Congressional Behaviour*, New York: Random House.

Purvis, H. (1984) 'Legislative-executive interaction', in H. Purvis and S.J. Baker (eds) *Legislating Foreign Policy*, Boulder: Westview.

Purvis, H. and Baker, S.J. (1984) *Legislating Foreign Policy*, Boulder: Westview.

Rieselbach, L. (1986) *Congressional Reform*, Washington D.C.: Congressional Quarterly.

Rossiter, C. (1960) *The American Presidency*, rev. edn., New York: Mentor.

Rourke, J. (1983) *Congress and the Presidency in U.S. Foreign Policymaking*, Boulder: Westview.

Schlesinger, A.M. (1974) *The Imperial Presidency*, London: Andre Deutsch.

Sidey, H. (1987) 'The speaker's itch for power', *Time* 30 November.

Smith, H. (1988) *The Power Game: How Washington Works*, London, Collins.

Spanier, J. (1981) 'Introduction – Congress and the Presidency: The weakest link in the policy process', in J. Spanier and J.L. Nogee (eds) *Congress, the Presidency and American Foreign Policy*, New York: Pergamon.

Spanier, J. and Nogee, J.L. (1981) *Congress, the Presidency and American Foreign Policy*, New York: Pergamon.

Spanier, J. and Uslaner, E.M. (1982) *Foreign Policy and the Democratic Dilemmas*, 3rd edn., New York: Holt, Rinehart and Winston.

Steiner, Z. (1987) 'Decision-making in American and British foreign policy: An open and shut case', *Review of International Studies* 13, 1: 1–18.

Sundquist, J.L. (1981) *The Decline and Resurgence of Congress*, Washington D.C.: Brookings.

Time (1987) 'The Good Soldier', 25 May.

Truman, D.B. (1959) *The Congressional Party: A Case Study*, New York: John Wiley.

United States v. Curtiss-Wright Export Corp. 299 US 304 (1936).

Wildavsky, A. (1968) 'The two Presidencies', in A. Wildavsky and N.W. Polsby (eds.) *American Governmental Institutions: A Reader in the Political Process*, Chicago: Rand McNally.

Woll, P. and Jones, R. (1981) *The Private World of Congress*, New York: Free Press.

Woll, P. (1985) *Congress*, Boston: Little, Brown.

X (1947) 'The Sources of Soviet Conduct', *Foreign Affairs* 25, 4: 566–82.

Yankelovich, D. (1979) 'Farewell to 'President knows best', *Foreign Affairs* 57, 3: 670–93.

Chapter six

Policy, process and power: understanding American bureaucracy

Robert Williams

The one thing that is crystal clear about the federal bureaucracy is that nobody likes it. Everybody attacks it and no one defends it. Many seem to share Ronald Reagan's view that the ten most frightening words in America are, 'I'm from the federal government and I'm here to help'. The federal bureaucracy is widely perceived as too large, too costly and too intrusive. It has become an issue which reaches across partisan divisions to unite Democrats and Republicans. In 1964, the actor Ronald Reagan claimed that America had 'a permanent structure so big and complex it is virtually beyond the control of Congress and the comprehension of the people' (Reagan 1988: 21). In 1981, the newly elected President Reagan pledged himself in his inaugural address 'to curb the size and influence of the federal establishment' (Reagan 1988: 35). But this was not a break with conventional wisdom because his predecessor, Jimmy Carter, had also spoken of the 'horrible, bloated bureaucracy' (Fawcett and Thomas 1983: 143) and his desire to cut it down to size.

The Founding Fathers thought that government was a 'necessary evil', but there are many Americans who are more persuaded of the latter than the former. Since the Second World War, the prestige and respect accorded political institutions has tended to decline. Politicians at all levels are unpopular as a breed even if locally successful in gaining re-election. Thus the fact that the federal bureaucracy enjoys particularly low esteem is not in itself extraordinary, though it is an interesting phenomenon requiring explanation, but the ubiquitous prejudice partly obscures more important and interesting issues concerning the proper role of and limits to the activities of the federal government. The recent revival of conservatism is discussed elsewhere in the book by Gillian Peele and it has given credence to the charge that the federal government and its bureaucracy intervenes in areas of social policy and economic regulation which are best left to market forces and private initiative. Conservatives strive to slow, halt or reverse the growth of government. To conservatives, bureaucratic answers to problems always involve higher taxes, recruiting more bureaucrats and exercising more government control over the lives of private citizens. Worse still, conservatives believe that governmental solutions to economic and social problems are usually counter-productive.

Reagan's conviction that the United States should become a bureaucracy-free zone is not something to be easily dismissed as campaign or administration rhetoric. While his tax and budget cuts understandably received most attention, as Joe Hogan's chapter explains, bureaucratic reform and de-regulation were also important elements in his domestic strategy. Thus, Reagan did not simply talk about the evils of big government and overweening bureaucracy, his administration made a serious and sustained effort to do something about it.

It is important to understand that beyond and behind ideological antipathy, the organization and operation of the federal bureaucracy have evoked much criticism from members of Congress, from the media, from the regulated interests and, of course, from successive occupants of the White House. These criticisms move beyond issues of legitimacy and focus more on issues of process, policy and structure. The most repeated complaints are about the alleged inefficiency and lack of responsiveness of bureaucracy. Doubts are often expressed about the accountability and control of bureaucracy and its apparent ability to resist, retard or deflect the political will of its constitutional masters. This frustration is particularly well illustrated by Franklin Roosevelt's evocative observation that

> To change anything in the Navy is like punching a feather bed. You punch it with your right and you punch it with your left, until you are finally exhausted, and then you find the damn bed just as it was before you started punching.
>
> (Hodgson 1984: 87)

Academics specializing in public administration have developed a more sophisticated if less colourful vocabulary to express their particular concerns. Eschewing the narrowly practical, academics tend both to develop models and to utilize methods of comparative analysis. Not only does the American federal bureaucracy fall sadly short of Weber's 'ideal type', but when set against North European comparators, it seems riddled with corruption and clientelism, troubled by issues of authority and autonomy, beset by problems of mission and morale and crippled by a profound lack of co-ordination and continuity. To most academic observers, the faults and weaknesses of the federal bureaucracy are manifold and manifest.

The central issues concerning the American federal bureaucracy are therefore the basic ones of legitimacy and performance. The United States possesses a large and costly bureacratic apparatus whose very existence is questioned and whose performance is found wanting. This chapter explores some of the reasons why there is a lack of political and public confidence in the bureaucracy and it further explores the reasons why repeated efforts, including President Reagan's, to produce significant change seem not to have been entirely successful.

The first question to address is why does the United States have the kind of bureaucracy it does? It was clearly not created by design if design is taken to mean constructed according to some kind of blueprint or master plan. The Founding Fathers had little or nothing to say about the organization and operation of the executive departments and it is therefore difficult to make any observations based on 'original intent'. The federal bureaucracy has grown in a sporadic, *ad hoc* way and its structures and activities have never been consciously integrated or co-ordinated. It was almost a hundred years after the constitutional and institutional framework of government was established that serious efforts were made to establish a national civil service. These belated efforts enjoyed only a limited success partly because political institutions were already well established and defined and partly because the effort was not wholehearted (Williams 1987: 122–4). In the 1880s, as in the 1980s, few Americans were prepared to concede much in the way of respect, status or priority to the federal bureaucracy.

Thus, bureaucracy in the United States lacks a sense of historical identity. It lacks any semblence of a noble tradition, any sense of continuity and any claim to have played a role in founding or securing the nation. Americans are said to be preoccupied with their 'roots' but, in the case of bureaucracy, they are difficult to locate. There are no linkages with pre-revolutionary forms of government and no evidence that the success of nation-building was dependent on bureaucratic efforts. The federal bureaucracy has then always been slightly detached from the mainstream of American institutional life. It was a late arrival at the institutional party and there are many who still wonder whether it was ever formally invited. The consequent lack of integration into the constitutional culture made it difficult for the federal bureaucracy to develop a distinctive and coherent identity and to defend itself effectively from the pressures exerted by the established political institutions whose own legitimacy derived both from the constitution and from their increasingly democratic forms.

In such an unwelcoming institutional environment, the likelihood of senior administrators being able to claim or retain elite status was always remote. With distinguished exceptions, the federal bureaucracy has not attracted 'the best and the brightest'. While some of the most able graduates in Britain and France compete strenuously to enter the higher civil service, there is no equivalent rush from the Ivy League universities to become career civil servants in the United States. The profession simply does not offer the prestige, power and material rewards that talented graduates can expect to obtain in other careers. The consequent lack of high quality recruitment naturally reinforces the image of the federal bureaucracy as a career to be avoided by high achievers.

The federal bureaucracy is then a sort of black sheep in the political family, whose existence is scarcely recognized and whose reputation is sullied without fear of contradiction. Lacking status, identity and legitimacy, it has difficulty attracting and retaining the sort of people capable of changing the image of bureaucracy. In the United States, young people seek to emulate successful businessmen, entertainers and athletes. To confess to your parents that you want to be a federal bureaucrat is almost to invite disinheritance. For these and other reasons, it is obvious that the federal bureaucracy in general and its higher levels in particular have failed to establish the presence in, or impact on, government that their Western European counterparts have achieved.

The failure of the federal bureaucracy to establish its presence, independence and prestige is hardly problematic because 'it is the absence of a sense of the state that has been the great hallmark of American political culture' (Skowronek 1982: 3). Marx and de Tocqueville, among others, have explained the absence or weakness of the formal, hierarchical institutional arrangements characteristic of European states as a consequence of the early development of democracy and attendant notions of political equality. These tendencies mitigated against state structures which reflected rigid social distinctions and produced a situation where the strength of political participation inhibited and even precluded the expansion of bureaucratic power.

Thus when demands on the governing capacity of the state increased in the late nineteenth century, due partly to continental expansion and industrialization, the institutional response was necessarily conditioned by the limits imposed by a democratic and decentralized polity. The bureaucratic advances of nineteenth-century Europe were therefore resisted in the United States until the twentieth century. The development of bureaucratic institutions was retarded by the strength of political parties, by the strength of local political affiliations and loyalties and by the strength of judicial control over the expansion of bureaucratic power.

As Skowronek's seminal study shows, the attempts to strengthen national administrative authority were resisted for as long as patchwork remedies were possible. Although ultimately resistance gave way to accommodation and the reconstruction of constitutional relationships, the political struggle ensured that the growth of bureaucratic power took place within an institutional environment characterized by conflict and division. In the context of a highly developed electoral democracy, the idea of building support for the insulation of bureaucratic power from political and public pressure was never likely to commend itself to governing elites.

In the nineteenth century, administrative patronage had grown to become the principal means of binding political parties together and encouraging co-operative action. Thus the passing of the 'spoils' system and the development of merit systems meant at one level a depoliticization of the federal bureaucracy, but at another level the organizing principle of party had been eroded without being adequately replaced. The new situation which emerged from the decline of party patronage can best be described as one of constitutional struggle and deadlock.

The need for a growth in bureaucratic power was finally acknowledged in the early twentieth century, but that agreement was not matched by a similar consensus defining and authoritatively allocating responsibility for controlling the federal bureaucracy. Thus political oversight of the new administrative state was characterized by parallel sets of controls which served to pull the bureaucracy in inconsistent and contrary directions. The ensuing constitutional and political conflicts have proved resistant to final resolution and therefore 'invitations to struggle' are built into the very fabric of government.

In such an institutional context, the needs and concerns of the federal bureaucracy have not impinged greatly on the political or public consciousness and, in consequence, 'the higher civil service, therefore, has been an outstanding ''nonsubject'' in the development of American central government' (Heclo 1984: 13). The reality is that there is no such thing as *the* federal service because each part is the product of a unique institutional skirmish. Instead, there is a collection of federal personnel systems which may be formally joined together but which in practice enjoy a high degree of effective autonomy. The links between, for example, the Forest Service and the Federal Bureau of Investigation are less than extensive.

The essence of the federal bureaucracy was and is that it is 'a many splintered thing'. It comprises not merely the well-known government departments, executive and independent agencies and commissions, but also all manner of boards, councils, advisory bodies, intergovernmental units, legislative organizations such as the General Accounting Office and quasi-public bodies such as the Corporation for Public Broadcasting. In consequence, determining who is and who is not a federal bureaucrat in the United States is very difficult because the line between the private and public sectors is both extremely blurred and constantly shifting.

While the size of the federal bureaucracy grew dramatically during the New Deal and the Second World War, it has remained at roughly the same level for the past forty years. Given the antipathy to bureaucracy, executive and legislative politicians of both parties have been keen to claim the credit for having contained the once apparently inexorable growth of the federal bureaucracy. But this 'achievement' conceals some major and striking developments in the organization and delivery of

101

public services in the United States. In the first place, while the size of the federal bureaucracy has remained broadly static, there have been substantial increases in the number of state and local level bureaucrats. This increase is largely associated with the increased dispersal of categorical, block grant and revenue sharing funds. In personnel terms, the scale of the increase is reflected in the growth in the number of local level bureaucrats from 6 million in 1960 to 10.8 million in 1981 (Stillman 1987: 13).

If bureaucratic growth has been stemmed at the centre, the increases in services, programmes and expenditure have produced a decentralized expansion in public employment. The second and related development is that, as an examination of the federal budget shows, 'the United States government is largely a funnel for passing money to individuals, other governments and contractors' (Newland 1988: 646). The job of the federal government is less and less to deliver services and more and more to contract others to implement government programmes. Although contracting has always been part of the federal bureaucracy's role, its scope and scale have greatly increased in recent years.

One consequence of the growth in contracting has been to accentuate the problem of determining the boundaries of government. The interaction between government and private business, between government and universities and between government and 'think-tanks', consultancy groups and the like are now so intensive and extensive as to make disentanglement virtually impossible. The relevant political conclusion is that, if the work undertaken by the contracted companies, groups and individuals were performed 'in house' by the federal bureaucracy, the claim to have contained the growth of bureaucracy would be exposed as being 'economical with the truth'. The reality is that government funded activities have greatly expanded in the past forty years and federal bureaucrats have increasingly taken on the role of contract managers. This development has brought not inconsiderable political benefits by allowing politicians to wage a popular war against the growth of the federal bureaucracy while, at the same time, ensuring that their constituents receive an expanding range of government benefits and services.

Both the real and the concealed growth in bureaucracy have taken place against a background of economic change and political upheaval. The belated appreciation of the need for a professional federal bureaucracy was accompanied by a variety of political strategies designed both to meet the new challenges of government while simultaneously avoiding undue accretions and concentrations of bureaucratic power. If the growth of the federal bureaucracy was ultimately inescapable, its shape, structure, composition, mission and procedures were all matters worthy of constant political struggle. The form and content of the struggles changed both over time and from issue to issue. On occasions, it took an institutional form pitting Congress against the White House while, at other times, the battles were partisan and personal. Whatever shape the struggles took one fact was clear, the advance of bureaucracy threatened the power positions of the other political players and those threatened with displacement sought to devise and implement strategies conducive to strengthening and defending their interests. Such strategies can be classified in a variety of ways but, for present purposes, they can be identified as functional specialization, legal constraints, review and reform, the administrative Presidency and bypass strategies.

Functional specialization

It has already been noted that one major characteristic of the American federal bureaucracy is its fragmentation. Functional specialization is a euphemism for saying that the United States came to terms with bureaucracy by dividing it on lines acceptable to legislative politicians. As Presidents recognized the need for enlarged and sophisticated bureaucratic organizations to handle the complex and burgeoning tasks of government, legislative politicians recognized the need to separate and divide bureaucracy along the functional lines already present in the legislature.

The fragmentation of bureaucracy is thus both a product and a source of congressional power. Bureaucratic structures have therefore to pass the twin tests of meeting the executive's needs without jeopardizing or threatening the position of Congress. The major weapon wielded by Congress in the early battles over the concentration of bureaucratic power was the independent regulatory commission and agency. In railroads and energy regulation, in broadcasting and telecommunications, in trade and financial markets, Congress came to recognize the need for a bureaucratic response to growing political and popular demands for effective action. The issue became one of how to respond to such pressures without giving up congressional prerogatives. The answer to the problem became known as the 'headless fourth branch of government', a set of independent, quasi-judicial bodies which enjoyed autonomy from presidential direction and which diffused bureaucratic authority in a commission rather than concentrated it in the hands of a single official.

The independent agency therefore became a convenient vehicle for exercising regulatory control. It had the double attraction of freeing Congress from its day to day responsibilities while avoiding any undesirable concentration of power in the executive branch. In concluding that regulation was a matter for experts and something to be taken 'out of politics', the advocates of the independent agency were able to fragment bureaucratic growth while further complicating the co-ordination of government activity and inhibiting the exercise of presidential control over administrative affairs. The creation of regulatory agencies was then both a consequence of the institutional struggle between the White House and Congress for control over the working of the federal government and a way of multiplying the arenas of contest. One major consequence is that the struggle for the control of bureaucracy is waged on many fronts simultaneously and, while fortunes may fluctuate, there are no final victories or defeats.

Legal constraints

If an enthusiasm for the commission form of organization represented in part an attempt to impose structural constraints on presidential and bureaucratic power, the enthusiasm for legal/formal controls reflected a continuing concern with the procedures and methods of bureaucratic government. In particular, the Administrative Procedure Act of 1946 involved a major effort to define process and to constrain the operations of the 'alphabetocracy', the numerous administrative entities created during the New Deal. It represented an attempt to develop a uniform process by imposing standard procedural requirements on all federal agencies which have, in consequence, adopted quasi-judicial procedures in their formal rule-making proceedings. Such proceedings are employed in situations where the issues are largely factual and the contending parties are few in number, for example, the granting of a licence or a franchise by one of the economic regulatory agencies.

Compelling an administrative entity to behave in a quasi-judicial manner serves not only the obvious purpose of providing a check on the unreasonable exercise of bureaucratic discretion, but it also acts as an obstacle to presidential involvement in agency decisions. As will be discussed below, recent Presidents have sought to centralize regulatory oversight, but the intention and impact of the Adminstrative Procedure Act was to make presidential control more rather than less difficult.

Regulatory commissions have also developed more informal procedures to meet cases where a quasi-legislative response is more appropriate, for example, where large numbers of individuals or companies are involved and where policy judgements rather than factual matters are at issue. But over time the distinction between formal and informal procedures has become blurred. Not only do interested parties have the right to seek review of agency decisions in the courts, but the informal procedures have become increasingly formal to protect further the interests of affected parties.

What clearly emerges from even a brief examination of agency rule-making procedures is that it contributes to the further fragmentation of federal government decisions. Judicial review of substantive and procedural propriety in individual decisions impedes the comparison and trading off of multiple regulatory objectives within and across agencies. The co-ordinating function of the White House is thus made more difficult and 'Above all, commission independence legitimates an autonomous capacity for action that enables boards to respond to preferences from sources outside the executive branch' (Chubb and Peterson 1989: 19).

If the creation of independent agencies and a reliance on judicial review of their operations served to fragment federal bureaucracy and helped to insulate it from presidential control, the fact remained that their congressional sponsors were still not enamoured of the growth in bureaucracy produced by the New Deal and World War II. Public opinion polls displayed conflicting attitudes in that they reflected support for New Deal policies and programmes, but hostility to those responsible for implementing them. A public opinion poll in 1945 indicated that 53 per cent regarded bureaucracy as an 'unmitigated evil' (Pemberton 1979: 30).

Reform and review

With the death of President Roosevelt and the resurgence of Republicans in the Congress, circumstances seemed propitious for an assault on bureaucracy and 'big government'. While President Truman did not share this ideological antipathy, he saw administrative reform and reorganization as important because they would remedy the administrative weaknesses and inefficiencies of the New Deal.

Anticipating the defeat of President Truman in 1948, the Republican Eightieth Congress created the Commission on the Organization of the Executive Branch (the Hoover Commission) to prepare the way for the Republican administration which would dismantle the institutional innovations of the New Deal. In a policy statement adopted on 20 October 1947, the commission declared that it was not just concerned with efficiency but was 'directed to exploring the boundaries of government functions in the light of their cost, their usefulness, their limitations, and their curtailment or elimination' (Pemberton 1979: 88). Truman's election in 1948 meant that the 'conservative revolution' was postponed, but even before that the nomination of Dewey rather than Taft as Republican candidate suggested that the new President was likely to be a moderate rather than a zealot in the cause of dismantling the federal bureaucracy. Recognizing the political realities, Hoover observed after the election that the job of his commission was 'to make every Government activity that now exists work efficiently. . . It is not our function to say whether it should exist or not' (Pemberton 1979: 90).

Thus the major congressionally located, conservative attempt to dismantle the greatly enlarged federal bureaucracy had failed. President Truman's reputation as the defender of the New Deal was secure and the conservative challenge was deflected into a non-partisan effort to improve the management and efficiency of the existing executive branch. This was not of course the end of the conservative challenge to 'big government', but the subsequent battles were largely waged from the White House rather than from Capitol Hill.

If the federal bureaucracy was held in low esteem by the White House in 1933 for its conservatism and resistance to change, it was held in equally low esteem in 1953 for exactly opposite reasons. Republicans viewed it with great suspicion as a haven for radical and activist liberals and they feared that it would be unsympathetic and uncooperative when faced with a conservative occupant of the White House.

The election of the first post-war Republican President, Dwight Eisenhower, did temporarily revive expectations that the federal bureaucracy would be cleansed of liberal Democrats, but in practice little effort was made to change the size, composition or responsibilities of the federal bureaucracy. Republican Congressmen's thirst for bureaucratic patronage was never assuaged and the brief effort to recruit party loyalists to civil service position caused such controversy that it was quickly abandoned.

What Eisenhower did introduce was a new category of senior civil service post called Schedule C for positions of a confidential or policy-determining character. The other main characteristic of these posts was that they carried no security of tenure. Many of the posts were filled by internal promotion and one irony of the Republican backlash against the bureaucracy is that 'having stamped many senior bureau posts as "political" by putting them in Schedule C, the new Administration promptly filled the majority of them with people who were in the federal service before they took over' (Spann 1956: 150) But despite this irony, Eisenhower was not prepared to allow liberal Democratic officials free rein in the executive branch. There were important changes of senior personnel in key areas dealing with new policies. Following the reforming zeal of the New and Fair Deal years, the 1950s witnessed an important division between presidential and bureaucratic values. President Eisenhower and his political appointees in the executive branch were striving to lead the nation in policy directions which most career bureaucrats opposed.

The tension between the White House and the bureaucracy was not as acute as it became under President Nixon and nor did Eisenhower's reform efforts match those of President Reagan. Eisenhower was by no means the creature of the Republican right and in practice he accepted that the increase in government functions and responsibilities which occurred under Truman and Roosevelt was largely inevitable. What did concern Eisenhower was both that presidential claims to authority over the federal bureaucracy were not readily conceded and that the increasing linkages between bureaucracy, interest groups and Congress were making government less responsive to White House policy initiatives and signals. Eisenhower's frustrations with the lack of bureaucratic responsiveness was shared by the next Republican President, Richard Nixon, who made a concerted attempt to solve the problem.

The administrative Presidency

The Nixon administration experienced a struggle with bureaucracy which 'was more intense, more calculated, and far more political in design than that of any previous President' (Cole and Caputo 1979: 399). To some observers, it was an intensified re-run of the Eisenhower experience in that a new Republican President was taking office after years of Democratic profligacy and liberalism. President Nixon was convinced that substantial elements in the bureaucracy were against him and he was probably right (Aberbach and Rockman 1976: 456–68).

The important difference was that, unlike Eisenhower, Nixon wanted to be an activist, radical President who initiated new policies and who eliminated redundant departments and extravagant programmes. His desire to change the federal bureaucracy was so strong that President Nixon found it difficult to accept the constraints on reform. His interest in bureaucratic reform and reorganization was such that he established a council under Roy Ash to make appropriate recommendations (Williams 1979: 55–69). President Nixon was impressed by Ash's maxim that 'organization is policy' and he increasingly interpreted administrative problems in political terms.

Nixon wanted to give domestic affairs a new direction by reducing central control and devolving more responsibilities to the states. In practice, his New Federalism was also an attack on the size, power and discretion of the federal bureaucracy. It was therefore unsurprising that such proposals would incur bureaucratic resistance, animosity and distrust. Unlike Eisenhower, Nixon thought he knew how to deal with such resistance, he would literally 'take over the bureaucracy' (Nathan 1975: 9).

His strategy had essentially two elements. In the first place, the White House staff would in effect become line managers and actually run government programmes in association with lower level bureaucrats. In this way, decisions would be made in accordance with presidential priorities and not those of senior officials or cabinet members. The second element was to place party loyalists in key bureaucratic positions both by placing more ideological Republicans in political executive posts, but also by using partisan considerations to fill senior civil service positions. The extent and success of this second element is not easy to determine, but one study has concluded that 'the Nixon White House extended the politicization of the bureaucracy further than any previous administration' (Cole and Caputo 1979: 410).

Nixon's so-called counter-bureaucracy approach met some obvious and intractable difficulties. In particular, White House staff became so immersed in implementation problems that policy issues were neglected. The absorption in administrative affairs meant that senior staff were gradually losing touch with the work of their subordinates and their struggles to subdue and control outlying bureaucracies took precedence over policy-making. In effect, the Nixon approach involved using the White House staff less to advise the President and more to administer the government. The consequence in some cases was to create a policy vacuum which bureaucrats moved to fill and the effect of the Watergate crisis was to reduce still further the President's control and influence over the federal bureaucracy.

If the Nixon offensive against bureaucracy was overwhelmed by the President's terminal political crisis, it is also important to note the limitations of the strategy itself. In Republican terms, Nixon was a pragmatist rather than an ideologue and, as a consequence, the bureaucratic responsiveness he sought was personal rather than programmatic. His concern was more with his immediate political standing and interests rather than with the diffusion of a particular world view. The attempt to make the bureaucracy more than a personal tool of an individual President and, more particularly, to make it the servant of an ideological crusade involved a more sustained and far-reaching approach than the Nixon administration ever managed or contemplated.

Bypass strategies

The collapse of Nixon's Administrative Pesidency, or what Nathan has called 'the plot that failed', did not deter a later Republican administration from striving to achieve even more ambitious goals. According to one recent analysis, 'the Reagan administration pursued a campaign to maximise presidential control over the federal bureaucracy that was more *self-conscious* in design and execution, and more *comprehensive* in scope, than that of any other administration of the modern era' (Benda and Levine 1988: 102).

Reagan was searching for mechanisms that would ensure bureaucratic responsiveness to a particular political and policy agenda. To overcome the resistance of Congress, it was decided to made extensive use of executive rather than legislative means to achieve policy goals and therefore the need to reconstruct the bureaucracy in line with presidential values and purposes was all the more important. Recent research suggests that the Reagan administration's efforts to staff both the political and career bureaucracies with conservative Republicans enjoyed much more success than the Nixon administration's earlier attempt (Rockman 1989: 12). While Nixon began his administration by allowing his Cabinet secretaries to choose their own staff and only later tried to assert central control and to politicize bureaucratic appointments, the Reagan administration had laid careful, thorough plans long before Reagan moved into the White House. As with the famous budget strategy of 1981, Reagan's war against bureaucracy 'hit the ground running' in pursuit of his major goal of securing *political* control and co-ordination of both policy-making and implementation.

The first task was to centralize control over appointments to ensure bureaucratic responsiveness. The presidential appointment strategy began well before Ronald Reagan had won even his party's nomination let alone the presidency itself. In April 1980 Pendleton James, a former White House official, was asked by Ed Meese to set up a personnel selection system. The challenge was to find suitable people to fill the 3,000 or so 'political' appointments available to a new President and, according to one recent study, the result was that the Reagan administration 'undertook transition personnel selection with more forethought, with a larger commitment of resources, and with more attention to detail than any other administration in the postwar period' (Mackenzie 1981: 24). The most important criteria for appointment were ideological compatibility with and personal loyalty to the President because Reagan was striving to ensure that his appointees did not 'go native', that is to say they would remain loyal to the White House agenda rather than act as spokesmen for departments, agencies or interest groups.

At the policy-making level, the development of Cabinet councils in Reagan's first term was clearly designed to minimize conflict between the White House and the departments and agencies. Although drastically modified in his second term, these councils demonstrated both Reagan's preference for settling policy disputes at sub-presidential level and his distrust of bureaucracy. During the Reagan administration, policy planning was a partisan preserve which mostly bypassed career officials and the role of Cabinet councils with their mixed White House/department membership was to reinforce loyalty to presidential goals. If 'going native' is a perennial problem, the Cabinet councils did help 'to insulate political executives from the permanent departmental bureaucracies and from the congressional committees' (Heclo 1983: 47). In Reagan's scheme of things, the role of bureaucracy was to implement presidential policy and not to make it (Williams 1987: 147–8). To ensure the former and prevent the latter, it became necessary both to bypass and obstruct the federal bureaucracy in a variety of ways.

Recognizing that control of appointments and the use of Cabinet councils were necessary but by no means sufficient conditions for ensuring bureaucratic submissiveness and responsiveness, the Reagan administration sought also to establish a central mechanism for shaping and timing the economic and regulatory decisions of departments and agencies. Its chosen vehicle was the Office of Management and Budget (OMB), which had originally been politicized by Nixon and which had consequently lost some of its once famous reputation for 'neutral competence' (Heclo 1975; Berman 1979).

Given that the administration's main policy goal in the regulatory field was to relieve business of what conservatives regarded as excessively burdensome and expensive controls, it might be thought that the obvious course of action was to repeal or amend the appropriate regulatory statutes. Yet this would have diverted presidential energies away from the crucial budget struggles; moreover, it enjoyed little prospect of congressional success. The Reagan strategy was therefore to employ administrative rather than statutory means to accomplish major reductions in federal regulatory activity and thus to bypass legislative opposition.

Having achieved significant cuts in the operating budgets of federal bureaucracies and having secured the appointment of political loyalists with anti-regulatory views to senior bureaucratic posts, the White House and OMB sought to develop other features of their 'war against bureaucracy'; these included re-examining existing federal regulations with a view to eliminating or modifying them, putting a brake on the publication of new rules and regulations, and relaxing the enforcement of existing regulations. Under the authority of Executive Order 12291, regulatory authority was concentrated in OMB, which performed vastly expanded regulatory clearance and oversight functions. The significance of this new central function has been likened to OMB's 'acquisition of control over agency budget decisions in 1921, or over agency legislative proposals in the 1930s' (Goodman and Wrightson 1987: 41).

If the administrative strategy toward de-regulation was aimed at bypassing Congress, the vesting of regulatory authority in OMB was intended to act as a road-block to delay and obstruct bureaucratic efforts to expand or intensify federal regulation. The overriding concerns were to keep bureaucracy in its subordinate place, to prevent policy-making emerging from below and to promote cohesion and co-ordination between the White House and the political heads of departments, agencies and bureaux. As far as the career bureaucrats were concerned, the Reagan administration seemed almost to favour the 'mushroom growing' approach – keep them in the dark, feed them a lot of bullshit and, if they stick their heads up, cut them off!

Conclusions

To those accustomed to centralized political systems, where the power to make and implement public policy is concentrated rather than diffused, the American political system seems strange, almost bizarre. To those familiar with societies where the permanent national bureaucracy enjoys great prestige and power, the American federal bureaucracy is a mystery. To every American President who believes that the title of chief executive means he should be able to guide and control the executive branch, the federal bureaucracy is the cause of great frustration. To legislative politicians anxious to respond to interest group pressure, the federal bureaucracy is a major political resource. To American public opinion, the federal bureaucracy is intrusive, ineffective and inefficient.

There seems to be a broad consensus that the federal bureaucracy is incurably politicized, inherently balkanized and irredeemably unpopular. In a society where the flame of private enterprise burns brightest, it is almost inevitable that public bureaucracy is seen as a threat, a danger, a problem, something to be curbed and controlled. But controlling bureaucracy in the United States is not the exclusive privilege of the powerful, the office-holders, but rather something everyone can and should do. As far as the federal bureaucracy is concerned, it is always open season.

But it has to be conceded that by North European standards, the organizational characteristics, operating procedures and general performance of the federal bureaucracy are not impressive. One interesting question is why is bureaucratic performance so disappointing, but a more illuminating question is why should anyone expect it to be any better? As Terry Moe has persuasively reminded us, 'American public bureaucracy is not designed to be effective' (Moe 1989: 267). The functioning of the bureaucracy is generally conditioned by the characteristics of the wider political system and the organization and processes of bureaucracy are immediately shaped by 'the politics of structural choice' (Moe 1989: 268), and those structural choices have major consequences for both the content and direction of policy.

Because the American system of government does not clearly allocate responsibility for directing and controlling the design and operation of the federal bureaucracy, the struggle between contending political interests extends beyond public policy disputes and popular concerns into the arcane world of administrative organization and procedure. The consequence is that bureaucratic structures and processes represent not so much expressions of any coherent theory of efficient organization or 'good government', but much more sets of compromises between the competing interests and strategies of those seeking to manipulate the levers of political power. To win the policy debate and lose the struggle over process and structure may mean trading symbolic victory for substantive defeat. In practice, structural choices may really be policy choices and that often makes the politics of structural choice as important as debates on principle and policy.

It was observed earlier that in the struggle for the control of bureaucracy there are no final, absolute victories. The fluid, dynamic character of American democracy, with its multiple access points, provides many opportunities to mitigate apparently grievous losses and even to snatch bureaucratic victory out of the jaws of policy defeat. In the American system, no single institution or interest group can assert unchallenged control of any significant issue for a prolonged period. If all political influence is temporary, it becomes important to consolidate short-term political advantage by shaping bureaucratic structures and processes in ways likely to perpetuate policy goals even after political power has been eroded.

Political uncertainty and insecurity encourages interest groups to seek ways of insulating bureaucratic agencies from political interference. Their concern is then not to maximize the immediate operational efficiency of the agency, but rather to protect it from anticipated and unwelcome sources of pressure in the future. As we have already seen, attempts to insert judicial forms of procedure not only serve to reduce bureaucratic discretion, but they may also help to limit presidential involvement. In some cases the rigidities and delays inherent in judicial procedures may be a price the sponsors of an agency, both interest groups and politicians, are willing to pay to help insulate it. Similarly, it may be thought desirable to ensure that enabling statutes are extremely detailed on the premise that it is always easier subsequently to block attempts to weaken statutes than it is to enact new legislation. Insofar as it makes sense to speak of the design of organizations within the federal bureaucracy, the design is often better understood as a means of minimizing political insecurity than as an attempt to ensure efficiency and effectiveness.

But not only is political control temporary, it is never complete. This means in practice that opposing forces both inside and outside of Congress have opportunities to help shape not only the mandate of an agency, but also the methods by which it is realized. As Terry Moe acutely observes

> Political compromise ushers the fox into the chicken coop. Opposing groups are dedicated to crippling the bureaucracy and gaining control over its decisions and they will pressure for fragmented authority, labyrinthine procedures, mechanisms of political intervention, and other structures that subvert the bureaucracy's performance and open it up to attack.
>
> (Moe 1989: 276)

The federal bureaucracy has grown like Topsy rather than being consciously designed. If it is clear that Presidents favour a rational, coherent and centrally directed bureaucracy, it is less clear why anyone should expect interest groups, bureaucrats and other politicians to accept presidential domination. From a congressional perspective, administrative efficiency and effectiveness are less important than responding to interest group demands. Responding piecemeal to such demands and developing compromises between them produces organizational gargoyles, which defy easy categorization. The federal bureaucracy has been built incrementally through a combination of congressional compromises and downward pressure from the White House. The results are, as in the cases of the Environmental Protection Agency (EPA) and the Occupational Safety and Health Administration (OSHA), that agencies are frequently endowed 'with organizational designs entirely ill suited to the effective pursuit of their policy goals' (Moe 1989: 305). The irony is, of course, that the politicians and interest groups who have created such ill-formed and hamstrung bureaucratic structures are often among the first to criticize the feeble performance of their own creations.

We have seen that, in comparative terms, the growth of bureaucracy in the United States was delayed and fragmented. We have also seen that, despite the growth of the positive and regulatory state and the development of the modern Presidency, power over the design and control of the federal bureaucracy is still a matter to be decided afresh as each new issue arises. The federal bureaucracy has been put together in small pieces without any over-riding concern for their integration or coherence. We can now see that the controversies over independent commissions, over judicialization of administrative procedures, over the Administrative Presidency and over the Reagan administration's bypass strategies are all manifestations of the continuing competition for power over American bureaucracy among interest groups, legislators and Presidents. This diffusion of power occurs in a highly competitive political democracy equipped with a fragmented state structure and seems unlikely to encourage or sustain bureaucratic excellence, coherence or consistency.

Academic reformers sometimes seem to want to take politics out of bureaucracy. They almost appear to see politicians as pollutants who despoil bureaucratic integrity and expertise (Seidman and Gilmour 1986; Mosher 1982). They seek to resurrect the notion of the national or public interest, which is assumed to be embodied in the office of the Presidency and in the disinterested hearts of career civil servants. Congress is portrayed as the bastion of parochial, particularistic interests, whose concerns are with the responsiveness of bureaucracy to selfish political needs rather than with developing a rational, coherent federal bureaucracy to secure the nation's purposes. It may well be that 'the fragmentation of Congress into a relatively undisciplined political arena and the segmentation of presidential and congressional politics have distorted the balance in the constitutional system' (Newland 1988: 653), but there are few indications of imminent change.

The Reagan administration well understood the futility of trying to take politics out of bureaucracy and it made a concerted effort to achieve the opposite objective, to take the bureaucracy out of politics. They went further than any other administration both in trying to ensure the loyalty of their political appointees and in excluding career civil servants from policy matters. But it still disappointed some of its conservative supporters and the right-wing Heritage Foundation concluded that Reagan appointees still 'went native' (Rector and Sanera 1987) and adopted a departmental or agency perspective rather than the President's. Adopting a departmental perspective is another way of saying that executive-branch politicians, like their legislative counterparts, are not immune or insensitive to particularistic pressures. The federal bureaucracy is incurably politicized, but there is clearly more than one source of the contagion. The need to respond to conflicting signals from more than one political master is hardly a recipe for rational, coherent administration.

The federal bureaucracy is necessarily the product of a distinctive political culture whose early attachment to political democracy inhibited the growth of a bureaucratic state. As President Reagan and his predecessors have discovered, a substantial, sustained change in the character and organization of the federal bureaucracy requires a major reform of American political institutions. The federal bureaucracy is the product of contending political and institutional forces and, if its performance is found wanting, the responsibility largely lies elsewhere. Too often the federal bureaucracy is used as the whipping boy for failures of policy and implementation when the structural and procedural constraints imposed by Congress and the President have made such failures almost inescapable. In the absence of major institutional reform, it seems inevitable that the federal bureaucracy will continue to serve as the scapegoat for the ills of the American political system.

References

Aberbach, J. and Rockman, B. (1976) 'Clashing Beliefs within the Executive Branch', *American Political Science Review*, Vol. 70, No. 2.

Benda, P.M. and Levine, C.H. (1988) 'Reagan and the Bureaucracy', in C.O. Jones (ed.) *The Reagan Legacy*, New Jersey: Chatham House: 102–42.

Berman, L. (1979) *The Office of Management and Budget and the Presidency, 1921–1979*, Princeton, New Jersey, Princeton University Press.

Chubb, J.F. and Peterson, P.F. (eds) (1989) *Can the Government Govern?*, Washington D.C.: Brookings.

Cole, R.L. and Caputo, D.A. (1979) 'Presidential Control of the Senior Civil Service', *American Political Science Review* 73, 2.

Fawcett, F. and Thomas, T. (1983) *America and the Americans*, London: Fontana.

Heclo, H. (1975) 'OMB and the Presidency: The Problem of Neutral Competence', *Public Interest* 38.

—— (1984) 'In Search of a Role: America's Higher Civil Service', in E. Suleiman *Bureaucrats and Policy Making*, New York: Homes and Meier: 8–34.

Hodgson, G. (1984) *All Things to All Men: The False Promise of the Modern American Presidency*, London: Penguin.

Goodman, M.R. and Wrightson, M.T. (1987) *Managing Regulatory Reform*, New York: Praeger.

King, A. (ed.) (1983) *Both Ends of the Avenue*, Washington D.C.: American Enterprise Institute.

Mackenzie, G.C. (1981) 'Cabinet and Sub-Cabinet Personnel Selection in Reagan's First Year' Paper to APSA, New York.

Moe, T.M. (1989) 'The Politics of Bureaucratic Structure', in J.E. Chubb and P.F. Peterson *Can the Government Govern?*, Washington D.C.: Brookings: 267–329.

Mosher, F.C. (1982) *Democracy and the Public Service*, 2nd ed., New York: O.U.P.

Nathan, R.P. (1975) *The Plot That Failed: Nixon and the Administrative Presidency*, New York: Wiley.

Newland, C.A. (1988) 'The American Senior Executive Service: Old Ideals and New Realities', *International Review of Administrative Sciences*, 54, 4: 625–60.

Pemberton, W.E. (1979) *Bureaucratic Politics: Executive Reorganization During the Truman Administration*, Columbia: University of Missouri Press.

Pfiffner, J.P. (1987) *The Strategic Presidency: Hitting the Ground Running*, Homewood, Illinois: Dorsey.

Reagan, R. (1988) *The Quest for Peace, the Cause of Freedom: Selected Speeches*, Washington D.C.: United States Information Agency.

Rector, R. and Sanera, M. (eds) (1987), *Steering the Elephant*, New York: Universe Books.

Rockman, B.A. (1988) 'The Style and Organization of the Reagan Presidency', in C.O. Jones (ed.) *The Reagan Legacy*, New Jersey: Chatham House: 3–29.

Seidman, H. and Gilmour, R. (1986) *Politics, Position and Power: From the Positive to the Regulatory State*, 4th ed., New York: Oxford University Press.

Skowronek, S.S. (1982) *Building a New American State*, New York: Cambridge University Press.

Spann, R.M. (1956) 'The Eisenhower Civil Service and the Reformers', *Public Administration*, 34.

Stillman, II, R.J. (1987) *The American Bureaucracy*, Chicago: Nelson-Hall.

Williams, R. (1979) 'Politics and Regulatory Reform: Some Aspects of the American Experience', *Public Administration*, 55–69.

—— (1987) 'The President and the Executive Branch', in M. Shaw (ed.) *Roosevelt to Reagan: The Development of the Modern Presidency*, London: Hurst: 119–58.

Chapter seven

Litigation and political action: making the Supreme Court activist

Richard Hodder-Williams

I

The controversy over Ronald Reagan's nomination of Judge Robert Bork to the Supreme Court is a reminder that the Supreme Court's significance is highly political and that passions are often raised because of the judgments it makes (Hodder-Williams 1988a: 613–37). The high saliency which this episode gave to the Court is not new; the Supreme Court is well-accustomed to being in the eye of political storms (Nagel 1965: 925–44; Handberg and Hill 1980–1: 309–22). This should not be surprising because the Court is frequently called upon to adjudicate in cases where tempers are inflamed and the stakes high. Every few years a particular judgment seems to generate especially articulate and concerted criticism and places the Court four square in the centre of the political arena. *Brown v. Board of Education of Topeka, Kansas*, the case that found segregated school systems unconstitutional, not only prompted the chief judges of the state supreme courts to issue a ringing denunciation of the Court; many a political career in the South depended upon extended, and active, opposition to that decision. The McCarthy period of communist witch-hunts, at least in its later stages, brought powerful political forces into conflict with the Court and attempts were made, ultimately unsuccessfully, to limit its authority (Pritchett 1961; Murphy 1962). A series of decisions radically extending the rights of suspects in state courts, and forcing upon the states electoral districts of equal size, generated a new wave of criticism, spawning in the late 1960s a widespread distribution of stickers calling for the Chief Justice's impeachment (Schmidhauser and Berg 1972). Indeed, at one stage, impeachment proceedings were actually commenced against the Court's most liberal member.

These passions reflect the political significance of the Supreme Court. They also raise several important issues which need addressing. First of all, it is necessary to be aware how, and why, the Court came to exercise political power and what, in fact, this political power in reality consists of. Second, it is essential to be aware that litigation is often used in the United States as part of a political strategy and that the courts are thereby drawn into disputes which, although presented as legal questions about the meaning of the Constitution, are actually conflicts about political goals. Third, it is vital to reflect on this fact and the part played by judges who are not directly accountable to the people, especially in the context of a political culture which publicly embraces the philosophy of democracy. These are the issues which this chapter addresses.

II

The political power of the contemporary Supreme Court is derived from several sources and it is important, from a political as well as an historical or legal perspective, to be aware of them. The starting point must be the Constitution itself. But this document is not entirely helpful. Article III purports to establish the judicial branch's remit and Article VI asserts the supremacy of the Constitution over any other laws, whether passed by the national legislature or the individual state legislatures. What is not set down, however, is any indication of who has the final say in establishing when a law contravenes the Constitution; nor is the Constitution so precisely drafted that questions of that kind are easily answered. Neither the proceedings of the Constitutional Convention (of which there is no verbatim record) nor the words of the Constitution itself, nor the debates in the individual states that ratified that Constitution are able to provide an unequivocal answer to either issue. The beauty of the United States Constitution, indeed, is its very imprecision; its plasticity, in fact, has enabled it to remain a living and relevant document two full centuries after it was produced as a compromise to resolve the philosophical and political disagreements represented by the delegates in Philadelphia in 1787. But there is also an inherent disadvantage; that same plasticity encourages disagreement over its precise application in specific situations.

The difficulty in deciding what the Constitution, as supreme law, actually *means* undergirds all the arguments about the Supreme Court's role. If it were clear, there would be no disputes. If it were not supreme law, it would not matter, because it would not bind, and hence limit, the actions of legislators and executives throughout the country. Because the Constitution's application to concrete factual situations is not always self-evident, there is necessarily the requirement that some person or body of people should have ultimate responsibility to say what the law is.

In retrospect, this question about the locus of ultimate authority was decided in 1803. In that year the Supreme Court, through Chief Justice John Marshall's opinion in *Marbury v. Madison*, claimed for itself that right (Garraty ed. 1964: 1–14). There are still some who argue that this

117

was an improper usurpation of power and, seen in a very narrow context, they may be right. Neither the Constitution nor the Founding Fathers during the Convention *explicitly* gave the Supreme Court this ultimate authority; but they did *not* give it to anybody else either (such as the President or the Congress, both of whom pledge to uphold the Constitution); nor were they unaware that in some states the courts did pronounce on what was, and what was not, constitutional. Marshall's opinion was deceptively, some would say ingenuously, simple, but it had an inner logic. A system of government bound by laws rather than the transient whims of the politically strong (which then, as now, was the predominant form of government in the world) necessarily requires an arbiter to decide when the limitations established by the written Constitution have been abridged. And it made sense to assume that it was the province of the courts, as Marshall firmly asserted, to say what the law was. The legislative, executive and judicial branches are thus each given their specific functions: in the language of modern political science, rule-making, rule-application and rule-adjudication.

Over the first half of the nineteenth century, this role for the Supreme Court came steadily to acquire nearly universal acceptance. The *Dred Scott* decision (which effectively asserted that a person, once a slave, was always a slave) had its profound political impact on the Civil War precisely because there was so widespread an acceptance that the Supreme Court was entitled to have the final word on the meaning of the Constitution. Thereafter, those who sought to justify their non-acceptance of the Court's decisions did so on grounds that the Constitution as a whole was inapplicable to them. But the Civil War had decided by force of arms that the United States was a single sovereign state composed of several states, many of which had originally given up their sovereignty (and hence their *right* to secede) when they joined the Union. It does not seem reasonable any longer, therefore, to engage in long argumentation over whether or not the Founding Fathers, however they may be defined, intended the Supreme Court to exercise this power of judicial review. The political reality is that the Supreme Court *is* the final arbiter of the Constitution.

For nearly a hundred years, this power was not a significant one. The passage of the Fourteenth Amendment in 1868 changed that. Until then, the focus of the Constitution was primarily on what the federal government in Washington could, or could not, do. With the exception of the First Amendment, the first ten amendments were drafted in a way that would make them applicable, if interpreted literally, to all levels of government, but they had always been exclusively applied to the national government (*Barron v. Baltimore* 1883; Friendly and Elliott 1984: 2–15). From 1868, however, the individual states were obliged to grant to all those who came under their jurisdiction 'the equal protection of the laws' and 'due process of law'. For the first time, individual citizens had a federal constitutional provision which gave them access to the federal courts, and therefore ultimately the Supreme Court, in disputes with individual state governments. Inevitably, this would rub on raw nerves in many states and raise the political visibility of the Court. It did.

A second development was simply the expanding use of governmental power itself. Regulations (of the railroads, of industrial combines, of working conditions, of injurious materials, of the environment itself) naturally curtailed the full exercise of power which the strong had enjoyed for much of the nineteenth century. The Great Crash and ensuing slump in the early 1930s gave a further impetus to regulation and President Franklin Roosevelt's New Deal was, in its early days, a regulatory onslaught on the inefficiencies of the market. These legislative attempts to limit laissez-faire unsurprisingly antagonized many of those whose free exercise of economic power was thereby constrained and, true to American tradition, they litigated. In the earlier period, they by and large prevailed; in the later period, they ultimately lost. In both cases, major battles over economic and social policy, with their enormous financial and human costs, were resolved in the courts.

The growth of government was not confined to Washington. The states themselves climbed onto the regulation bandwagon but the complaints this time related to claimed infringements of individual rights. The issue of the 1950s and the two decades thereafter thus shifted to civil rights and to the limitations imposed upon the states in this area by the Fourteenth Amendment. In essence the 'due process of law' clause, almost certainly under the influence of the centuries-old belief in natural rights or a higher law preceding the Constitution itself, was used to protect fundamental rights against state government encroachment (Abraham 1972: 29–88). The process was incremental as the due process clause gradually covered many, then most, of the rights first set down as of primary importance in 1791 and ultimately protected them against encroachment by state actors. Later, rights not specifically mentioned in the original Bill of Rights were distilled from the due process clause, such as the right to travel or, more recently, the right of a woman to decide whether or not to abort a foetus in its early months (*U.S. v. Guest* 1966; *Roe v. Wade* 1973).

Whether those who drafted the Fourteenth Amendment, voted for it in Congress or ratified it in the states intended this precise development is highly unlikely (Berger 1977). But the American people, through litigation and the decisions of their federal judges, have developed the Constitution to the point where it is generally (although not universally) accepted that the Fourteenth Amendment applies against the states virtually all the rights assigned to citizens against the federal government in the first nine amendments. Precisely what *they* may cover is a matter of continuing disagreement and so the Supreme Court is regularly drawn into conflicts between state governments, who believe that their laws are necessary and proper for the general welfare of their people, and individuals, who believe that those same laws impinge unconstitutionally upon their rights and liberties.

Nobody pretends now that the Supreme Court does not exercise political power. I have already mentioned *Brown v. Board of Education*, but it is simple to think of other cases establishing principles and practices which, in most other countries, would have been set by the legislatures. In *Miranda v. Arizona*, the court effectively set down detailed rules for law enforcement officers to follow when interrogating suspects; in *United States v. Nixon* it rejected President Nixon's claim that the tape recordings of White House conversations were protected by executive privilege and, therefore, need not be handed over to a grand jury examining criminal charges; in *Furman v. Georgia*, it struck down the death penalty as then practised throughout the Union. That is an impressive exercise of power at first sight; but it is also importantly misleading.

Consider again for a moment these selected, and well known, cases. *Brown* did not immediately open the doors of schoolhouses to black children; far from it. For at least a decade, most of the states of the deep South sought by every means available, including the harassment of judges and activists, to prevent the purpose of *Brown* and in the process many people were actually killed (Wilkinson III 1979; Peltason 1961; Brass 1981). It needed the 1964 Civil Rights Act, passed by an elected Congress and signed into law by the President of the United States, to turn the promise of de-segregated schools into reality. That is not to say that *Brown* played little part in the process of de-segregation; this would be quite wrong. That famous decision forced onto the public agenda the question of the equal treatment of black Americans and was a catalyst for the dramatic changes in the law which have transformed so much of the American South. But the courts could not by themselves transform society.

Look again at *Miranda*, too. Although it took several years for the detailed requirements of the decisions to filter down to the patrolmen in the hundreds of independent police forces in the United States, within a few years there had been a radical change in the treatment of suspects by law enforcement officers throughout the country. This was helped by a further Supreme Court decision (*Mapp v. Ohio*), which ruled that evidence improperly gathered had to be excluded from a trial; not unnaturally, police chiefs sought to minimize the use of evidence which could possibly be described by a defence lawyer as tainted. But there was a clear backlash, especially as crime statistics seemed to indicate an ever increasing number of offences, particularly violent ones. Nor was Ernesto Miranda an individual with whom it was easy to empathize, as Linda Brown had been; he was later convicted of murder again. What happened was a legislative response, most notably in the Omnibus Crime Control Act of 1968, which weakened the *Miranda* requirements and, as more Republican judges were added to the federal courts during the Presidencies of Richard Nixon (1969–74) and Ronald Reagan (1981–9), the judges themselves began to carve out 'good faith' exceptions to the *Miranda* rule, attempting thereby to preserve tainted evidence for trials when that evidence had been obtained without an obvious and premeditated breach of the spirit of the *Miranda* rulings (Kamisar in Schwartz ed. 1987: 143–68). What is particularly interesting about this area of constitutional law is not that the Reagan administration sought to reverse *Miranda* itself (and, as importantly, *Mapp*), although it did (Report to Attorney General 1986), but that the senior policemen in most of the country still seek to preserve *Miranda*. They find that the decision, as Chief Justice Earl Warren had hoped in 1966, led to more professional policing.

United States v. Nixon is often credited with the final pressure leading to the resignation of Richard Nixon as President of the United States. There is no doubt that the response to the decision did hasten his demise. Once the grand jury considering criminal charges against Nixon heard the tapes, they had little doubt that he had been involved in a 'cover-up' and therefore had impeded the course of justice. But it should be observed that it was only after much anguished consideration that Nixon actually gave up the tapes; nobody could compel him since, in the end, it is the executive branch itself which has the power to enforce the decrees of the federal courts. Presidents in the past, on occasions, have refused to accept the judgment of the Court, although, as a general rule, the justices have looked kindly on presidential claims (Hodder-Williams in Shaw ed. 1987: 11–45). Nevertheless, since the Court has no police or coercive powers of its own, it must depend ultimately on popular acceptance or presidential willingness to enforce its edicts. In Nixon's case, however, *another* political force was at work; the Congress was moving inexorably towards impeachment proceedings. The thrust, then, of the judgment in *Nixon v. United States* was decisively enhanced by what was going on in another part of the political system, just as the Congress's determination was decisively hardened by what the Court had decided.

My final instance was the case of *Furman v. Georgia*, which many observers believed had put an end altogether to the death penalty in the United States. They were wrong. *Furman* had not actually found that the death penalty was *per se* 'cruel and unusual punishment' forbidden by the Eighth Amendment; rather, a majority of the Court had found merely that the death penalty, as then *practised*, for a number of

121

differing reasons contravened the Constitution's requirements. Thereafter no less than thirty-seven states redrafted their laws to meet what they believed to be the Court's requirements. And in *Gregg v. Georgia* a majority of the Court accepted as constitutional certain carefully crafted laws which at least distinguished between the process of deciding upon guilt or innocence and the process of deciding upon the punishment (Zimring and Hawkins 1986). Action in the states, therefore, responded to the Court's initial judgment and put the death penalty back on the statute book.

The purpose of looking, however briefly, at these famous cases is to place the notion of judicial power firmly in its political context. Although these cases plainly all had significant consequences, they were neither the premeditated actions of goal-oriented individuals (the essence of the behaviour of professional politicians) nor the final and immutable statement of the law. The working out of the Constitution's application in the real world is complex and many actors other than the justices of the Supreme Court actually contribute to its operation (Fisher 1988).

It is also a reminder that the areas of public action in which the Court is intimately involved are only one part of the domain of public authorities. Fiscal and monetary policy, welfare provisions, foreign policy and business policy remain the province of the legislatures and executives of the United States. On occasions some aspects of them may reach the Supreme Court, especially for statutory interpretations, but its substantive involvement is slight. Indeed, it could be argued that some wrangles in these areas (over, say executive agreements or the discretionary power of the executive in the Iran-Contra imbroglio) were exacerbated precisely because the Court had restrained itself from authoritative intervention. The Supreme Court is not the most powerful branch of government, as some commentators have recently held; for ordinary Americans, the decisions that most affect them and their families are still unquestionably decisions taken by the elected branches, normally at the level of state or even local government. But there is no escaping the fact that cases are litigated in the federal courts which profoundly affect large numbers of Americans. It is this readiness to litigate which needs more extended examination because it lies at the heart of any understanding (and many misunderstandings) of the Court's role in the political process. The central reality is that American citizens and corporations employ their Constitution when they can to provide a legal underpinning to their political goals.

III

Courts do not initiate litigation; Americans do. And they are a litigious people (Lieberman 1981); they always have been. It was, after all,

Alexis de Tocqueville who observed a century and a half ago that 'Americans have the strange custom of seeking to settle any political or social problem by a lawsuit instead of using the political process as do people in most countries' (Fein 1984: 1). All the great issues of American history, from slavery through governmental regulation to individual rights, have ultimately reached the Supreme Court. Whether that body has resolved them wisely or successfully is another matter. This overworked perspective needs to be put in a wider political context. These same issues, it should be remembered, were contested in the political branches, both at state level and in Washington, *as well as* in the courts, but the special and confusing characteristic of the American political system is its multiple points of access. The courts, both state and federal, provide some of those points.

In this respect, three significant developments have occurred in the last fifty years. One has been the growth of litigation as an interest group strategy and a consequent growth in public interest law. The National Association for the Advancement of Colored People, through its Legal, Education and Defence Fund, had for many years lent its support, both financial and legal, to individual litigants whose claims were of interest to blacks generally (Kluger 1975). With the much publicized victories in *Shelley v. Kraemer*, the 1947 case that outlawed restrictive covenants on property, and *Brown v. Board of Education of Topeka*, the 1954 case that outlawed segregated schools in the state educational system, other groups began to see litigation as a strategy to be employed in pressing their concerns. The American Civil Liberties Union, which had, like the NAACP, been active in the inter-war years, was now joined by a host of groups pressing liberal conclusions onto the Court. It should not be thought that liberal groups enjoyed a monopoly of interest-group input. Business and other conservative groups had been active before the Second World War and, after a period of comparative inactivity in the 1950s and early 1960s, began again to press their causes, increasingly supported by organizations whose interests were more social than economic (Epstein 1985). Professionalization of these interest groups and a growth in the teaching of public interest law in American law schools combined to create a large constituency of highly articulate and able lawyers ready to use their expertise, and the Constitution, to prosecute policy in the court system.

A second development, whose origins predate *Brown* but which was strongly reinforced by that decision, was an enhanced concern for individual rights. This powerful ideological movement, generated in part by the war against Nazi Germany, turned people's attention anew to the Bill of Rights and the possible reach of the Fourteenth Amendment's command that the states ensure the equal protection of the laws and due process of law to all people. Although the American culture is profoundly conservative, claims for individual rights and equal treatment nevertheless matched the conception of equality of status and the emphasis on individualism which was shared by most conservatives and liberals alike. Since it was the states whose laws mostly affected the day-to-day lives of the people, it was the states which were mostly taken to court when the abridgement of rights was claimed. There was, therefore, a certain inevitability in the clash between a Supreme Court intent on establishing national rights applicable across the country under the Fourteenth Amendment and state governments concerned to protect their autonomy in a federal system predicated on differences. The Court, hence, was embroiled in two contradictions: an emphasis on individualism and individual rights will always clash with the populist belief in the legitimacy of majoritarianism and the nationwide rights will always clash with the particularism protected by federal institutions. It would have been impossible, therefore, for the Court to have satisfied all the Americans all of the time. It was, on the contrary, inevitable that it become a source of political division.

A third development, which may well have encouraged the others, was the readiness of the courts to allow access to a wider range of litigants than before and to look carefully at the substance of the claims brought to it. The classic form of litigation involves two parties who have an adversarial relationship in which one has already suffered a measurable loss. Nobody else is involved. This simple model has been modified over time, largely for perfectly logical reasons. If the freedom of the press, guaranteed by the First and Fourteenth Amendments, is to mean anything, governments should not be permitted to restrain an author or publisher prior to publication; in other words, editors should be allowed to go to court *before* suffering any tangible limitations on their freedom to publish and run the risk of the libel laws. Similarly, prisoners condemned to death should be able to raise their claims that, say, evidence against them had been unconstitutionally gathered or the jury which found them guilty had been improperly impanelled, *before* suffering the very tangible, and finite, punishment of death. Legal form gradually ceded its primacy to equitable justice.

This opening of the courts was also observable where the question of standing was concerned. Increasingly the Court permitted one individual to have standing to sue on behalf of all others similarly situated (the so-called class action suit) rather than require each individual claiming the same denial of rights to initiate a case. This is what happened in the *Brown* case which was prosecuted on behalf of Linda Brown *and* other black children similarly deprived of the equal protection of the laws. Furthermore, the definition of a tangible loss was extended so that individuals could, as tax payers, sue governments for the unconstitutional use of their revenues. Organizations, too, could sue on behalf of their members, but the Burger Court was particularly concerned to ensure that there was a direct link between the litigator and the challenged action. Hence the Sierra Club, because it had not itself suffered a tangible loss as a club, was deemed not have standing to represent its members' interests in cases involving environmental matters (*Sierra Club v. Morton* 1972). Questions of standing are complex and in fact take up a surprisingly large amount of the Supreme Court's time. There are always lawyers, and some judges, ready to argue that one of the parties does not have standing, or that the case is moot because the passage of time had made the resolution of the dispute irrelevant in immediate practical terms, or that the issues are political and not amenable to judicial resolution at all. The Warren and the early Burger Courts had a relatively liberal attitude towards those who wished to bring cases before the courts. The later Burger Court, partly for policy reasons and partly to reduce its enormous caseload, tried to tighten the conventions (Rathjen and Spaeth 1979: 360–82).

These developments reflect two important points. First is the acceptance by a majority of the Court that its role should not be bound by technicalities but should develop to perform the wider function of achieving the abstract ideal of justice. Any case involving the constitutionality of anti-abortion laws would be moot by the time it reached the Supreme Court, because the pregnancy would inevitably have been completed and having a legal abortion would no longer be a possibility. In such a case, technicalities had to be set aside, since a genuine constitutional issue, worthy of consideration, had been raised. Second, the Court has come to reflect developing social attitudes in the wider community from which the Justices themselves have been drawn. The widely held belief that a principal function of the Supreme Court was to protect the constitutional rights of individuals against governmental action, for example, was accepted by the justices themselves and, once some rights had been extended, it proved, as it always does, extremely difficult to cut back upon them.

The growth of Court involvement in social and political matters, in the rights of suspects, the equality of women, the treatment of criminals, the structure of the educational system, and so on, was thus incremental and stretched over time. But it clearly created a momentum of its own. *Brown* encouraged liberal groups generally while the liberalization of the rules about standing encouraged the participation of public-interest groups and concerned individuals; law school training and the eruption of a liberal conscience in the days of the civil rights movement and the Vietnam War provided a generation of lawyers concerned to promote the 'public interest' and protect the disadvantaged. Precedents suggested new avenues to explore and new rights to claim. When Earl Warren stepped down from the Chief Justiceship in 1969, he had left the groundwork for a more activist Supreme Court still to come. It was, after all, a Court with four nominees of Republican Richard Nixon which introduced notions of sexual equality (*Reed v. Reed* 1970), a limited right to an abortion (*Roe v. Wade* 1973), the unconstitutionality of the death penalty as then practised (*Furman v. Georgia* 1972), and the constitutional propriety of affirmative action programmes (*Regents of the University of California v. Bakke*) 1978). Litigation is a leisurely matter, so changes in the legal culture take time; papers were filed on behalf of Norma McCorvey, the 'Jane Roe' of *Roe v. Wade*, on 3 March 1970 and the Supreme Court decided on 22 January 1973 (Faux 1988). Jagdish Chadha began his litigation against his deportation order on 11 January 1974 and only received Supreme Court support on 23 June 1983 (Craig 1988). The point, then, is that the burgeoning rights industry (Morgan 1984) of the late 1970s has its roots in the developments of an earlier decade, and it cast its shadow over the 1980s, as the passions aroused over the nomination of Judge Robert Bork revealed. Rights, once granted, are rarely taken away, except in revolutionary circumstances or war. There *was* no counter-revolution, even though conservative Republicans like Nixon, Ford and Reagan controlled the process of nomination (Blasi ed. 1983).

Seen in this perspective, there may be a presumption that the Supreme Court has no choice but to involve itself in these matters. This is not entirely true. Although some appeals are required by law to be granted, the practice has been that the justices choose which of the cases before them they will hear. Over 4,000 are appealed but a writ of *certiorari*, the formal method of granting an appeal, is given to only about 150. The vast majority of cases do not deserve a further hearing; they have already been once reviewed and probably raise no major principles of law. Even so, choices have to be made and, if five justices act in concert, whole classes of cases could be denied review. But the justices very rarely behave in this way. Although they naturally differ over what they think are the significant cases, there are some issues which they all come to realize must be faced. In the early 1960s, it became clear that malapportionment was one such issue. The lower courts were dealing with an increasing number of such cases and their judgments were not all in the same direction. Although Justices Frankfurter and Douglas disagreed on what the judgment should be, they agreed that the Court was required to address the question (*Baker v. Carr* 1962; Schwartz 1983: 410–28). Broadly the same was true with the abortion cases, although the actual case, *Roe v. Wade*, was granted *certiorari* almost by chance (Woodward and Armstrong 1979: 169).

The lower courts are obliged to hear the cases properly brought to them. Their dockets, therefore, reflect the concerns that trouble Americans enough to make them litigate. When such an issue becomes salient, it generally appears in lawsuits in many courts over the country. As communications have improved and public interest lawyers have pro- liferated these new issues soon generate co-ordinated and carefully structured strategies of litigation. There is, I would argue, something very democratic about this process which the Supreme Court is uniquely well prepared to observe. In the process of sifting the petitions for *certiorari* the justices come to see the flow of litigation and learn at first hand what the prevalent issues are. Most of them see it as their respon- sibility, as the court of last resort, to attend, when the moment seems ripe to them and when the facts of the case are appropriate, to what should be seen as the jurisprudential demands of the wider public.

The landmark cases of the Warren Court were usually concerned with a set of facts which were both common (and therefore in need of action) and which also clearly indicated where justice lay (and therefore relatively easy to decide). The absolute, legally sanctioned separation of white children from black children into segregated schools presented the Court with stark choices. It could refuse to hear the cases on the grounds that *Plessy v. Ferguson*, the 1896 case which sanctioned the principle of 'separate-but-equal', still ruled; it could take the case and publicly reaffirm *Plessy*; or it could take the case and demand the end of segregated schools. Politics (and most of the justices had been politicians and understood what was needed for the good of the wider polity) demanded the last course of action. In some ways, *Brown* was an easy decision. Certainly, at one level, there was a rightness about Warren's opinion which was demanded by the post World War II morality; the segregated south *was* an anachronism. But the decision was a sharp break with the past, overruling a long-standing precedent and interpreted the equal protection clause of the Fourteenth Amendment in a novel way. Although there were cases which pointed towards the *Brown* decision, they did not lead inexorably to it. The justices agonized over the case and acted as they did precisely because they situated the dispute in the contemporary ideological and political context of the 1950s (Schwartz 1983: 72–127; Kluger 1975: 657–99). Justice and politics required the result. But it created philosophical concern among many commentators, seeming to be an instance of 'policy in search of law' (Maidment 1975: 301–20). More obviously, it stirred bitter and determined political opposition and placed the lower court judges, who were obliged to put the decision into effect, into positions of physical danger and social ostracism.

What was more problematical – and this was a difficulty which the Burger Court had to face in the 1970s – was to define the point at which segregation had ended and integration begun: at what level of racial mix was the command of equal protection satisfied?

The same kind of analysis could be followed in most of the other areas in which the Court set out on bold new courses. The treatment of suspects (let alone criminals) was, frankly, scandalous in much of the United States, especially in the South. Forced confessions and rigged juries were normal fare. Given the specificity of the facts in the early cases, the Court, although always divided, nevertheless felt it comparatively easy to advance the cause of justice by using its authority to outlaw certain practices. Similarly, the refusal of some states to redistrict had left constituencies of unbelievable inequality and had genuinely devalued the votes of urban and suburban dwellers in relation to rural inhabitants. A voter in Moore County, Tennessee, for example, had twenty-three times as much influence in choosing a state representative as a voter in Shelby County, the seat of the city of Memphis; one district had a population of 2,340 and the other 312,345 (*Baker v. Carr* 1962). A clear majority of the justices thought that, if equal protection was to mean anything, it required action on their part.

The second generation of cases proved much less easy. *Reynolds v. Sims*, which mandated that states electoral districts should be of equal size as possible, clearly enhanced democracy. But, when the population differences of districts were less than one per cent (even though the disparity was technically avoidable), the issue was less clear-cut.[1] When policemen failed to abide quite by the letter of the new constitutional requirements when dealing with suspects, the Court had to choose between enforcing their rules rigorously, even if the results seemed wrong, or bending their rules to allow practices which were technically improper (*Brewer v. Williams* 1977). The consequence of these later decisions was to encourage some sectors of American political society to complain publicly that the justices had ceased to be judges and had become politicians. What right, they demanded, had they to decide that one per cent was too great a discrepancy between constituencies, or that states should consciously advance the employment interests of blacks or women, or that the difficult but important work of policemen was being frustrated by mere technicalities? This was an interesting shift in argument. The right had, in the 1950s and early 1960s, attacked the Court for not strictly abiding by the narrow technicalities of the law. In the 1970s and 1980s, it was the liberals who wanted the Court to abide by the precise principles it had set down earlier and not to take wider considerations into account.

Establishing a right does not necessarily establish a remedy; yet a right that cannot be exercised is hardly worth establishing. This was a problem which faced the courts and which often brought them into the political limelight. Let me take two instances (Cooper 1988). As is well known, the southern states were deliberately slow in translating the principle of *Brown* into practice. In January 1965, nearly ten years after the Supreme Court's decision that school boards should move 'with all deliberate speed' to end segregation, a case was filed in North Carolina demanding that the Charlotte-Mecklenberg school district, in which only 490 of more than 20,000 black children attended schools with white children, should disestablish the segregated system that was *still* in force. It was more than four years after this that the federal district court in Charlotte actually held a trial on the merits. The judge, a pillar of the southern social establishment nominated by Richard Nixon, found, to his admitted astonishment, that at least 14,000 black children were going to all black schools fifteen years after *Brown* had been handed down. He therefore instructed the school board to devise a 'plan for effective desegregation of pupil population, to be predominantly effective in the fall of 1969 and to be completed by the fall of 1970' (Schwartz 1986: 16).

The school board, by a consistent 5-4 vote, refused to accept this invitation to change. After several proddings from the judge, they instigated some minimal alterations which would still leave at least two-thirds of the black children in single race schools. Judge McMillan felt he had no option. He arranged for an expert to design plans for the desegregation and imposed that plan. Otherwise, he argued, the black children had no remedy against the school board which was denying them their rights. Part of the plan involved the busing of children from their neighbourhoods to schools some distance away. It was this busing requirement that sparked off the most vocal opposition, despite the long tradition of busing in public education in the United States. But the Supreme court authorized it as one constitutionally proper way of desegregating schools (*Swann v. Charlotte-Mecklenburg School District* 1970). It was a decision forced upon it by the recalcitrance of local politicians; but it was a decision which conservatives constantly employed as an example of judicial legislation.

The second example concerns prisons. Litigation began in the Arizona courts in 1965 claiming that the conditions in the major state penitentiary amounted to cruel and unusual punishment. Certainly the record indicated an appalling state of affairs. The inmates slept in huge 100-man barracks in which some convicts would crawl along the floor at night to stab their enemies, seventeen being stabbed in one eighteen-month period; homosexual rape was so common that some potential victims feared to sleep and spent the night clinging to the bars nearest the guard room; inmates were lashed with a wooden-handled leather strap until their skin was bloody and bruised; a hand-cranked device was used to administer electrical shocks to sensitive parts of the body; gruel such as Oliver Twist might have recognized was a staple food; inmates could obtain access to medical treatment only if they bribed the guard in charge of the sick bay; at the heart of it all, the guards were mostly nothing more than inmates who had been issued with guns (*Finney v. Hutto* 1978). Confronted with these facts, the district judge had invited the Department of Correction in 1969 to improve conditions. A later hearing, finding once again that conditions remained 'cruel and unusual', yet again let the Department of Corrections provide a remedy, although this time indication was given as to where improvements had to be made. In 1976 the district court found that in some respects conditions had seriously deteriorated; there were, for example, twice as many inmates as beds. The court this time entered specific orders to eradicate some of the worst practices, especially those concerned with punitive isolation.

My point in this section is that the courts, if they are to ensure that the rights they assert are actually granted, must on occasions involve themselves in the nitty-gritty of writing regulations, devising remedial actions, drawing district boundaries. In an ideal world, no doubt, this would not be necessary. But the United States is far from an ideal world and elected officials do deny to some of those over whom they rule the rights that are properly theirs. Some, but by no means all, of those whose rights are abridged then take to the courts and draw them into political disagreements with constituted authority. On occasions, those authorities, despite the supremacy of the Constitution and the convention that the Supreme Court is its authoritative expositor, refuse to act in accordance with the principles established by the Supreme Court. The blame for the Court's intrusion into regulation-making should properly be laid at the door of public officials, whose behaviour must leave the courts with the choice between abdicating their responsibilities or taking it upon themselves to force, usually by detailed oversight, the recalcitrant bodies to comply. Non-compliance is in fact rare; but it takes place on the most salient and politically explosive issues where the personal and political costs for the losers of obedience may well be very high. It is little wonder, then, that the courts get sucked into political controversy. They cannot avoid it.

IV

The Supreme Court is political in the sense that its decisions have political consequences. By affecting the distribution of power and advantages within the United States, it performs some of the functions associated with the overtly political parts of the political system.[2] It is nevertheless unquestionably a judicial body, bound in theory by legal norms. Political actors have policy goals and their behaviour is determined by their estimation of the best way to achieve such goals. Judicial actors, by contrast, should not have their behaviour prescribed by previously determined policy goals. Judges are certainly not political eunuchs, entirely devoid of political convictions, but the motive force behind their decisions should not be those convictions. They should in a very real sense be bound by the law and the accepted canons of legal reasoning. There are some commentators in the United States who claim that too many of the nation's judges breach this rule and are nothing more than politicians in judicial robes (McGuigan and O'Connell eds 1987). Given that so many judges in the United States are elevated to the bench from active political careers, it would not be altogether surprising if there were a handful who never made the transition properly. But those errant individuals are few in number. The reason many commentators think otherwise is their failure to comprehend the process of judging itself.

The process of judging is not simple.[3] The language of judging the judges, by contrast, is often too simple. The lexicon of evaluation is dominated by two concepts: self-restraint, the characteristic of the true judge, and activism, the characteristic of the judicial politician. It is worth pausing a moment to examine those two ideas, because they hide a great deal (Halpern and Lamb eds 1982). Within those notions lie at least four components. The first refers to a judge's personal and subjective preferences. Self-restrained judges, by definition, restrain their own values so that these do not determine their judging; they operate primarily as objective technicians, discovering the law through their well-honed skills which have been developed by training and experience. In the constitutional sphere, this was famously expressed by Justice Owen Roberts in 1936 with the following words: 'The judicial branch of the Government has only one duty: to lay the article of the Constitution which is invoked beside the statute which is challenged and to decide whether the latter squares with the former' (*United States v. Butler* 1936). The central problem with this kind of approach is obvious. Leading legal scholars themselves disagree on the proper way of deciding many disputes because, quite simply, they are not amenable to technical solutions in the same way that disputes over the length of a particular piece of string always are.

Laws are often imprecise; precedents frequently point in more than one direction; constitutional provisions are mostly generalized statements of principle, the precise application of which is often unclear. In short, there can be no such thing as a completely self-restrained, entirely technical judge. In many cases the decision *must* rest on the self choosing one interpretation over another, one competing value in preference to another, one claimed right in favour of another. In saying this, it is essential to be aware of what I am *not* saying. I am not denying that some cases before judges, even the hard cases which face the Supreme Court, clearly demand only one result. The laws of the land would have to be unimaginably badly drafted if this were not the case. The fact that a very considerable proportion of the cases chosen by the Supreme Court for a full hearing are decided unanimously, on average thirty-two per cent in the decade 1977–86, is an indication that there is much that all the justices agree upon. Nor am I saying that judges, when they choose between alternatives, have no principles outside their personal preferences

131

to guide those choices. All I am saying at this stage is that all judges, and especially Supreme Court justices, are faced with sets of facts which require them to make choices; or, to put it another way, they must actively select the most appropriate principles on which to decide the case and cannot restrain their need to make this subjective selection.

A second theme is the preference to avoid making a judgment, and thus exercising power, whenever possible. This self-imposed restraint thus consciously reduces the role to be played by the judiciary in the settlement of disputes. If there are technical devices which can be used (such as mootness, or lack of standing, or the political questions doctrine, or the possibility of other routes to be followed), they should be. The presumption underlying this view is that the courts are not the proper place in which certain types of dispute should be brought, let alone resolved. Particularly in the United States, with its tradition of the separation of powers, there are many channels through which an individual or a group can prosecute their interests, in the state political system as well as in the federal one. It is in those arenas, so the argument goes, that struggles over civil rights or the freedom of individuals should be fought. Where there is a political process, there alone lies the road to legitimacy. It is a seductive argument, but it is not a wholly convincing one. Americans pride themselves on operating a system of 'government of laws, not of men', implying thereby the superiority and vitality of a rule of law. Inevitably, and rightly, citizens therefore take to the law to ensure the protection of their claimed rights against mere men, the politicians whose narrow interests can dominate legislatures and whose bureaucratic prejudices can skew administrations. The political culture calls for the law to be tested, as I have already described, and a natural corollary of that is that the function of judges is not to restrain their power but to use it actively.

Once again, it is important to be clear about what is *not* being said. I am not arguing that judges should refuse to ensure that a genuine dispute is before them or that the procedures set down in the laws of the states or the federal government have been duly followed. Nor am I suggesting that judges should impose upon the facts before them issues which the parties have failed to raise. There are well-known rules and practices of that kind which any organized system of law must follow. But what I am arguing is that a central, in most ways *the* central, function of the judiciary is to hear and adjudicate the cases brought to the courts in proper manner. And it is 'We, the People', in whose name the Constitution originated, who initiate litigation. This, then, may require judges to be activist in the sense that their judgments will inevitably impinge on the acts of the overtly political institutions. But the cause of such political involvement is not the justices' personal wills so much as the people's wishes. Section III made this point a central one to any full comprehension of the Supreme Court's role. My argument here is that the self-restraint of deciding only the minimum number of cases ignores the fact – and it is a fact – that the courts are now used openly by individuals and groups to advance their political interests. Limiting litigation, although in an ideal world possibly desirable, is not an expression of confidence in democracy, as is often made out, but a denial of the democratic right of citizens to choose an effective method of political action. Judicial self-restraint, in this light, becomes a negation of democracy.

The third way of thinking about the activist/self-restraint argument follows directly from this. To many people, the courts, by definition, should not instigate public policy because the legitimacy for such policies rests in the political branches alone. Since federal judges are not elected and are accountable to no electorate, they are, again by definition, undemocratic in one strict sense. Indeed, to Justice Felix Frankfurter, the American people should learn to be good democrats through the public exposition of their venality in Court decisions consciously refusing to intervene where rights have been abridged.[4] So a double dilution of the democratic ideal is achieved when non-elected judges decide political cases. The good judge, therefore, has a duty to eschew decisions which run counter to the deliberate choices of legislatures or executives. Deference to elected bodies should be the guiding principle.

Of course, there is much to be said for such an argument. Where a challenged policy may seem unwise or unnecessary or unattractive to the judge, it does not thereby become unconstitutional. The Constitution may contain many broad generalities, but it is not merely a compendium of generalities inviting judges to write into it *any* policy outcome which they might prefer. Supporters of activist judges never hold such a silly view (although their opponents are not averse to implying that they do).[5] But what really cannot pass without comment is the assumption that legislative or executive supremacy is the central essence of American democracy. An enduring central feature of the nation's political culture shared by the Founding Fathers themselves is a deep-seated suspicion of governments and a readiness to limit their powers. The Constitution, although it grants powers, is largely about the limitations of government. The Bill of Rights and the post-Civil War Amendments were self-conscious and public statements of this philosophy. Hence, to deny elected officials the full fruits of their power (and it is only recently that *they* can claim the legitimacy that flows from achieving positions of authority through free and fair elections) is to emphasize one central tenet of the American variety of democracy. For there is a conflict at the heart of American democracy. On the one hand, there is a strong populist streak which holds fiercely to the belief that legitimacy flows from popular backing ('no taxation without representation'); on the other hand, there is a powerful individualism which challenges the state and asserts rights against it. A majoritarian ethos side by side with a commitment to individual rights must generate conflicts and Americans have generated a great many. The Supreme Court is inevitably caught in the centre of that paradox. Hence, once again, the Court is forced, by the political culture and the nature of American democracy, to be activist. That is what the political system calls upon it to do.

I would argue thus far that the Supreme Court must be activist. My position depends upon an acceptance that this means no more than these three things: first, the Court's duty to adjudicate in hard cases necessitates choosing between different, and often almost equally defensible, positions. Second, the American people quite properly have chosen to use their Constitution, and therefore the Court, to advance their political interests. Third, the American political culture, expressed in the Constitution itself, requires the Court on occasions to defend unpopular individuals and groups against the decisions of elected politicians. Two points must be emphasized. The first, and already much repeated, is that the Court is forced into its political role by the political process itself. The second point is that this enforced role inevitably antagonizes some sections of the American public who would have preferred judgments to be different. There are some legal scholars, perhaps, whose criticism of the Court is genuinely based upon a resentment that it has not been able to defend the role of law in the limited and private form they would ideally have liked. The vast majority of critics, however, just do not like its results (McGuigan and O'Connell eds 1987). Liberals berated its jurisprudence in the 1930s (Pearson and Allen 1936; Corwin 1938; Jackson 1941); conservatives have in recent years led the protest (Kurland 1970; Glazer 1975: 104–23; Graglia 1976; Wolfe 1986).

This brings us to the fourth, and most problematic, theme of activism and self-restraint. Decisions in discrete cases flow from a justice's conception of what the legal dispute is and from the principles they apply to the facts before them. From a judge's perspective, the most difficult task is to find a set of principles that will protect him from the exercise of subjective choices at this stage. Because the vast majority of judges not only believe that the law should be as impartially administered as is humanly possible but also that decisions which authoritatively bind citizens to particular courses of action should ideally be taken by elected politicians. They seek to articulate for themselves a philosophy, a jurisprudence if you will, which reduces to the absolute minimum their need to resort to subjective choice. The search for some universally accepted and objective guidelines, however, has so far proven unsuccessful.

The conception which came to dominate discussions in the 1980s, especially since it was espoused by both Attorney-General Edwin Meese III and Judge Robert Bork, was that of 'original intention' (Meese III

1985: 701–4; Bork 1971–2: 1–35). Obviously, the intention of those who drafted constitutional provisions and those who ratified them is a sensible starting point in any search for the meaning, and hence application, of the Constitution. It is a sensible starting point, but it can be no more than that. As I have already had occasion to mention, we do not know precisely what the Founding Fathers intended, still less what the ratifiers intended. Of course, we can, with little difficulty, discover what policies they almost certainly did *not* at the time have in mind. But that does not necessarily mean that they positively intended that such policies should not occur. Unable to foresee the future, most of the Founding Fathers were aware that the document they were producing was a general guide, not an itemized set of instructions.[6]

Those who hold to the doctrine of original intention admit that it cannot manage to resolve every dispute before the courts, but they maintain that in most instances the litigation can be managed by reference to what the Founding Fathers and their contemporaries most probably would have thought. But this position, based upon guesswork as it must be in many cases, ignores two important points; those same Founding Fathers, if they were alive today, would be quite unlikely to hold views identical to those they may have entertained 200 years earlier. And, second, the role of a constitution is not necessarily to preserve in political aspic the assumptions particular to one period. Neither of these arguments will persuade the original-intent school of the errors of its ways; but they must be faced. My own view is that the Founding Fathers were well aware that changing conditions create new problems and fresh ideas and that the constitutional framework was designed to absorb such developments and adapt to them (Hodder-Williams in Bogdanor ed. 1988b: 73–102). In other words, except for a handful of very special provisions, the Constitution provided an enduring set of principles which set down a structure of governmental power, not a policy programme, and that whatever was not denied was entirely legitimate so long as it did not contravene a principle of the Constitution. The right to privacy is not explicitly mentioned in the Constitution; but it is not denied either. Hence the creation of such a right may well be a legitimate interpretation of general phrases as they evolve over time.

It is not implausible to argue that several of the early leaders were ready to give to the courts, as arbiters of the Constitution, a special role to play over and above the obvious one of resolving the day-to-day disputes that arise in any political system attempting to practise the rule of law. This view found expression nearly half a century ago in a famous footnote of Justice Stone's opinion in what was otherwise a case of only average importance. In *United States v. Carolene Products Co.*, Stone set down three areas in which courts should feel particularly eligible to be activist. Although usually taken together, they are actually three

135

distinct perspectives. The first holds that, since the legitimacy of legislative and executive acts flows from their democratic base, courts have a special duty to ensure that access to the vote, to a range of political views and to political institutions must be as open as possible. Activism that enhances democracy must, therefore, be legitimate (Ely 1980; Choper 1980; Perry 1982). Second, the Philadelphia Convention was not the last word on the Constitution. A number of amendments were added with due deliberation, implying thereby that the American people, in whose name the amendments were ratified, believed the original document to be less than perfect. These later amendments, many of which were concerned with the protection of individual rights against governments, enjoy, therefore, a superior status when conflict arises and the responsibility of the courts is to ensure that these rights are fully preserved. Third, and growing most obviously out of the post-Civil War amendments, the special position given to race in the Constitution demands a special protection, which only the courts can provide.

Hence Stone, and many who followed in his footsteps, saw the function of the courts in some areas as being necessarily active. Otherwise, it would be impossible to advance the democratic ideal, protect individual rights, and provide a substantive bulwark for 'insular minorities'. This conception of the judicial role clearly requires an activist stance on occasions, but it does not really manage to establish either clear principles to guide justices in fulfilling that role or guidelines for cases which do not fall within this special responsibility of the courts. The presumption of official innocence will not cope with conflicts between the branches or between the federal and state governments, for example. Here, judicial choice is required.

Those who claimed that they were self-restrained in the 1930s, 1940s, and 1950s flirted with Stone's preferred freedoms but would not embrace them, arguing quite rightly that nothing in the Constitution expressly gave them preference. This was, of course, correct. But, where rights and legitimate power collide, one litigant must be preferred and the Constitution is, alas, disturbingly silent on which should prevail. Justices like Benjamin Cardozo and Felix Frankfurter, torn between their preference for legislative supremacy and their commitment to justice, began to use the due process clause of the Fourteenth Amendment to write into the Constitution an 'honor role' of rights, as Cardozo put it, using judicial power on occasions to strike down the most egregious misuses of power by state governments (*Palko v. Connecticut* 1937). The problem with this was its essential subjectivity. What constituted 'ordered liberty' or 'seared the conscience' (*Rochin v. California* 1952) was not written into the Constitution; and this worried people like, for example, Justice Hugo Black (Black and Black 1986).

Black's answer, once again, was deceptively simple. In order to avoid the subjectivity inherent in the position held by Cardozo and Frankfurter, Black elected to incorporate into the Fourteenth Amendment all the rights enumerated in the original Bill of Rights and give them all the status of preferred freedoms (Black 1968). This had two important consequences. Initially, it led Black into a series of positions in which judicial power was used to strike down state actions over a wide area of religious, criminal and free speech issues. Ultimately, however, it led him to break with his erstwhile liberal colleagues by refusing to read into the Fourteenth Amendment rights that were not mentioned in, or which could not be easily deduced from, the Constitution.

Black is customarily thought of as a leading activist; but I would argue that he was more self-restrained than Frankfurter (Redlich 1975–6: 20–46). At issue here is the context of those two categories. It is useful to distinguish between substantive activism and procedural activism. Substantive activism refers to the consequences of particular judgments and is applicable whenever the decisions of executives or legislatures are overthrown. Whether or not, and in what form it occurs, depends upon the nature of the political decisions being challenged in the courts. In the period before 1937, when substantive due process incorporated a preferred position for property rights and the sanctity of contracts, liberal legislation was overturned. In the post-1954 period, when substantive equal protection dominated, conservative legislation was overturned. So activism is the prerogative of neither conservatives nor liberals; the ideological colour of activism depends upon the dominant coalitions against which it is directed.

Procedural activism, by contrast, refers to the methods by which judges decide the difficult cases before them. If they embrace a philosophy which allows very little of what Holmes called 'the sovereign prerogative of choice', they may be termed self-restrained. Black's quasi-literalism (he was not always consistent) or an extreme form of original intent (i.e. whatever was not explicitly intended cannot be done) would be procedurally self-restrained. But the balancing of issues, the search for the essence of ordered liberty, in short the jurisprudence of men like Felix Frankfurter, the second John Harlan and Lewis Powell, are procedurally activist. It just is not possible to bring mere techniques, whether a deference to past decisions or a set of simple rules, to bear on many of the cases that are brought to the federal courts.

The literature on American jurisprudence is vast and the arguments subtle and complex. But from the perspective of political science, the situation is clear and ambiguous at the same time. It is clear that a system of government that respects the rule of law and the centrality of a written constitution in particular will inevitably pit those who interpret and apply that constitution against elected officials. The nature of American democracy is not merely plebiscitary and populist; it incorporates conscious limitations upon the elected. Furthermore, the wording of the Constitution and the development of constitutional law has meant that many disputes do not have a clear resolution. One should not underestimate how many do. The level of agreement amongst the Circuit Courts of Appeal and the degree of unanimity in the Supreme Court, given its propensity only to take potentially divisive cases, is testimony to that. There is ambiguity, however, on how best to resolve the obvious conflict between the culture that embraces both an ethos of electoral accountability and the principle of entrenched individual rights. Political scientists, steeped in the pragmatic study of human behaviour, should not be surprised that no theory has emerged which satisfies all persons and provides solutions to problems which are, at heart, not soluble. What judges can, and ought to do is to make clear their conception of the role of the judge and to provide as many consistent rules as practicable in setting out principled reasons for each judgment they make.

V

The 1980s saw a renewed attack upon the federal courts. It differed from many earlier attacks in that the leading figures were often members of the executive branch itself. Attorney-General Edwin Meese was the most outspoken critic; but veiled attacks on the Court are to be found in the Republican Party platforms in both 1980 and 1984 (Meese III 1985: 701–4; 1985–6: 22–30; 1986–7: 979–90) and Bradford Reynolds, who headed the civil rights division of the Department of Justice, also made it clear that he disapproved of the Court's jurisprudence (*Congressional Quarterly Weekly* 38, 1980; 42, 1984). The Solicitor-General, who has the responsibility to present the Administration's case in litigation before the Supreme Court, regularly presented briefs and arguments which challenged existing precedents (*New York Times* 1986). Administrations have always tried to persuade the justices that their view of the Constitution is the correct one, but this has traditionally been done in a much more deferential way, normally by suggesting extensions or new lines for existing precedents. The request to overrule several landmark decisions of the 1960s and 1970s was qualitatively different.

Aware that a majority of the nine justices of the Supreme Court could not easily be persuaded to follow the administration's line of argument, the Department of Justice, with President Reagan's encouragement, tried to ensure that the lower courts were filled with judges who shared its jurisprudence (Caplan 1987). The struggle over Robert Bork's nomination was unique in its intensity and in the extent to which interest groups acted openly and passionately to persuade Senators to vote the nomination down (Schwartz 1988; O'Brien in Jones ed. 1988: 60–101). But it was not unique as an instance where liberals and conservatives clashed over the propriety of Senatorial confirmation for some of the Reagan nominations. There has certainly been a politicization of the judiciary to an unparalleled extent; but it has been the administration, quite as much as its concerned opponents, that has made the judiciary a major political issue. It makes sense for it to do so, since much of its social agenda has failed in the legislative and executive branches of the federal government (Hodder-Williams 1988b). But it only makes sense if it is accepted, as surely it must be, that the courts are in the thick of the political process.

This is the very essence of the 'problem' about the Supreme Court. There is in many quarters a longing for an imagined golden age when courts were not sullied by politics (Hodder-Williams forthcoming). Perhaps, from time to time, the federal courts have in the long-distant past approximated to this ideal, but only very rarely has this been the case. A political structure that invites contestation between state and federal government, between executive and legislative branches, between individual and government, is bound to spawn political litigation, especially when the Constitution is so revered. Control over the meaning of that Constitution is power indeed. The Supreme Court, if it is to fulfil the role forced upon it by Americans, must be activist. Yet this is only half the issue, for there are more principled and less principled ways to be activist. That imagined golden age created the model of a judge dispensing justice and equity impersonally and objectively. It is an impossible model to realize, but it is a model after which judges are required to strive. The difficulties facing justices derive not only from the very nature of their task but from the fecund minds of lawyers and political actors who use litigation openly as a resource to achieve political goals. Supreme Court justices are called upon to be idealized judges in the reality of a deeply divided polity. This surely demands that only people of great distinction be nominated to the Court.

Notes

1 *White v. Weiser* (1973) 412 US 783, which held this difference impermissible, concerned congressional districting. A greater tolerance was shown in state districting cases; see *Mahan v. Howell* (1973) 410 US 315, *Karcher v. Daggett* (1983) 462 US 725.

2 On the political nature of courts, see Richard Hodder-Williams, 'Courts of last resort', in Richard Hodder-Williams and James Ceaser (eds), *Politics in Britain and the United States: comparative perspectives*, Chapel Hill, Duke University Press, 1986, pp. 142–72 and Richard Hodder-Williams, 'Political power and the modern Supreme Court', in R.C. Simmons (ed.), *The United States Constitution: the first 200 years*, Manchester, (Manchester University Press, 1989), pp. 150–7.

3 The difficulties are well put by the current Chief Justice William

Richard Hodder-Williams

Rehnquist in his *The Supreme Court: how it was, how it is*, New York, Morrow, 1987, pp. 253–304.

4 Felix Frankfurter to Harlan Fiske Stone, 27 May 1940, in Thomas Alpheus Mason, *Harlan Fiske Stone: pillar of the law*, New York, Viking, 1956, p. 526. See also similar sentiments expressed by the historian Henry Steele Commager and the constitutional scholar James Thayer and cited in David F. Forte (ed.), *The Supreme Court in American Politics: judicial activism v. judicial restraint*, Lexington, MA, Heath, 1972, p. 85.

5 For example Walter Berns's comment in 'The least dangerous branch, but only if . . .', in Leonard J. Theberge (ed.), *The Judiciary in a Democratic Society* Brookfield, VT, Gower, 1979, p. 15: The Justices use the Constitution 'as a kind of letter of marque authorising them to set sail at will among laws, striking down any they find displeasing'.

6 See Edmund Randolph's clear advice to his fellow members of the Committee of Detail, reproduced in C. Rossiter, *1787: the Grand Convention*, New York, Macmillan, 1966, pp. 201–2.

References

Abraham, H.J. (1972) *Freedom and the Court: civil rights and liberties in the United States*, 2nd Ed., Oxford: Oxford University Press: 29–88.
Baker v. Carr, (1962) 369 US 186.
Barron v. Baltimore, (1833) 7 Peters 243.
Berger, R. (1977) *Government by Judiciary: the transformation of the Fourteenth Amendment*, Cambridge, Mass.: Harvard University Press.
Black, H.L. (1968) *A Constitutional Faith*, New York: Knopf.
Black, H.L. and Black, E. (1986) *Mr. Justice Black and Mrs. Black: the memoirs of Hugo L. Black and Elizabeth Black*, New York: Random House.
Blasi, V. (ed.) (1983) *The Burger Court: the counter-revolution that wasn't*, New Haven: Yale University Press.
Brown v. Board of Education of Topeka, (1954) 347 US 483.
Brown v. Board of Education of Topeka, (1955) 349 US 294.
Bork, R.H. (1971–2) 'Neutral principles and some First Amendment problems', *Indiana Law Journal* 47: 1–35.
Brass, J. (1981) *Unlikely Heroes*, New York: Simon and Schuster.
Brewer v. Williams, (1977) 430 US 387.
Caplan, L. (1987) *The Tenth Justice: the Solicitor-General and the rule of law*, New York: Knopf.
Choper, J. (1980) *Judicial Review and the National Political Process*, Chicago: Chicago University Press.
Congressional Quarterly Weekly (1980) 38: 2034, 2035, 2046 and (1984) 42: 2105, 2107, 2108 and 2110.
Cooper, P.J. (1988) *Hard Judicial Choices: federal district court judges and state and local officials*, Oxford: Oxford University Press.
Corwin, E.S. (1938) *Court over Constitution: a study of judicial review as an instrument of popular government*, Princeton: Princeton University Press.

140

Craig, B.H. (1988) *Chadha: the story of an epic constitutional struggle*, Oxford: Oxford University Press.

Dred Scott v. Sandford (1857) 19 Howard 393.

Ely, J.H. (1980) *Democracy and Distrust; a theory of judicial review*, Cambridge, Mass.: Harvard University Press.

Epstein, L. (1985) *Conservatives in Court*, Knoxville: University of Tennessee Press.

Faux, M. (1988) *Roe v. Wade; the untold story of the landmark Supreme Court decision that made abortion legal*, New York: Macmillan.

Fein, B. (Nov/Dec 1984) 'Selecting a Supreme Court Justice devoted to judicial restraint', *Benchmark* 1: 1 (citing Alexis de Tocqueville, *Democracy in America*).

Finney v. Hutto (1978) 437 US 678.

Fisher, L. (1988) *Constitutional Dialogues: interpretation as political process*, Princeton: Princeton University Press.

Forte, D.F. (ed.) (1972) *The Supreme Court in American Politics: judicial activism v. judicial restraint*, Lexington, Mass.: Heath: 85.

Friendly, F.W. and Elliot, M. (1984) *The Constitution that delicate balance*, New York: Random House.

Furman v. Georgia (1972) 408 US 238.

Garraty, J.A. (ed.) (1964) *Quarrels that have Shaped the Court*, New York: Harper, Row: 1–14.

Glazer, N. (Fall 1975) 'Towards an imperial judiciary', *The Public Interest* 40: 104–123.

Graglia, L.A. (1976) *Disaster by Decree: the Supreme Court decisions on race and the schools*, Ithaca, N.Y.: Cornell University Press.

Gregg v. Georgia (1976) 428 US 153.

Halpern, S.C. and Lamb, C.M. (eds) (1982) *Supreme Court Activism and Restraint*, Lexington, Mass.: Lexington Books.

Handberg, R. and Hill, H.F. jnr, (1980–1) 'Court curbing, Court reversals and judicial review: the Supreme Court versus Congress', *Law and Society Review* 14: 309–322.

Hodder-Williams, R. (1986) 'Courts of last resort, in R. Hodder-Williams and J. Ceaser (eds) *Politics in Britain and the United States: comparative perspectives*, Chapel Hill, North Carolina: Duke University Press: 142–72.

—— (1987) 'The President and the Constitution', in Malcolm Shaw (ed.) *Roosevelt to Reagan: the development of the modern presidency*, London: Hurst: 11–45.

—— (1988a) 'The strange story of Judge Robert Bork and a vacancy on the Supreme Court', *Political Studies* 33: 613–37.

—— (1988b) 'The Constitution (1787) and modern American Government', in Vernon Bogdanor (ed.) *Constitutions in Democratic Politics*, Aldershot, Hampshire: Gower: 73–102.

—— (1989) 'Political power and the modern Supreme Court', in R.C. Simmons (ed.) *The United States Constitution: The first 200 years*, Fulbright Papers No. 6, Manchester: Manchester University Press.

—— (Forthcoming) 'The Supreme Court and the Reagan Administration', in

Joseph Hogan (ed.) *The Reagan Presidency*, Manchester: Manchester University Press.

Jackson, R.H. (1941) *The Struggle for Judicial Supremacy: a study of a crisis in American power politics*, New York: Knopf.

Karcher v. Daggett (1983), 462 US 725.

Kamisar, Y. (1987) 'The "police practice" phases of the criminal process and three phases of the Burger Court', in Herman Schwartz (ed.) *The Burger Years*, New York: Viking: 143–168.

Kluger, R. (1975) *Simple Justice*, New York: Random House.

Kurland, P.B. (1970) *Politics, the Court and the Warren Court*, Chicago: University of Chicago Press.

Lieberman, J.K. (1981) *The Litigious Society*, New York: Basic Books.

Mahan v. Howell(1973), 410 US 315.

Maidment, R. (1975) 'Policy in search of law, *Journal of American Studies* 9: 301–20.

Mapp v. Ohio (1961), 367 US 643.

Marbury v. Madison (1803), 1 Cranch 137.

Mason, T.A. (1956) *Harlan Fiske Stone: pillar of the law*, New York: Viking: 526

McGuigan, P. and O'Connell, J. (eds) (1987) *The Judges War: The Senate, Legal Culture, Political Ideology and Judicial Confirmation*, Washington D.C.: Institute for Government and Free Congress Research and Education Foundation.

Meese III, E. (1985) 'The Attorney-General's view of the Supreme Court: towards a jurisprudence of original intention', *Public Administration Review* 45: 701–4.

—— (1985–6) 'Construing the Constitution', *UC Davis Law Review* 19: 22–30.

—— (1986–7) 'The law of the Constitution', *Tulane Law Review* 61: 979–990.

Miranda v. Arizona (1966) 384 US 436.

Morgan, R.E. (1984) *Disabling America: the 'rights industry' in our time*, New York: Basic Books.

Murphy, W.H. (1962) *Congress and the Court: a case study in the American political process*, Chicago: Chicago University Press.

Nagel, S. (1965) 'Court-curbing periods in American history', *Vanderbilt Law Review* 18: 925–944.

New York Times (13 September 1986) see report on the Solicitor-General's lecture at the University of Missouri Law School.

O'Brien, D. (1988) 'The Reagan judges: his most enduring legacy?', in Charles O. Jones (ed.) *The Reagan Legacy: promise and performance*, Chatham, New Jersey: Chatham House: 60–101.

Palko v. Connecticut (1937) 302 US 319.

Pearson, D. and Allen, R.S. (1936) *The Nine Old Men*, New York: Doubleday, Doran.

Peltason, J. (1961) *Fifty-Eight Lonely Men: southern federal judges and school desegregation*, New York: Harcourt, Brace.

Perry, M. (1982) *The Constitution, the Courts and Human Rights*, New Haven: Yale University Press.

Plessy v. Ferguson, (1896) 163 US 537.

Pritchett, C.H. (1961) *Congress versus the Supreme Court, 1957–1960* Minneapolis: University of Minnesota Press.

Rathjen, G.J. and Spaeth, H.J. (1979) 'Access to the federal courts: an analysis of Burger Court policy-making', *American Journal of Political Science* 22: 360–382.

Reed v. Reed (1971) 404 US 71.

Redlich, N. (1975–6) 'A Black-Harlan dialogue on due process and equal protection: overheard in Heaven and dedicated to Robert B. McKay', *New York University Law Review* 50: 20–46.

Regents of the University of California v. Bakke (1978) 438 US 265.

Rehnquist, W. (1987) *The Supreme Court: how it was, how it is*, New York: Morrow.

Report to the Attorney-General on the Law of Pre-Trial Interrogation, (1986), Washington D.C.: Office of Legal Policy.

Reynolds v. Sims (1964) 377 US 533.

Rochin v. California (1952) 342 US 165.

Roe v. Wade, (1973) 410 US 113.

Rossiter, (1966) *1787: the Grand Convention*, New York: Macmillan.

Schmidhauser, J.R. and Berg, L. (1972) *The Supreme Court and Congress: conflict and interaction 1945–1968*, New York: Free Press.

Schwartz, B. (1983) *Super Chief: Earl Warren and his Supreme Court*, New York: New York University Press: 72–127; 410–428.

—— (1986) *Swann's Way: the school busing case and the Supreme Court*, Oxford: Oxford University Press.

—— (1988) *Packing the Courts: the conservative campaign to rewrite the Constitution*, New York: Scribner.

Shelley v. Kraemer (1948) 334 US 1.

Sierra Club v. Morton, (1972) 405 US 707.

Swann v. Charlotte-Mecklenburg School District (1970) 420 US 1.

Theberge, R.J. (ed.) (1979) *The Judiciary in a Democratic Society*, Brookfield, Vermont: Gower.

United States v. Butler, (1936) 297 US 1.

United States v. Carolene Products Corp. (1938) 304 US 144.

US v. Guest (1966) 383 US 745.

United States v. Nixon (1974) 418 US 683.

White v. Weiser (1973) 412 US 783.

Wilkinson III, H. (1979) *From Brown to Bakke: the Supreme Court and school integration, 1954–1978*, Oxford University Press.

Wolfe, C. (1986) *The Rise of Modern Judicial Review: from constitutional interpretation to judge-made law*, New York: Basic Books.

Woodward, R. and Armstrong S. (1979) *The Brethren: inside the Supreme Court*, New York: Simon and Shuster.

Zimring, F.E. and Hawkins, G. (1986) *Capital Punishment and the American Agenda*, Cambridge: Cambridge University Press.

Chapter eight

Is the party over? Decline and revival in the American party system

Dean McSweeney

Beginning in the late 1960s titles of books, chapters and articles reflected a pervasive belief amongst scholars that parties were losing their influence in the American political system. Originating with Burnham's 1969 article 'The End of Party Politics', this strain of writing proliferated into the 1980s reflected in titles such as *The Party's Over, Dismantling the Parties, Parties in Crisis, American Parties in Decline.* Within a decade of the appearance of Burnham's article the decline of parties was part of the conventional wisdom of American political science.

Compared with Western Europe, America has never had parties which were strong as organizations or instruments of government, but they were said to have performed numerous necessary functions (Key 1964; Sorauf 1980). They simplified the choices for an electorate faced with numerous opportunities for use of the franchise by providing cues to voters. They influenced the selection of candidates competing for elective office and they mounted election campaigns. They provided the personnel for many appointive positions in government. Through both party personnel and programmes they provided a degree of cohesion in a governmental system in which power is fragmented between institutions.

Party decline entailed impairment in the performance of these traditional functions. From the late 1960s and 1970s (hereafter known as the decline period) parties degenerated in their command of voters' loyalties, as guides to the vote, as recruitment agencies for public office, as election campaign organizations and as sources of cohesion in Government. Parties were less dominant and less effective than before, capacity had diminished and competition from non-party structures to perform functions had increased.

Four aspects of the party decline thesis are reviewed in this chapter. First, the evidence for decline is presented. Second, the causes of decline are detailed. Third, the consequences of decline are outlined. Finally, the evidence for party revival is analysed. Replicating the emphasis in the literature, most attention will be devoted to the evidence of decline.

Evidence

The atrophy of party occurred in three contexts – electoral, organizational, governmental. For convenience the evidence of decline will be presented under these three headings. While most of the literature deals with decline in a single context, only a handful of studies deal with decline in general (Pomper 1977; Scott and Hrebnar 1979; Fiorina 1980; Crotty 1984). There is also a great disparity in the volume and precision of the evidence available for the three contexts. At one extreme stands the abundance of data on voting behaviour with which to measure electoral decline. For over thirty years surveys of voters conducted under the auspices of the University of Michigan's Centre for Political Research (formerly the Survey Research Centre) have provided a detailed profile of the American electorate. Such materials facilitate precise measurement of change in the electorate over time. On the other hand, studies of party organization are sparse and consist principally of case studies of particular locales, frequently of big city machine-style parties. The shortage of research is compounded by the unrepresentativeness of those studies that have been conducted. Few studies have been conducted of the same locale at different points in time. In consequence assessments of the nature and magnitude of organizational changes are necessarily impressionistic.

The electorate

Virtually all discussions of decline refer to the attenuation of party in the electorate, and numerous studies concentrate on it exclusively (Burnham 1969; 1982; Nei *et al.* 1976; Wattenberg 1984). Party decline amongst the electorate entails a depletion of the quantity and strengths of voters' attachments to parties and their impact on the vote. The weakening of the bonds between party and voter forms part of the trend known as dealignment. Its second component is the break-up of the party electoral coalitions forged in the realignment of the 1930s (for further discussion see the chapter by John Zvesper in this volume).

Studies in the 1950s found a large majority of the electorate expressing an attachment to one of the two major parties (Campbell *et al.* 1960). This attachment, known as party identification, was a reliable guide to voting behaviour. Most identifiers most of the time were party-line voters.

Surveys into the early 1960s reveal a stability in the volume and strength of party identification in the electorate. In retrospect the years 1952–64 came to be known as the 'steady state period' (Converse 1976). From the later 1960s this stability unravelled with the number of voters expressing a party identification falling from three-quarters of the

145

Table 8.1 Party Identification, 1952–80 (in percentages)

	1952–64	1968	1972	1976	1980
Party Identifiers	74	69	64	63	63
Independents	23	29	35	36	34
Apoliticals, Don't Knows	3	2	1	1	3

Source: Stanley, H.W. and Niemi, R. (1988) *Vital Statistics on American Politics*, Washington D.C.: Congressional Quarterly Press.

electorate to under two-thirds (Table 8.1). Most independents do lean towards one of the parties but the minority of 'pure' independents (those who lean towards neither party) also underwent an increase, doubling between the steady state period and 1976.

During the same years the strength of attachment to the parties diminished (Table 8.2). In the steady state period strong and weak identifiers were roughly equal in numbers. By 1976 the latter outnumbered the former by two to one.

Table 8.2 Strength of Party Identification, 1952–80 (in percentages)

	1952–64	1968	1972	1976	1980
Strong Identifiers	36	30	25	23	26
Strong Identifiers of all Identifiers	48	43	39	37	41

Source: Stanley, H.W. and Niemi, R. (1988) *Vital Statistics on American Politics*, Washington D.C.: Congressional Quarterly Press.

The erosion of party identification had behavioural consequences. First, election turnout declined. The propensity to vote is associated with party identification. Strong party identifiers have the highest rates of turnout, independents the lowest. As the magnitude and strength of party identification waned so did the stimuli to voting and turnout declined progressively in the five presidential elections after 1960. By 1980 only 53 per cent of American adults voted in the presidential election and turnout in non-presidential years was under 40 per cent.

Declining party identification also registered in the votes that were cast. Party weakened as a voting cue with increasing numbers casting votes contrary to their party identification. The trend towards greater defection occurred in both presidential and congressional contests. (Table 8.3).

Split-ticket voting (switching between parties for different offices on the same ballot) became more common (Table 8.4). Coattail effects virtually disappeared as congressional contests became insulated from the effects of the presidential race (Calvert and Ferejohn 1983). Beginning in 1968 Republicans won three out of four presidential contests to 1980 but the House of Representatives remained under Democratic control throughout. Even the Nixon landslide of 1972 was accompanied by the

Table 8.3 Voting Defection from Party Identification, 1952–80 (in percentages)

	1952–64	*1968*	*1972*	*1976*	*1980*
Presidential Vote	15	23	27	17	21
Congressional Vote	12	18	18	21	23

Source: Wattenberg, M.P. (1986) *The Decline of American Political Parties, 1952–1984*, Cambridge, MA: Harvard University Press

re-election of House with a comfortable Democratic majority. In the past, prior to 1956, instances of divided control were the exceptions. They were the result of mid-term elections in which the President's party lost control of Congress. In the decline period the divided control occurred in presidential election years, the subsequent mid-term election merely confirmed the division, enlarging the Democratic House majority facing the Republican President. In the decline period divided control became the norm. At state level a similar trend was apparent, divided control becoming more frequent.

Table 8.4 Ticket-splitting, 1952–80 (in percentages)

	1952–64	*1968*	*1972*	*1976*	*1980*
President-Congress Ticket Splitters	14	26	30	25	30
State-Local Ticket Splitters	22	48	61	NA	59

Source: Wattenberg, M.P. (1986) *The Decline of American Political Parties, 1952–1984*, Cambridge, MA: Harvard University Press

Fewer voters remained consistent party supporters in successive elections. In the 1950s two-thirds of voters claimed to have always voted for the same party's presidential candidates. By the 1970s less than half the voters made this claim to consistency. At the aggregate level greater fluidity of the vote was apparent in the volatility in consecutive presidential elections and much greater shifts occurred than in the past (Flanigan and Zingale 1985).

Organization

Compared to electoral decline few authors have specialized in the organizational atrophy of parties (Ranney 1978; Kirkpatrick 1978; Ware 1985). The literature has also been selective in its coverage, much of it concerned with the weakened impact of party on presidential nominations whilst other levels of organization such as local parties have received little attention.

The decline of party organizations entails their loss of resources and partial displacements from the electoral process. Declining resources entailed a loss of manpower and money. Manpower, that is, activists, diminished for several reasons related to the incentives to participation in organizations. These have been defined as material (jobs, money), solidary (social contacts, friendships) and purposive, entailing the pursuit of policy goals or good government (Clark and Wilson 1961). Incentives of all three types were harder to generate for parties by the end of the 1960s. Pressures on time or alternative leisure time attractions reduced involvement. Other avenues of political participation such as candidates' organizations and single-issue campaigns grew in availability and attractiveness.

Party money diminished as a resource for campaign funds in the 1970s. Existing trends towards candidates' financial autonomy from parties accelerated with the 1974 and 1976 amendments to the Federal Election Campaign Act (FECA) of 1971. Party financing of campaigns was circumscribed in three ways. First, ceilings were placed on the amounts parties could contribute to candidates or spend on their behalf. By the early 1980s contributions from parties (national and state) were restricted to $30,000 for House contests and $27,500 for Senate races though larger amounts for co-ordinated expenditures on behalf of candidates were allowed.

Second, candidates for presidential nominations obtained a new source of funds, the federal government. After raising $5,000 in each of twenty states, candidates became eligible for federal matching funds for all individual contributions under $250 dollars. Third, non-party fund-raising organizations, political action committees (PACs), were encouraged by the legislation as they could contribute more to candidates than individuals could ($5,000 compared to $1,000). For general elections PACs could contribute as much as any one party committee (though several different party committees are entitled to contribute).

By circumscribing party capacity to contribute and by promoting alternative sources of finance, FECA amendments immediately reduced candidates' dependence on parties for funds. In 1972, the last national elections prior to the enactment of the amendments, congressional candidates received 17 per cent of their funds from parties. In 1974 the party contribution fell to 5 per cent of the total. By 1980 PACs accounted for approximately a third of all contributions to candidates in House races and a fifth in Senatorial campaigns. Contributions are not the full extent of the parties' financial assistance, owing to the allowance for co-ordinated expenditures but, after co-ordinated expenditures are included, parties could legally provide only a quarter of the funds required to finance a typical competitive House campaign (Jacobson 1984).

In the electoral process party displacement occurred at both the nomination and general election stages. In the 1960s and 1970s control over state and congressional nominations was diminished for more parties with the continued spread of the direct primary and even redoubts of the convention system such as Indiana switched to primaries.

The most striking erosion of party control over nominations occurred at presidential level. Presidential nominations had retained an immunity from popular control that was unusual for major offices by the 1960s. For presidential nominations primaries had been added to the convention system rather than replacing it, so state party organizations continued to be the dominant influences over the selection of delegates to national conventions and the presidential nominations made there. Only a minority of states held presidential primaries; they accounted for only a minority of total national convention delegates and a smaller minority were mandated by their results.

The Democrats' selection of Vice President Hubert Humphrey in 1968, despite the support in primaries for Senators Eugene McCarthy and Robert Kennedy, who opposed the administration over the Vietnam War, marks the final triumph of party dominance of a presidential nomination. Controversy surrounded the delegate selection process in 1968. McCarthy supporters charged that it was biased against them, denying them access to participate, under-representing their strength and in other ways producing a result which was an inaccurate reflection of popular choice. Prompted by these charges the 1968 national convention authorized the establishment of a committee to review delegate selection procedures and make recommendations for change.

The resulting report of the Commission on Party Structure and Delegate Selection, commonly known after its successive chairmen as McGovern-Fraser, advocated a more participatory delegate selection process whilst retaining national conventions (Shafer 1984). Caucuses (delegate selection meetings) were to be made accessible to those who wanted to participate and more accurate in representing their preferences. Specific proposals included the requirement of adequate public notice of delegate selection meetings, the abandonment of ex-officio delegates, proxy voting and winner-take-all systems of allocating delegates in caucuses. State delegations at national conventions were to represent women, young people (defined as aged eighteen to thirty) and minorities in proportion to their numbers in state populations, effectively a quota system (Commission on Party Structure and Delegate Selection 1970).

Most states complied with the report's recommendations. Several reforms required changes in state laws which thus also altered the way the Republican Party conducted its presidential nominations. Whilst the commission made no proposal for increased use of presidential primaries several states did opt to widen participation introducing them by laws which usually were mandatory upon both the Democratic and Republican parties.

That changing the rules changes the game was proven by the 1972

149

Democratic nominating contest. Participation doubled that for 1968. Edmund Muskie, the favourite of party leaders, performed disappointingly in early primaries and withdrew. The nomination was won by George McGovern despite the paucity of his support among party notables, his criticisms of the Washington establishment and stances on issues which placed him to the left of most of the public. At the national convention women, minorities and young people were represented roughly in proportion to their numbers in the population. Party notables – governors, senators, representatives – were conspicuously lacking.

Though successor commissions adjusted the rules, a participatory process was retained. The quota system was eliminated but in many other respects the procedures introduced by the McGovern-Fraser Commission were preserved. Without encouragement from the later commissions, primaries continued to multiply and by 1980, there were more primaries and a larger proportion of delegates chosen in or mandated by them than ever before (Table 8.5).

Table 8.5 Democratic Presidential Primaries, 1968–80

	1968	1972	1976	1980
Number of states holding primaries	17	23	29	31
% Delegates chosen in/bound by Primaries	37.5	60.5	72.6	74.7

Source: Author's calculations (based on various sources)

Contests continued to reflect the altered balance of power within the nominating process. Candidates lacking support from party leaders continued to flourish, exemplified in the victory of Jimmy Carter in 1976. The reduced asset that support from party notables had become was evident in the struggles to win the nomination of incumbent Presidents Ford and Carter.

In general elections, formerly traditional party campaign activities fell into disuse or were undertaken by non-party structures. Door-to-door canvassing receded and public meetings addressed by the candidates became rarer. New methods developed for conducting the campaign. Where once party officials provided impressionistic assessments of election prospects, pollsters now offered more precise profiles of voter sentiment.

The provision of campaign services became commercialized (Sabato 1981) and professional pollsters, media advisors, campaign managers and fund raisers grew in number. More significantly, they offered services to individual candidates rather than to party organizations. They became rivals to the latter in the provision of campaign services and their professionalism implied a sophistication of technique which parties usually lacked.

Commercialized campaign services facilitated the development of individual candidate organizations to conduct electioneering. Independent of party structures, candidate organizations were staffed by personal supporters and contracted campaign specialists. The best-known candidate organizations appeared in presidential contests but they were not peculiar to elections at that level. John Kennedy's 1960 presidential campaign, based on family, personal associates, a commercial pollster and one prominent figure in the Democratic Party, is an early instance of the trend towards candidate organizations. Much more sophisticated and infamous (owing to its involvement in the Watergate affair) is Nixon's 1972 Committee for the Re-election of the President, alias CREEP. Organizationally separate from the Republican Party, devoted solely to winning the presidential contest, the CREEP empire included an advertising agency, a direct-mail operation, regional, state and local branches.

Television advertising provided an alternative to parties for reaching voters. As early as 1956 television had become the most widely used of the mass media because it offered a device for penetrating into voters' homes without the manpower of a party organization and with more potent effect. Television advertising and media relations became part of commercialized campaigning and by the 1970s spending on media accounted for over half the total of expenditure in congressional contests. In 1978 in districts where campaign managers considered party organizations to be weak, 73 per cent of expenditure was devoted to media (Wattenberg 1984: 105–6).

Government

There are three elements to the literature on the decline of party in government. First, there are studies of the erosion of party cohesion in Congress (Deckard 1976; Collie and Brady 1985). Second, there is work discussing the decline of party as a link between the legislative and executive branches of government (Edwards 1983; Light 1982). Third, there are studies of the decline of party in the executive branch, particularly relating to the appointment process (Polsby 1978; Brown 1982).

Voting along party lines in Congress reaches an all-time low in the late 1960s and early 1970s. At that time only one vote in three divided a majority of Democrats against a majority of Republicans in the House compared to one vote in two a decade earlier (Table 8.6). A less precipitous decline, but one starting from a lower base, occurred in the frequency of party votes in the Senate.

Party leaders in Congress no longer possessed the resources to produce the modest party cohesion of the past. Negotiating compromises between members to generate party unity was harder than before because members were more individualistic, less deferential to leaders, and more sensitive

151

Table 8.6 Party votes in Congress, 1957–75 (percentage of all votes)

	1956–65	*1966–75*
House	50.3	35.4
Senate	44.6	39.8

Source: Compiled from *Congressional Quarterly Almanac* (various years), Washington, D.C.: Congressional Quarterly Press

to constituency pressures. Constituency service rather than party loyalty was seen as the key to re-election and where constituency and party pressures pointed in contrary directions the former was frequently the dominant influence over members' decisions.

Increased conflict between Congress and the President reduced the unity generated by party between the two branches. Congress, less internally cohesive, became more assertive in its dealings with the executive. Three Supreme Court nominations were defeated or withdrawn between 1968 and 1970. Congress sought to institutionalize its capacity for assertiveness by reining in the President by legislation. The War Powers Act of 1973 and the Budget and Impoundment Control Act of 1974 symbolize a Congress intent on restraining presidential power. Votes in Congress showed a reduced deference towards the President, their success on roll calls falling (Table 8.7). Vetoes also grew in number and so did the frequency with which they were over-ridden.

Table 8.7 Presidential success on votes in Congress, 1953–80 (in percentage)

	Victories
1953–66	77.9
1967–80	69.0

Source: Compiled from *Congressional Quarterly Almanac* (various years), Washington, D.C.: Congressional Quarterly Press

The intensification of legislative-executive conflict is not explicable solely by the divided control that characterized most of the decline period because Republican Presidents Nixon and Ford were less successful than Eisenhower had been in working with a Democratic Congress. (For further discussions of the relations between President and Congress see the chapters in this volume by Michael Foley and Joe Hogan). When united control was restored following the 1976 elections, presidential victories in Congress did not return to the level achieved in the Kennedy-Johnson years when Democrats had last controlled both branches of government. Democratic members of Congress frequently voiced their discontent over the treatment they received from the Carter White

House. The lack of a working relationship between the two branches registered in the congressional reception given to President Carter's proposals. Major items of his domestic agenda – hospital cost containment, the energy programme, restructuring of the tax and welfare systems – were either severely amended or defeated.

In forming administrations partisan connections diminished as criteria for appointment. Patronage positions were in shorter supply than formerly owing to the extension of permanent appointments. In making those appointments that remained discretionary, recent Presidents were less inclined than their predecessors to rely on the national party to act as a recruiting agency for the administration. In consequence appointments diminished as methods of rewarding party loyalists or representing the various blocs which constituted the parties' electoral coalitions. Presidents established organizations in the White House to seek out potential recruits (Bass 1983). The national party ratified rather than initiated appointments. A large majority of top appointees lacked even a party identification in common with the President. Recent cabinet secretaries have tended to be technocrats or generalist administrators rather than former elected or appointed party officials. Carter's first Cabinet contained seven Ph.Ds but only four former governors or members of Congress.

There was also a drift of decision-making power from Cabinet secretaries to the White House staff. In the latter, party connections tended to be fewer and weaker than in the former. Often long-term associates of the President, the White House staff had a personal rather than party loyalty. Their selection is less responsive to party pressures and less representative of the party blocs than the traditional Cabinet.

Causes

Much less attention has been devoted to explaining the causes of decline than in demonstrating its occurrence. References to causation have frequently been fleeting consisting of lists more than argument. Detail, debate and the testing of rival hypotheses of decline is sparse.

A minority of authors see some aspects of decline as long-term phenomena. In one account party decline in the electorate originated in the 1890s, was temporarily interrupted by the New Deal realignment in the 1930s but then recommenced in the 1950s (Burnham 1970). For Burnham, party decline, though not a linear process, has been a lengthy one which predates the twentieth century.

The trend towards presidential independence of party has been traced to the 1930s (Milkis 1985). Franklin Roosevelt attempted to centralize power in the executive branch. He also sought to institutionalize that power, making it less dependent upon party through measures such as prohibitions on political activity by federal employees (the Hatch

Act). Roosevelt both anticipated party decline and contributed to it.

However, most writers located the causes of decline more recently. Its causes originate in the period post-1945 and many of them are concentrated in the decline period. Thus most authors argue that in the last quarter of a century change was occurring either in the parties or the environment in which they operated of such a magnitude as to transform the way they performed their traditional functions.

A variety of explanations for decline have been proposed. Most accounts are multi-causal and even those authors who have preferred monocausal explanations have been inconsistent about which cause it is (see Ladd and Hadley 1975; Ladd 1978). Reflecting the imbalance in the sources on the evidence of decline, most efforts to explain its causes have been concerned with efforts to comprehend the erosion of party in the electorate though this is often then seen as producing a chain-reaction which is transmitted into government.

For simplicity, attempts to explain decline can be collapsed into six sets of causes. They involve change in respectively, society, political controversy, values and orientations, technology and mass communications, generations, and institutions ('reform').

Society

The battery of social changes entailed in the evolution from industrialism to post-industrialism has been employed to account for the destruction of the old party system (Ladd and Hadley 1975). Relevant to political change in this process has been the reshaping of the class structure, the development of the knowledge professions (the intelligentsia) and the spread of affluence.

The New Deal realignment occurred in a mature industrial society. Partisan loyalties forged in that period were a reflection of the social cleavages of industrialism. The evolution to post-industrialism reduced the salience of earlier cleavages. New Deal Democratic blocs such as manual workers, trade unionists and Catholics ceased to be 'have nots'. Less sympathetic to redistribution than in the 1930s, these groups lost their attachment to the Democratic Party.

The decline in union membership accompanying post-industrialism also undermined Democratic party organization. In many northern urban areas unions had been adjuncts to the Democratic party or substitutes for it. Loss of union members correspondingly depleted the manpower available to the party in industrial centres (Ware 1985).

Generalized affluence also reduced participation in party organizations muting material incentives to activism. Service in party organizations had once provided economic security in a society in which poverty was widespread. Amidst post-war affluence, a welfare state and a decline

154

in mass immigration from its peak early in the century diminished the numbers that could be motivated by material benefits.

Social changes peripheral to conceptions of post-industrialism have also been adduced to account for some aspects of party decline. For example, the post-war baby boom produced a disproportionately large influx of young voters in the 1960s. Customarily weak in rates of voting turnout and partisan identification, young voters were a larger share of the electorate than in the recent past and diluted its partisanship (Miller and Levitin 1976).

Growing proportions of blacks in central city populations increased the size of a racial group weakly integrated into urban party organizations (Ware 1985). Despite their growing voting strength, many Democratic party organizations remained unresponsive to blacks. First, white-dominated parties resisted the integration of blacks. Second, where white resistance was not mounted, the growth of militancy amongst blacks proved difficult to channel into the conventional electoral politics practised by parties.

Political controversy

Politics became more conflictual, intense and divisive in the 1960s and 1970s compared to the placidity of the 1950s (the latter partially induced by the intimidation of the liberal-left by the anti-communist witch-hunts). New issues emerged to dominate the political agenda – race, the Vietnam war, law and order. These issues stood outside the New Deal divide over economic management and the welfare state and their emergence heightened political awareness whilst reducing the relevance of the New Deal alignment to voting choice. On issues that concerned voters the parties either were not differentiated (Vietnam) or they were distinguished in ways that fractured the established party coalitions exemplified in the Democrats adoption of a strong civil rights stance with consequent losses of white southerners and gains amongst blacks (Nei et al. 1976; Carmines and Stimson 1982, 1984).

The new issue agenda disrupted party in Congress because members were compelled to attend to controversies that stood outside the New Deal divide between Republicans and Democrats. Economic management and social welfare issues were poorer sources of votes than in the recent past. Confronted with a new agenda on which partisan cues were lacking or contradictory, as on racial matters for southern and northern Democrats, less partisan voting patterns emerged (Deckard 1976).

For the Democrats the divisive issues diminished the party's activist base (Ware 1985). The intensity of internal party conflict, particularly over Vietnam, alienated many Democrats motivated by purposive incentives from partisan activity. Other avenues of participation such as candidate organization, interest groups, campaigns for initiatives gained in attractiveness by comparison.

Values and orientations

Many of the changes in values and orientations that have occurred derive from the social and political transformation detailed above. Four aspects of change in values and orientations have been related to party decline. Post-material values displaced material ones. Uncompromising attachment to candidates and issue stances ('purism') gained more opportunities for expression in internal party affairs. Disenchantment with political institutions grew and parties were devalued in the thinking of key political actors.

Post-material values were the attitudinal accompaniment to post-industrialism (Inglehard 1977). Economic security lost its primacy as a concern for voters amidst affluence. Issues concerning the quality of life became paramount for some voters rather than the standard of living and the growing concern for civil rights for blacks, women's rights, drug use and environmental protection illustrate the shift to a non-material agenda. For voters concerned with these issues, the economic partisan divide originating from the New Deal was not a pertinent voting cue or a source of loyalty.

Social change promoted the growth of the white-collar professional strata who became politically active, penetrating the Democratic Party. Espousing distinctive stances on foreign policy and socio-cultural issues, the new elite captured the party in 1972, alienating many traditional Democratic voters (Kirkpatrick 1975: 1976; Miller et al. 1976). Division within the Democratic Party on socio-cultural issues threatened its electoral coalitions (Ladd 1976–7).

Purism, the uncompromising attachment to candidates and issues, gained a greater voice in party affairs following reform of the presidential nominating process. Purist stances, often embraced by new class professionals, distinguished the new breed of activist from the old. The new activitists wanted parties and candidates who stood for moral principles. They wanted electoral coalitions of like-minded people. They disavowed compromise to widen electoral appeal. They sought the translation of their own preferences into election platforms rather than designing programmes to appeal to the largest possible number of voters (Kirkpatrick 1976; Polsby and Wildavsky 1976). Parties controlled by purists, as the Democrats were in 1972, failed as representative institutions because their appeal was narrow in a diverse society.

Confidence in American political institutions diminished from the later 1960s through the 1970s (Lipset and Schneider 1983). The reasons for the loss of faith cannot be precisely determined but they are probably related to the divisiveness of issues, the ineffectiveness of government in resolving pressing problems like the Vietnam war and racial tension, and the corruption in high office of the Watergate affair leading to the resignation of President Nixon. Parties were among the victims of this disenchantment and polls revealed a negative trend in the public's evaluation of parties. They were seen as increasingly self-interested and decreasingly important to democracy (Dennis 1980). Such judgements were unconducive to the forging of loyalties and encouraging participation.

The devaluation of party refers more to inadvertence than conscious choice. When parties were reformed from the late 1960s there was a failure to appreciate either their significance for democracy or the destructiveness of the changes (Pomper 1977; Ladd 1978: 1981). In particular, such authors argue, there was lack of judgement involved in trying to encourage contradictory objectives of internally democratic parties and parties capable of sufficient internal cohesion to be mechanisms of accountable government.

Technology and mass communication

Technological innovations transformed the conduct of elections and the transmission of political information. Computerization facilitated the expansion of opinion polling and the contacting of voters by post. Television commercials provided a new means for reaching voters. Television also became the principal source of news for most of the population.

These innovations reduced the dependence of candidates and voters upon parties (Sabato 1981). Campaign organizations, voting cues and political information increasingly derived from non-party sources. The mechanization of electioneering facilitated escape from labour-intensive campaigns mounted by parties. The manpower that the parties once provided became dispensable and candidates developed their own campaign organizations. The content of campaigns launched from such organizations stressed the candidate's issues and personality rather than party affiliation. In office, successful candidates, owing little to party for their election, persisted in their independence from it and, as a consequence, voters received few partisan cues from elections or government.

Generations

Generational explanations of party decline stress the qualitative differences between the new voters of the 1960s and 1970s compared with older members of the electorate (Abramson 1974; Beck 1974). New voters grew to political maturity when the socializing impact of party was waning. Candidate-centred campaigns were growing more common, and the last six years of the Eisenhower Presidency entailed divided party control in national government. Partisan influences in elections and government were both weak.

New voters of the decline era were distant from the experience of the Depression and New Deal, the events which had been formative political experiences for the new voters of the 1930s, being so profound as to lock many of them into a party identification for life. By the 1960s young voters were two generations removed from the realignment era and neither they nor their parents had lived through a period that forged political affiliations durably. In consequence neither personal experience nor family socialization tended towards partisanship for the new generation of voters in the decline period.

Institutions

Several conscious efforts to change institutions in the 1960s and 1970s diminished the parties (Ladd 1978; Kirkpatrick 1978; Polsby 1983). Reformist intentions found expression in internal party rules, public laws, judicial interpretations, the procedures and working practices of Congress. It was not the manifest intention of these initiatives to weaken parties but rather parties fell victim to the reforms' unintended effects.

Reforms of the Democrats' presidential nominating process were designed to reinvigorate the party by promoting participation within it. Enlarged citizen involvement and influence necessarily reduced the control over the outcome exerted by party elites. The size of the reduction was magnified by the proliferation of presidential primaries which the McGovern-Fraser commission and its successors rejected. The switch from low turnout party-run meetings (caucuses) to mass turnout, election-like forums demolished the prospects for elite control to survive. Caucuses might have been susceptible to elite leadership, primaries were not. Party organizations lacked the numbers and the influence to control primaries. The delegate selection process became a succession of state intra-party election contests. Candidates adopted election-style campaigns, they assembled personal organizations, recruited paid consultants and appealed to voters through the mass media. National convention delegates were candidate supporters additionally bound by the voters' mandates delivered in the primaries rather than party elites prepared to bargain to obtain benefits for themselves and their parties.

Reforms of campaign financing aimed at eliminating electoral corruption. Contributions were to be restricted in size and publicized. By including parties in the restriction, candidates' financial dependence upon them was also curbed. The trend toward candidate financial independence from party was accentuated by the promotion of alternative sources of funds as the federal government, for the first time, and political action committees, to a greater extent than formerly, moved into the funding gap vacated by party.

Within Congress, changes to promote the effectiveness of individual members undermined the collective influence of party. Devolution of decision-making to subcommittees fragmented power, rendering it less susceptible to the centralized control exerted by party leaders. The increase in members' personal staffs and constituency offices, allied with devolution to heighten the scope for individuals to serve their localities, strengthened their re-election chances. The exploitation of these opportunities enhanced the electoral security of incumbents. Electoral security became more personal and less partisan. In consequence, the incentives for incumbents to emphasize party in Congress or in campaigns diminished.

Consequences

Few authors have devoted sustained attention to the operation of the political system in which parties are losing their former effectiveness. Most discussions of impact are cursory comments in passing. The neglect of detailed discussion of consequences reflects the constraints of the American political science discipline. There is a behaviourist preoccupation with documenting the quantitative 'facts' of recent history rather than speculating upon the future. Narrow specialization also deters evaluation of 'the system' as a whole.

Where the consequences of decline have been discussed, the tone is invariably pessimistic even apocalyptic. Proponents of party dominate the literature and the decline trend is widely viewed as harmful. Amongst the damaging results of party decline that have been identified are: the erosion of citizen influence in government, the strengthening of special interests and mass media, demagoguery, governmental immobilism and diminished effectiveness.

Many authors view parties as essential components of mass democracy. Parties have been the pre-eminent mechanism for linking citizens to government, enforcing the responsiveness of the latter to the former. They have been a device for spreading influence:

> political parties, with all their well-known human and structural shortcomings, are the only devices invented by the wit of western man which with some effectiveness can generate countervailing collective power on behalf of the many individually powerless against the relatively few who are individually – or organisationally – powerful.
>
> (Burnham 1970: 133)

Party decline lowers the obstacles to concentrated power and hinders popular responsiveness. The ultimate loss from this trend is democracy itself (Pomper 1977; 1980).

The rise of the organizationally powerful registers in the growing influence of special interests (Burnham 1970; Banfield 1980; Fiorina 1980; Polsby 1983). By representing the many, parties provide organizational competitors to interest groups and they also provide the electoral backing for officeholders enabling them to resist interest-group pressures. The decline of parties diminished the insulation of government from interest-group pressures. Insofar as parties no longer aggregate and modify group demands, they no longer protect officeholders.

As parties have declined as sources of political information, the mass media have grown. There are baleful effects in this transition. The media, unlike parties, are unaccountable and possess power but not responsibility. Nor is the media neutral. It is biased towards particular interests. Reflecting their new class origins, journalists are favourable towards groups such as blacks, women, Hispanics and self-appointed defenders of the public interest such as Ralph Nader and Common Cause (Polsby 1983).

By promoting cohesion parties fulfilled a pre-condition of action in government. The unity generated by common party allegiance provided the legislative majorities to enact programmes and the executive commitment and cohesion necessary for implementation. The weakening of parties tends towards deadlock (Broder 1972; King 1978; Fiorina 1980). Governmental capacity for identifying and responding to major social problems has diminished because the driving force of party has waned, and no unifying alternative has replaced it.

Governmental capacity has also shrunk through the lowered effectiveness of Presidents produced by the participatory process. Presidents are unversed in and unaware of the need for bargaining with political elites (King 1981; Polsby 1983; Lowi 1985). Nominations (and elections) are won without the support of party elites. But presidential effectiveness cannot be attained only by mass support. A contradiction exists between the qualities necessary to be nominated and elected, and to be effective in office.

Demagoguery is facilitated by weak parties (Ceasar 1978: 1979). Where parties are strong, the ambitions of the individuals within them are curbed. Parties provide a career structure through which those who provide responsible service advance. They moderate the excesses of individuals. The latter, their political careers necessarily short, might risk irresponsible behaviour for temporary advantage. Parties, with a potential for long-term survival, depend upon the provision of stable, responsible government. Extremism, divisiveness, utopianism, and the ruthless careerism of individuals risk the party's destruction. Leaders processed through party channels are responsible moderates. The removal of party from control over leadership succession has reduced the obstacles to demogoguery. Peer review has been removed from the presidential selection process. Elites concerned for the parties' long-term prospects have been removed as actors and their moderating influence on Presidents in office has suffered accordingly.

Party revival

The thesis of party decline quickly became the conventional wisdom without resistance. Criticisms of the decline thesis were conspicuously few. Some dissenting voices were raised about the ahistorical nature of the decline thesis by authors who argued that the conventional wisdom embraced an assumption of a golden age of party which was empirically invalid (Nelson 1982; Joseph 1982). A systematic challenge to one aspect of decline appeared in the evidence that state parties were organizationally more developed at the end of the 1970s than they were before the decline period commenced (Gibson *et al.* 1983: 1984). The number of state parties with full-time staff and permanent headquarters had grown. Budgets, staff numbers and the range of activities undertaken all grew during the decline period.

How much decline had occurred and whether its impact warranted the at times apocalyptic treatment it received is worth considering. Characteristics of American parties such as the shortage of activity at the grass roots, nomination by primary, lack of cohesion in Congress and candidates' dependence on non-party sources of campaign funds are not new. All of these characteristics pertained (despite greater stability to voters' loyalties to parties) in the past indicating some insulation of different spheres of party activity from others.

As the quantiative indicators reveal, the decline was a relative one. Even in the pre-decline era there were substantial numbers of independents and ticket-splitters. Though their numbers grew from the later 1960s, the increase was not spectacular in magnitude.

The preoccupation with decline and change also neglects the signs of strength and continuity. Most voters remained party identifiers, most identifiers continued to support their party's candidates in presidential and congressional elections, parties continued to mount election campaigns and partisanship remained the single best explanation of votes cast in Congress. Even where the evidence of change was more substantial, as in the erosion of the party organizations' hold over presidential nominations, this has been seen as an accentuation of the trend towards popular control over nominations that had been underway since the Second World War (Reiter 1985).

The explanations of such decline as had occurred also suffered from a typically American insularity. Rarely was there a recognition of change in parties and party systems in other democracies. Yet several other political systems revealed changes similar to those in the United States, such as the erosion of loyalty to a party among voters, the fall in participation in party activities and the growth of interest-group activism and influence (Dalton, Flanagan and Beck 1984; Bartolini and Mair 1985; Crewe and Denver 1985). These common trends are suggestive of the impact of trends at work in post-industrial society rather than influences peculiar to the United States. However, though the sources of declined may not be unique it may be that their impact was greater in the United States than elsewhere. In a system where power was already fragmented and unifying forces weak the decline of parties was more profound in its effect on government, exaggerating the existing tendencies towards deadlock and inertia.

By the 1980s a revisionist literature emerged, arguing that parties, having declined, were undergoing a revival (Kayden and Mahe 1985; Reichley 1985; Miller and Jennings 1986). Parties responded to the decline period, adapted to the changed environment and established new roles or ways of performing traditional functions. The focus of the revival thesis is often the role of national party organizations, particularly that of the Republicans. From the late 1970s the Republican National Committee became more heavily involved in elections below the presidential level than ever before. It raised and distributed large sums of money, seconded staff to state parties, provided services to candidates such as polling and training in campaign management. Similar innovations, more modest in scale, were undertaken by the Democratic National Committee. After 1980 the Democrats undertook a modest reversal of the participatory trend in presidential nominations. Ex-officio delegates were re-established at Democratic national conventions in the form of 'superdelegates', consisting of party officials and members of Congress who were not bound by primary or caucus results. In 1984 there was one less Democratic presidential primary than in 1980 (though the number rose again in 1988). The result of these changes in 1984 was that delegates selected in or bound by primaries constituted a little over half of the total, and more Senators and Representatives served as delegates than at any time since the reform era began (Ranney 1987). Despite these changes, the dynamics of the nominating process continued to pivot around the primary results. But the last two elections have seen an end to the insurgent victories that characterized the early post-reform era. In 1984 ex-Vice-President Mondale, a candidate popular with the party hierarchy, won the nomination. In 1988 the nominees of both parties, Vice-President Bush (for the Republicans) and Governor Dukakis for the Democrats, were the type of centrist candidates acceptable to party leaders who usually won nominations in the pre-reform era.

Several other signs of party revival apparent in the 1980s have still to find their academic champions. The 1984 presidential election saw the lowest defection rate amongst party identifiers since the Michigan surveys began. The marginal recovery in party identification registered in 1980 also continued in 1984. In Congress the years 1985–7 saw a marked increase in party voting. In 1987 party votes contributed to 64 per cent of the total in the House, the highest proportion for more than thirty years. Whether party revival is a temporary deviation in a few facets of party or a more general, long-term resurgence remains to be seen.

References

Abramson, P. (1974) 'Generational Change in American Electoral Behavioural', *American Political Science Review* 68, 1: 93–105

Banfield, E. (1980) 'Party Reform in Retrospect', in R. Goldwin (ed.) *Political Parties in the Eighties*, Washington DC: American Enterprise Institute: 20–37.

Bartolini, S. and Mair, P. (1985) *Party Politics in Contemporary Western Europe*, London: Frank Cass.

Bass, H. (1983) 'The President and the National Party Organization' in R. Harmel (ed.) *Presidents and their Parties: Leadership or Neglect*, New York: Praeger: 59–89.

Beck, P. (1974) 'A Socialization Theory of Partisan Realignment', in R. Niemi *et al.* (eds) *The Politics of Future Citizens*, San Francisco: Jossey-Bass Publishers.

Broder, D. (1972) *The Party's Over: the Failure of Politics in America*, New York: Harper and Row.

Brown, R. (1982) 'Party and Bureaucracy: From Kennedy to Reagan', *Political Science Quarterly* 97, 2: 279–94.

Burnham, W. (1965) 'The Changing Shape of the American Political Universe', *American Political Science Review* 59, 1: 7–28.

—— (1969) 'The End of American Party Politics', *Trans Action* 7, 2: 12–22.

—— (1970) *Critical Elections and the Mainsprings of American Politics*, New York: Norton.

—— (1982) *The Current Crisis in American Politics*, New York: Oxford University Press.

Calvert, R. and Ferejohn, J. (1983) 'Coattail Voting in Recent Presidential Elections', *American Political Science Review* 77, 2: 407–19.

Campbell, A., Converse, P. and Stokes, D. (1960) *The American Voter*, New York: John Wiley.

Carmines, E. and Stimson, J. (1982) 'Racial Issues and the Structure of Mass Belief Systems', *Journal of Politics* 44, 1: 2–20.

Carmines, E. and Stimson, J. (1984) 'The Dynamics of Issue Evolution: the United States', in R. Dalton, S. Flanagan and P. Beck (eds) *Electoral Change in Advanced Industrial Democracies: Realignment or Dealignment*, Princeton NJ: Princeton University Press: 134–58.

Ceasar, J. (1978) 'Political Parties and Presidential Ambition', *Journal of Politics* 40, 3: 208–41.
—— (1979) *Presidential Selection: Theory and Development*, Princeton NJ: Princeton University Press.
Clark, P. and Wilson, J. (1961) 'Incentive Systems: a Theory of Organization', *Administrative Science Quarterly* 6, 2: 129–66.
Collie, M. and Brady, D. (1985) 'The Decline of Partisan Voting Coalitions in the House of Representatives', in L. Dodd and B. Oppenheimer (eds.) *Congress Reconsidered*, 3rd edition, Washington DC: Congressional Quarterly Press.
Commission on Party Structure and Delegate Selection (1970) *Mandate for Reform*, Washington DC: Democratic National Committee.
Converse, P. (1976) *The Dynamics of Party Support: Cohort-Analysing Party Identification*, Beverley Hills, California: Sage Publications.
Crewe, I. and Denver, D. (1985) *Electoral Change in Western Democracies: Patterns and Sources of Electoral Volatility*, Beckenham: Croom Helm.
Crotty, W. (1984) *American Parties in Decline*, 2nd edition, Boston: Little Brown.
Dalton, R., Flanagan, S. and Beck, P. (1984) *Electoral Change in Advanced Industrial Societies: Realignment or Dealignment*, Princeton NJ: Princeton University Press.
Deckard, B. (1976) 'Political Upheaval and Congressional Voting the Effects of the 1960s on Voting Patterns in the House of Representatives, *Journal of Politics* 38, 2: 326–45.
Dennis, J. (1980) 'Changing Public Support for the American Party System', in W. Crotty (ed.) *Paths to Political Reform*, Lexington, Massachussets: DC Heath.
Edwards, G. (1983) 'Presidential Party Leadership in Congress', in R. Harmel (ed.) *Presidents and their Parties: Leadership or Neglect*, New York: Praeger.
Fiorina, M. (1980) 'The Decline of Collective Responsibility in American Politics', *Daedalus* 109, 3: 25–45.
Flanigan W. and Zingale, N. (1985) 'United States', in I. Crewe and D. Denver (eds) *Electoral Change in Western Democracies: Patterns and Sources of Electoral Volatility*, Beckenham: Croom Helm: 23–49.
Gibson, J., Cotter, C. Bibby, J. and Huckshorn, R. (1983) 'Assessing Party Organization Strength', *American Journal of Political Science* 27, 2: 192–222.
—— (1984) *Party Organization in American Politics*, New York: Praeger.
Inglehart, R. (1977) *The Silent Revolution: Changing Values and Styles Among Western Publics*, Princeton NJ: Princeton University Press.
Jacobson, G. (1984) 'Money in the 1980 and 1982 Congressional Elections', in M. Malbin (ed.) *Money and Politics in the United States: Financing Elections in the 1980s*, Washington DC: American Enterprise Institute: 38–69.
Joseph, L. (1982) 'Neo-Conservatism in Contemporary Political Science: Democratic Theory and the Party System', *Journal of Politics* 44, 4: 955–82.

Kayden, X. and Mahe Jr., E. (1985) *The Party Goes On*, New York, Basic Books.

Key, V. (1964) *Politics, Parties and Pressure Groups*, 5th edition, New York: Thomas Y. Crowell.

Kirkpatrick, J. (1975) 'Representation in American National Conventions: the Case of 1972', *British Journal of Political Science* 5, 3: 265–322.

— (1976) *The New Presidential Elite: Men and Women in National Politics*, New York: Russell Sage Foundation and the Twentieth Century Fund.

— (1978) *Dismantling the Parties: Reflections on Party Reform and Party Decomposition*, Washington DC: American Enterprise Institute.

King, A. (1978) 'The American Polity in the Late 1970s: Building Coalitions in the Sand', in A. King (ed.) *The New American Political System*, Washington DC: American Enterprise Institute: 371–95.

— (1981) 'How Not to Select Presidential Candidates: A View from Europe', in A. Ranney (ed.) *The American Elections of 1980*, Washington DC: American Enterprise Institute: 303–28.

Ladd, E. (1976) 'Liberalism Upside Down: The Inversion of the New Deal Order', *Political Science Quarterly* 91, 4: 577–600.

Ladd, E. (1978) *Where Have All the Voters Gone?*, New York: Norton.

— (1981) 'Party "Reforms" Since 1968: a Case Study in Intellectual Failure', in P. Bonomi, J. McGregor Burns and A. Ranney (eds) *The American Constitutional System Under Strong and Weak Parties*, New York: Praeger.

Ladd, E. and Hadley, C. (1975) *Transformation of the American Party System: Political Coalitions from the New Deal to the 1970s*, New York: Norton.

Light, P. (1982) *The President's Agenda*, Baltimore: Johns Hopkins University Press.

Lipset, S. and Schneider, W. (1983) *The Confidence Gap*, New York: Free Press.

Lowi, T. (1985) *The Personal President: Power Invested, Promise Unfulfilled*, Ithaca, NY: Cornell University Press.

Milkis, S. (1985) 'Franklin Roosevelt and the Transcendence of Partisan Politics', *Political Science Quarterly* 100, 3: 479–504.

Miller, A., Miller, W., Raine, A. and Brown, T. (1976) 'A Majority Party in Disarray: Policy Polarization in the 1972 Election', *American Political Science Review* 70, 3: 753: 78.

Miller, W. and Jennings, M. (1986) *Parties in Transition*, New York: Russell Sage Foundation.

Miller, W. and Levitin, T. (1976) *Leadership and Change: the New Politics and the American Electorate*, Cambridge, Mass: Winthrop.

Nelson, M. (1982) 'Sentimental Science: Recent Essays on the Politics of Presidential Selection', *Congress and the Presidency* 9, 2: 99–106.

Nie, N., Verba, S. and Petrocik, J. (1976) *The Changing American Voter*, Cambridge, Massachussets: Harvard University Press.

Polsby, N. (1978) 'Presidential Cabinet Making: Lessons for the Political System', *Political Science Quarterly* 93, 1: 15–25.

—— (1983) *Consequences of Party Reform*, New York: Oxford University Press.

Polsby, N. and Wildavsky, A. (1976) *Presidential Elections: Strategies of American Electoral Politics*, 4th edition, New York: Scribner's.

Pomper, G. (1977) 'The Decline of Party in American Elections', *Political Science Quarterly* 92, 1: 21–44.

—— (1980) 'The Contribution of Political Parties to American Democracy', in G. Pomper (ed.) *Party Renewal in America, Theory and Practice*, New York: Praeger.

Ranney, A. (1978) 'The Political Parties: Reform and Decline, in A. King (ed.) *The New American Political System*, Washington DC: American Enterprise Institute: 213–47.

—— (1987) 'A Farewell to Reform – Almost', in K. Schlozman (ed.) *Elections in America*, Boston: Allen and Unwin.

Reichley, J. (1985) 'The Rise of National Parties', in J. Chubb and P. Peterson (eds.) *The New Direction in American Politics*, Washington DC: Brookings Institution: 175–200.

Reiter, H. (1985) *Selecting the President: the Nominating Process in Transition*, Philadelphia: University of Pennsylvania Press.

Sabato, L. (1981) *The Rise of Political Consultants: New Ways of Winning Elections*, New York: Basic Books.

Scott, R.K. and Hrebnar, R.J. (1979) *Parties in Crisis: Party Politics in America*, New York, Wiley.

Shafer, B. (1983) *Quiet Revolution: The Struggle for the Democratic Party and the Shaping of Post-Reform Politics*, New York: Russell Sage Foundation.

Sorauf, F. (1980) *Party Politics in America*, 4th edition, Boston: Little Brown.

Ware, A. (1985) *The Breakdown of Democratic Party Organisation, 1940–1980*, Oxford: Oxford University Press.

Wattenberg, M. (1984) *The Decline of American Political Parties, 1952–1980*, Cambridge, Mass: Harvard University Press.

Chapter nine

Party realignment: a past without a future?

John Zvesper

A Greek historian of Rome once claimed that history is philosophy teaching by example. For many observers of the American party system, history has become political science teaching by example. Instead of studying the party system by concentrating only on recent events, political scientists in the last two or three decades have learned to benefit from what some of them call 'longitudinal analysis' – which simpler folk might call historical awareness – going back into party history a century or two rather than merely a year or two. By doing this, they have become aware – some would say all too aware (for there is no guarantee that the past will be repeated) – that the American party system has gone through several cycles, punctuated by what have become known in the trade as 'critical elections'.

Just as in British electoral studies, the first 'scientific' accounts of voting in the United States were done during a period when there was relatively little deep disagreement between the two major parties and therefore not much evidence either of such dramatic events as critical, realigning elections, or of the levels of voters' and leaders' interest and ideological polarization that accompany such events. In 1960, *the* study of *The American Voter*, (Campbell *et al.* 1960) was based mainly on the elections of 1952–8 (and especially on information about the American electorate in 1956, gathered by the Survey Research Center at Ann Arbor, Michigan, in the first of its series of national sample surveys). Not surprisingly, that study did not report the kind of electoral awareness, excitement and division that was to come to the fore in the 1960s and 1970s. But by the 1970s, political scientists had to begin talking about *The Changing American Voter* (Nie *et al.* 1976): the political times had changed, and electoral apathy and ignorance reigned less widely in the Johnson and Nixon years (1963–75) than in the Eisenhower years (1953–61). It is always dangerous to take a snapshot of a political system at a certain point in time and assume that it accurately captures the character of the system. This proved to be particularly the case with the paradigm of the American voter and party system constructed by

167

many readers of the first 'scientific' studies of the American electorate, which were done at a time when the critical realigning potential of this electorate was not much in evidence. The authors of those studies themselves were rightly cautious about inferring too much from their 'observations . . . of a relatively brief interval' in American party history (Campbell *et al.* 1960: 43; see also 531–38).

The concept of major critical (or realigning) elections and the recognition of the cyclical character of American party history, the tempo of which has been determined by such elections, has trickled into the world of journalism and practical politics, so that today not only academic political scientists and historians but also American politicians themselves frequently reflect or at least speculate upon the presence of or the prospects for major realigning elections in the current political scene. This is one development in the academic study of politics that has been taken notice of by practising politicians, who naturally do not want to miss out on any opportunities that such significant shifts in electoral alignments and party fortunes might be offering, and do want to avoid any dangers that these events might be threatening. They do not want to miss the boat.

Much of the recent literature on American political parties has aimed to add precision to the understanding of critical elections and realignments in the past. This effort has naturally been associated with the attempt to discern the posssibilities of realignments in the present and future. More recently, there have also been attempts to explain why such possibilities, in spite of all the wishes of some American voters and politicians to the contrary, seem slighter today than they might have been in similar circumstances in the past; even if the pattern of post realignments cannot or will not repeat itself today, knowing the reasons why this is so can illuminate our understanding of contemporary American politics.

The American one-party system

Although the American party system is and has been largely a two-party system, there is an important sense in which this system is actually a one-party system. This can be seen in Table 9.1, which summarizes the results of elections to federal offices for the entire history of the American party system.

Since the electoral 'Revolution of 1800', the dominance of federal office holding by one of the two major parties has been striking. In the twenty-eight years from 1801 to 1829, the Republicans (or National Republicans) controlled the Presidency, House and Senate together for twenty-six years. In the following thirty-two years (1829–61), the Democrats held all three bodies for eighteen years, their opponents only for two years. In the seventy-two years from the election of Lincoln to

Table 9.1 Partisan control of the federal government*

Presidents	Years	Presidency	House	Senate
Washington, Adams:	1789–93	——— non-partisan ———		
	1793–5	F	R	F
	1795–1801	F	F	F
Jefferson, Madison, Monroe:	1801–25	R	R	R
J.Q. Adams:	1825–7	NR	NR	NR
	1827–9	NR	D	D
Jackson, Van Buren:	1829–41	D	D	D
W.H. Harrison, Tyler:	1841–3	W	W	W
	1843–5	W	D	D
Polk:	1845–7	D	D	D
	1847–9	D	W	D
Taylor, Fillmore	1849–53	W	D	D
Pierce:	1853–5	D	D	D
	1855–7	D	R	D
Buchanan:	1857–9	D	D	D
	1859–61	D	R	D
Lincoln, Johnson, Grant:	1861–75	R	R	R
Grant, Hayes:	1875–9	R	D	R
	1879–81	R	D	D
Garfield, Arthur:	1881–3	R	R	R
	1883–5	R	D	R
Cleveland:	1885–9	D	D	D
B. Harrison:	1889–91	R	R	R
	1891–3	R	D	R
Cleveland:	1893–5	D	D	D
	1895–7	D	R	R
McKinley, T. Roosevelt, Taft:	1897–1911	R	R	R
	1911–13	R	D	R
Wilson:	1913–19	D	D	D
	1919–21	D	R	R
Harding, Coolidge, Hoover:	1921–31	R	R	R
	1931–3	R	D	R
F.D. Roosevelt, Truman:	1933–47	D	D	D
	1947–9	D	R	R
	1949–53	D	D	D
Eisenhower:	1953–5	R	R	R
	1955–61	R	D	D
Kennedy, Johnson:	1961–9	D	D	D
Nixon, Ford:	1969–77	R	D	D
Carter:	1977–81	D	D	D
Reagan, Bush:	1981–7	R	D	R
	1987–91	R	D	D

Source:

Note:
*F = Federalist
R = Republican
NR = National Republican
D = Democrat
W = Whig

Elections occur in even-numbered years, preceding the years in which presidential administrations and Congresses begin the election of Franklin Roosevelt, the Republicans controlled all three for forty-two years, their opponents for only ten. Finally, in the fifty-eight years from 1933 to 1991, the Democrats will have held all three for thirty years, their opponents for only two years. In other words, the dominant parties in each of these periods (the Republicans from 1801 to 1829, the Democrats from 1829 to 1861, the Republicans from 1861 to 1933, and the Democrats since 1933 – although their failure to dominate the Presidency since 1968 is a notable fact which we shall consider in the last section of this chapter) have elected the President and majorities in the House and Senate for a total of 114 years; their opponents have done this for only fourteen years. (The continuity in the names of the parties is of course a little misleading: the Republican Party from 1860 was a new party, not the same as the Jeffersonian Republicans, and the New Deal Democratic party from the 1930s became a new coalition, organized on different principles from the Democratic Party of previous periods).

More importantly, the dominant party in each period of party history has managed the policy-making agenda, and the subordinate major party in each period has had to learn to conform to the policy preferences established by the dominant party. The subordinate parties have had to offer an echo, not a choice, in order to survive as well as they can. In presidential contests, they have been well advised to nominate military heroes with rather obscure party loyalties rather than party regulars with ideologies too readily identified with energetic opposition to the dominant party. (This was the successful formula of the Whigs in 1840 and the Republicans in 1952; in 1964, with the nomination of Goldwater, the Republicans neglected this strategy and were soundly defeated. By 1980, the dominant Democratic Party was no longer dominant in presidential elections, so the advice no longer applied.)

In the study first published in 1951, Samuel Lubell described this feature of the American party conflict in the following terms:

> Our political solar systems . . . has been characterized not by two equally competing suns, but by a sun and a moon. It is within the majority party that the issues of any particular period are fought out; while the minority party shines in reflected radiance of the heat thus generated.
>
> (Lubell 1965: 191–2)

One finds in the writings of American politicians from the first party conflict onwards a recognition of this fact, and of the justice of this fact. For example, Thomas Jefferson referred to the electoral 'Revolution of 1800', as a decisive establishment of true republican principles. If only one party is true to American republicanism, then it deserves to enjoy a hegemony over the other party. In a deep and important sense, the American political system has not experienced *The Rise of Legitimate Opposition*, the somewhat misleading subtitle of Richard Hofstadter's study of the American attitude towards party politics in the first half-century of the republic (Hofstadter 1969). In their origins, each of the dominant major parties – the Republicans under Jefferson, the Democrats under Jackson, the new Republicans under Lincoln, and the new Democrats under Franklin Roosevelt – has claimed superior legitimacy over its rival and therefore a right to a dominant position in the political system.

Lubell argued that the transition from one period to another occurred when the majority party coalition, always subject to the centrifugal pull of its various elements, flew apart. 'The more heated the frictions within the majority sun . . . , the more luminous are the chances of victory for the minority moon'; and when the majority sun party is 'shattered to its core . . . , both parties are reshuffled and a wholly new political solar system is created.' (Lubell 1965: 194–5). While this focus on the problems faced by the majority party in maintaining its coalition of diverse elements does help to explain what has happened in those elections in which the subordinate party has been *temporarily* victorious (for example, the presidential victories of the Whigs in 1848 and of the Democrats in 1884, 1892, 1912 and 1916), it is less helpful in understanding those few elections (or series of elections) in which the dominant party coalition has been established in the first place (1792–1800, 1828–32, 1860, and 1932–6). In the case of these elections, more attention has to be focused on the appeal of the emergent new dominant party than on the troubles of the old one, in order to understand what has happened. Understanding these rare but era-forming elections is the primary aim of the theory of critical elections.

Theories of critical elections and critical realignments

The American political scientist V.O. Key was the first to propose 'A Theory of Critical Elections', in an article published in the *Journal of Politics* (Key 1955). As we have seen, other writers and politicians had been aware of the significance of certain watershed elections in American political history. In fact, Key cited in support of his theory the 1947 American Political Science Association Presidential Address by Arthur MacMahon, with its discussion of the rarely disturbed consensual context of conflict between major American parties (MacMahon 1948). And another American political scientist, E.E. Schattschneider, published almost simultaneously with Key's article an important essay (later expanded into part of a widely read book on American party politics (Schattschneider 1960) that discussed the revolutionary character of certain elections, focusing on the durable redefinition of the cleavage between the major parties that occurred in these revolutionary elections (Schattschneider 1956). But the academic theory of critical elections begins with Key's succinct statement of the characteristics of these elections, and by his giving them the pregnant label, 'critical'.

Key differed from many of his more 'scientific' colleagues in the political science profession by his conviction that the American electorate was more rational and responsible than some of the voting studies paradigms gave them credit for being (Key 1966). The theory of critical elections thus has implications for democratic theory. 'Realistic' critics of the 'classical' view of democracy follow in the footsteps of Machiavelli, who argued that democracy is an impossible regime because most people are too apolitical to be active citizens. The 'realistic' portrait of American voters offered by the new voting studies of the 1950s encouraged this scepticism about the possibility of democracy, even democracy by means of elections; if voting is largely an irrational act based on unthinking, habitual identification of voters with one party or another, electoral direction and control of government can hardly be described as an attractively democratic process. Yet if in some elections, at least some voters act in a way that addresses and resolves a political crisis, then democracy looks more actual. Critical election theory offers 'to redefine democracy as a process which is more continual than continuous; more periodic than constant; more sudden, dramatic, abrupt, shattering, and monumental than smooth and incremental' (Trilling and Campbell 1980: 4). In fact, one could go further; the democratic cast given to American politics by critical elections could be seen not only in the critical periods themselves, in which habits of party identification are established, but also in the stable periods that follow the crises, since even in these periods the democratic decision made in the critical period is maintained by means of elections, albeit voters are then acting more habitually.

Key argued that voters' own recognition that some elections are much more important than others made their inconsistent levels of interest and excitment, and their usual dependence on habitual party identification, seem quite reasonable. Key's theoretical account of the deservedly exciting 'critical' elections pointed to five characteristic features of these elections: the durable transfer of dominance from one party to another, durable changes in the loyalties of the groups that comprise each party's usual coalition, a marked increase in the intensity of interparty and intraparty conflict (often associated with the mobilization of new groups of voters and an increase in turnout), the emergence of a new set of issues as the basis of conflict, and the loosening of inherited party loyalties in the face of these new issues. A few years after his first article on critical elections and realignments appeared, Key published an addendum on 'secular' realignments (Key 1959), which emphasized the point that realignments of the electorate sometimes occurred in slower motion than they did in critical realignments, as long-term drifts rather than as sudden waves. Critical elections are associated with critical realignments; secular realignments occur more gradually and more frequently.

The comprehensiveness of Key's theory probably helped make it the starting point for so many later studies, not all of which were as comprehensive or as sensible as his. Yet even Key's theory probably paid too little attention to two things: (1) the role of political leaders in making or failing to make elections critical – a point explored by later theorists, and one which seems particularly germane when contemplating the absence of critical elections in the 1980s; and (2) the very distinctive, evangelical quality of the political appeals made by leaders such as Jefferson, Jackson, Lincoln and Roosevelt during their critical election periods. This point deserves wider investigation than it has received. It has been noticed that the similarity of the rhetoric voiced by the winners of all of the critical elections makes more reasonable the continuity in the names of these parties; they are all called Democrats or Republicans – or in the case of Jackson's party, both – because only democratic republicans win these decisive contests in American politics. What is at issue in these elections is the meaning of loyalty to democratic republican principles. The American party system is thus in an even more profound sense a one-party system (Jaffa 1965).

Key's typology of elections – the division into critical and uncritical elections – has been elaborated by later writers. A few pages of *The American Voter* were devoted to Angus Campbell's 'Classification of Presidential Elections' (Campbell *et al*. 1960: 531–8), which divided the category of uncritical elections into 'maintaining' and 'deviating' elections. Maintaining elections – a category that includes the large majority of American elections – are those 'in which the pattern of partisan attachments prevailing in the preceding period persists and is the primary influence on forces governing the vote'; whereas in deviating elections, although 'the basic division of partisan loyalties is not seriously disturbed', the majority party is nevertheless defeated, because personalities or events change voters' attitudes sufficiently to produce 'a temporary reversal' in the fortunes of this party that nevertheless continues to hold 'a clear advantage in the long-term preferences of the electorate'. In 1961, having been reminded of a further possibility by the results of the 1960 presidential election, Campbell and his colleagues added to their scheme of classification a third type of uncritical election: 'reinstating' elections, those in which 'the party enjoying a majority of party identifiers returns to power' (Converse *et al*. 1961). In 1967, Gerald Pomper argued in favour of a further category of uncritical elections, to reflect a distinction between critical elections proper and merely 'converting' elections, which resemble critical elections in the intensity and quality of the conflict and in the durability of their effects, but result (as in 1896, called a critical election by some) not in the displacement of the currently dominant party, but merely in the reassertion or strengthening of its dominant position (Pomper 1967). The presidential election of 1964, in which the Republicans offered in their nominee Barry Goldwater a 'choice' rather than an 'echo' who was, however, over-whelmingly rejected by the voters, and the presidential election of 1972, in which the 'deviating' result of 1968 was increased to landslide proportions by the voters' rejection of the Democrats' candidate, George McGovern (felt by many voters to be out of the mainstream of the Democratic Party), provided examples of a third type of election: a 'reinforcing' election, which can be basically either maintaining (as in 1964) or deviating (as in 1972), but which punishes whichever party offers a choice perceived to be too far out of step with the underlying consensus established in the last critical realignment.

In addition to expanding and polishing the terminology of critical realignment theory, political scientists have tried to define more precisely the essence of the object of their studies. What is necessary, and what is sufficient, to constitute a critical election or realignment? Everyone agrees that these phenomena are marked by durable change in the electoral universe. But what must durably change?

In one of the best studies of realignments of the American electoral system, in a work that traced the changing contours of this system since the 1840s, James Sundquist argued in favour of Schattschneider's emphasis on the effects of critical realigning elections on 'the agenda of American politics' (Sundquist 1983: 13, citing Schattschneider 1960: 88). Key's criteria for critical realignments concentrated too much, according to Sundquist, on changes in the composition of the parties and too little on the terms of political conflict. Sundquist proposed to reserve the term 'realignment' to those elections or periods when there has occurred 'a change in the structure of the party conflict and hence the establishment of a new line of partisan cleavage on a different axis within the electorate'. He argued that such 'conflict displacement', rather than shifts either in relative party strength or in changes in the parties' group coalitions – both of which could be expected to be associated with such displacement – is best regarded as '*the* characteristic that identifies a party realignment' (Sundquist 1983: 13).

Treating conflict displacement as the essence of the thing makes the line between critical realignment and secular realignment less necessary to draw. Sundquist pointed out that

> much of what appears as secular realignment is simply a later stage, or a later series of stages, of a preceding critical realignment – the aftershocks, so to speak, as the fault lines created by the initial political earthquake settle into place.
>
> (Sundquist 1973: 8)

This happened during several decades following the New Deal realignment. Thus the perfectly reasonable tendency of commentators to talk of 'realigning periods' or 'eras' rather than a single 'realignment election'. Even critical realignments have their 'secular' phases, if by that is meant simply that they have some important long-term manifestations, such as northern liberals finally getting around to identifying and registering with the Democratic Party, and southern conservatives with the Republican party, thirty years after the New Deal elections that defined the Democrats as the home of these northerners' kind of liberalism and the Republicans as the home of these southerners' kind of conservatism. It can be confusing, therefore, to focus our attention on the pace of the realignment process.

Sundquist also argued that the magnitude and geographic scope of the change were inessential features. As to magnitude, 'how significant is significant enough?' and as to geographic scope, why insist – against everything we know about the decentralized and geographically uneven way that the American party system functions – that the change takes place nationwide? Even durability as a criterion of realignment needs to be qualified by the recognition that there are some realignments that might have been durable if events had not intervened to shorten their lives – such as when the Great Depression obliterated or at least drastically modified the realignment of 1928 (Sundquist 1983: 6–10). So Sundquist concludes that it is better to follow Schattschneider's lead and to define a critical realignment – or any party realignment strictly speaking (as opposed to a mere 'shift in the party balance within an established and continuing alignment') – 'in terms of the nature of the phenomenon rather than the electoral consequences that the phenomenon produces, in terms of the underlying process rather than its surface manifestations', in other words, by the movement of 'the line of cleavage between the parties' to 'cut across the electorate in a new direction', so that the party system has 'shifted on its axis'. (Sundquist 1983: 13–14).

Even if one does not follow Sundquist's advice in every particular, his argument that realignments should be defined with reference to changes in the major issues that the party system deals with is persuasive. It is this kind of change that has made it plausible for historians and political scientists to talk of an essentially new party system coming into being with every critical election period, and to look at American political party history as a series of four or five such 'party systems' (Chambers and Burnham 1967, Burnham 1970, Kleppner *et al.* 1981). Critical elections are 'constituent acts' that redefine 'the broad boundaries of the politically possible' (Burnham, 1970: 10), and thereby usher in a new party system.

175

Applying and Elaborating the Theories

Sundquist's attempt to clarify what he called 'the muddied concept of party realignment' by restricting it to changes in the line dividing the major parties on key issues is supported not only by Schattschneider's and others' earlier thinking but also by much of the subsequent and current writing on realignment and critical elections. Among political scientists, there are always those who would never miss any opportunity to count things, and testing the theory of critical elections by examining past and present American party politics has provided plenty of such opportunity. Voting figures are available in some form for the whole history of the party system. However, voting figures alone do not tell the whole story. And modern scientific survey techniques, which can help flesh out the story, have been deployed only since the Second World War (and party registration figures are available only for the twentieth century – and even then not universally). So the most comprehensive and sensible studies have combined quantitative and non-quantitative techniques, looking at 'the content of partisan conflict from year to year, and the behaviour of party leaders, conventions, caucuses, and candidates and their organizations and supporters' (Sundquist 1983: 15). This approach has been so successful that one sometimes wonders whether the data provided by the more 'scientific' techniques enhance the study of party realignment more than they risk bogging it down in somewhat sterile quarrels over methods of measurement (Nexon 1980). Here as elsewhere in political studies, it is helpful to pay heed to Aristotle's advice about not demanding more precision than is appropriate in political science. The character and the broad outlines of the phenomena of critical elections and realignments are perfectly visible without going overboard on calculations. In realignment studies, some very sophisticated statistical techniques have yielded at best only confirmation and elaboration of the basic theory, rather than fundamental corrections of it.

While many realignment studies have been concerned simply to define precisely when and where realigning elections have occurred, others have extended their field of vision, in three distinct ways. These broader studies have measured and described, in the first place, the changes that realigning elections have brought to the substance of interparty conflict (Ginsberg 1972). They have also demonstrated the significant changes in government policies that have followed from realigning elections (Beck 1979; Brady 1980; Clubb *et al*. 1980; Hansen 1980; Stewart 1980; Brady and Stewart 1982). Finally, they have related these changes in party competition and government policy to changes in the staffs who formulate and administer policy, at both federal and state levels, and in legislatures, judicial courts and bureaucracies, as well as in executive offices (Burnham 1970; Funston 1975; Sinclair 1977, 1978 and 1982; Beck 1979; Adamany

1980; Brady 1980; Clubb *et al*. 1980; Meier and Kramer 1980; Seligman and King 1980; Brady and Stewart 1982; Lasser 1985).

Studies of the electoral, policy and personal contours of realignments have noted some interesting variations among the major realignment eras. For example, a recent account of the public policy dimension of congressional party realignment in the 1860s, the 1890s and the 1930s, found differences in the degree to which realigning issues polarized voters and their representatives in Congress. Specifically, it found less polarization during the New Deal realignment of the 1930s than during the two previous periods. (Brady and Stewart 1982). Partly, the authors note, this was simply because the New Deal Democrats enjoyed such an overwhelming majority in the House of Representatives that party polarization was dampened down. One might also wonder whether their findings reflect the overall decline of party politics in the twentieth century, *versus* the nineteenth (the notorious '*de*lignment' of voters and politicians, discussed below). But the main point to notice here is that such findings do not alter the basic portrait of critical elections and realignments so much as they add local colour and shading.

Like students of other political phenomena, students of party realignment are divided on the question of the extent to which political phenomena should be explained in terms of socio-economic causes. Are critical elections and realignments, which everyone admits have great effects on the course of partisan conflict and public policy, fundamentally political events, involving a fair degree of conscious choice by individual voters and politicians? Or are they results of less rational changes in the arrangements of the parties' group coalitions, with the interests of some groups shifting them into one party and those of other groups shifting them into the other party, resulting in a net change in the balance between the parties? That is how the classic post-war studies of American voting behaviour preferred to see durable electoral changes occurring, because individual voters' judgement of the issues of the day seemed less likely to influence their long-term party loyalty than did the socially-reinforced attitudes of their group's opinion: 'Attitudes rooted in social groups are likely to be more stable than are attitudes that are denied the status of group norms', and changes in groups' party loyalties 'tend to be associated with issues that persist through time', such as the issues linked to economic class (Campbell *et al*. 1960: 536). Moreover, although V.O. Key tended to be less cynical about the rationality and responsibility of voters than some of his colleagues in the political science profession, his own statement of the critical election process had emphasized the extent to which these important events in American party politics are associated with durable changes in the loyalties of the groups that make up the parties' coalitions.

It has proved possible to write the history of American party policies with an emphasis on this underlying coalitional dynamics. Such a history can recognize the different historical 'party systems' that have emerged during that history, but must trace these different systems to underlying socioeconomic changes, rather than to autonomous political choices made by the electorate or some considerable portion of the electorate. In this account of the history of American party politics in terms of *Social Change and Political Response* (the subtitle of Everett Carll Ladd's study of *American Political Parties*: Ladd 1970), each successive party system appears not as the result of political issues decided by critical elections but as the natural political expression of the current state of socioeconomic development. Parties in the 'rural republic' give way gradually to parties in the 'industrializing nation'; these in turn to the parties of the 'industrial state', and finally perhaps to the 'postindustrial state'. The emphasis shifts from political changes (such as those produced by elections) to social changes. What appears to be a critical election turns out to be merely an election that happens to occur during a social crisis: 'the election is but one current in the sweeping tide of sociopolitical change. Critical realignments take place primarily as *effects of* other major changes occurring in the society' (Ladd and Hadley 1975: 25 – original emphasis).

This subordination of politics to sociology may seem natural and necessary in a society like the United States 'which has achieved a high measure of consensus around its constitutional arrangements'; with no fundamental political conflict,

> The source of lasting change in the structure of conflict must be transformation of the social system . . . the appearance of broad new sets of political interests, drastically altered expectations within the citizenry, marked increase in the numerical strength of established interest groups, and the like.
>
> (Ladd and Hadley 1975: 90).

But the American experience of critical elections throws doubt on the hypothesis that such a consensus has been achieved. What is at issue in the critical elections if not precisely the shape of that consensus itself, or in other words the meaning of democratic republicanism? The 'consensus' view of American political history is today widely (and rightly) questioned. Those who are more impressed with the depth of political conflict in the United States in certain periods, and with the importance of certain decisive elections, emphasize with Sundquist (here explicitly disagreeing with Ladd) the fact that social changes 'do not in themselves produce realignments. They must first give rise to genuine *political* issues'. Sundquist (who as a former speech writer for Harry Truman might well be expected to know something about the existence and importance of controversy in American politics) points out that a 'profound change in the structure of society, particularly one that occurred gradually, might never produce a political issue of realigning force; on the other hand, a major political issue might arise in the absence of fundamental structural change' (Sundquist 1983: 299). The realignment that elevated the parties of Jefferson, Jackson and Lincoln and Franklin Roosevelt all involved quick political actions, rather than merely political reactions to slow socio-economic developments. Only the combination of interest group politics with ideological politics describes and explains critical elections. Interest-group politics does not disappear in critical elections, but it is accompanied by principled conflict.

In fact, such conflicts are not absent in other periods of American party history, and one of the most interesting questions pursued by realignment studies is why the rise of principled conflicts has not always led to critical elections. How have critical elections been avoided in many cases, in spite of the existence of cross-cutting issues of realigning potential? Addressing this question should help relieve the uneasiness felt by some that critical elections and realignment studies must neglect long periods of American party history to concentrate only on actual critical elections, which have been very few in number. It should also bring more into the centre of the picture the importance of political leaders' actions and failures to act, instead of leaving the behaviour of the electorate to dominate the scene on its own. Doubtless there have been occasions in American political history – perhaps particularly in cases of ethnic or religious quarrels – when potentially realigning issues deserved to be ignored or suppressed, in spite of their actual or potential appeal to the electorate. Political leaders deserve to be judged on (among other things) how well they perceived such occasions and acted accordingly, as well as on how skilfully or how badly they have exploited realigning issues that deserved to be effective. When the times cry out for inaction, cooling the electorate's passions can be as praiseworthy as warming them up can be at other times. Statesmanship does not always have to deal in the stuff of tragedy. Uncritical elections can in this way be as interesting and as demanding as critical ones.

It has been noticed by some studies that the exploitation of realigning issues by political leaders has occurred not only in critical elections themselves, but also in government policies afterwards, which in at least some cases have helped make the preceding elections durably critical. Electoral victories have simply provided the opportunity for 'decisive and innovative policy actions', and it is these actions that have been necessary 'to convert temporary electoral strength into lasting partisan support and loyalty' (Clubb *et al.* 1980: 32). Like vintage wines, critical elections can be proclaimed only in retrospect, when the durability of the changes they bring has been seen; but perhaps they depend even more than good wines on the way they are handled after the harvest. After the votes are counted, it remains to be seen what the victors will make of their spoils. 'Vigorous policy action . . . can be seen as reinforcing and, indeed, rewarding voting behaviour and as necessary for the final element of [a] realignment, the formation of a new and lasting distribution of partisan loyalties . . .' (Clubb *et al.* 1980: 260). This perspective can help to resolve conflicting interpretations of the significance of the mobilization of new voters *versus* the conversion of existing ones, in a given realignment. (Such conflicting interpretations have been especially evident in the literature on the New Deal realignment Anderson 1979; Erikson and Tedin 1981; Sundquist 1983: 229–39). Even newly mobilized voters need to be 'converted' in the sense that they need to become party loyalists rather than merely instrumental voters for the party for the time being.

These last two points – the absence of critical elections and realignments in certain times of principled political conflicts, and the importance of political leaders' action both during and after potentially critical elections – have figured prominently in studies of party conflict in the last twenty years, and in considerations of the prospects for realignment today.

Waiting for realignment

From Table 9.1, it can be seen that the legislative branch of the federal government – the House of Representatives and Senate – has been controlled by the Democratic Party since 1955, with the exception of the first six years of Reagan's Presidency, when the Democrats lost control of the Senate. During the same period, the Republican Party has controlled the White House for all but twelve years. Divided party control of the federal government seems to have become the normal situation. The Republican's apparent 'lock' on the presidential Electoral College is more than matched by the Democrats' 'lock' on congressional elections. During this period, all but the twelve years of Democratic Presidents have been years of divided government; in other words, there has been divided government about 65 per cent of the time. During the previous 164 years of American party politics, one can calculate from Table 9.1 that there was divided government for only about 20 per cent of the time.

The Republican presidential victories of Eisenhower in 1952 and 1956 could (and still can) be seen mainly as deviating elections, in which a military hero *not* known as 'Mr Republican' helped the subordinate Republican Party temporarily to defeat the presidential ambitions of the dominant Democrats (and, even more temporarily, their congressional ambitions). But the victories of Richard Nixon in 1968 and 1972 were accompanied by greater speculation about the possibilities of lasting shifts of the electorate towards identification with the Republican Party.

Some observers discerned an *Emerging Republican Majority* (Phillips 1970). The Watergate scandals checked any such emergence, at least for a few years, but the victories of Ronald Reagan in 1980 and 1984 (and Republican victories in Senatorial elections in 1980, 1982 and 1984) led to further speculation about a major realignment of the party system. Academics immediately voiced much scepticism about the existence of such a realignment, pointing out that the Democrats maintained firm control of the House (as well as of the majority of state legislative branches), and that the exit polls in 1980 and other indicators of public opinion showed little evidence that voters thought they were giving the Republicans a conservative mandate (e.g. Ladd 1981; Schneider 1981). More evident than any realignment trend was a continuing trend towards party *de*alignment and decline. Burham (1970) and others had pointed out the evidence of a long-term decomposition of the party system, stretching back to the end of the nineteenth century, and such dealigning trends as low levels of partisanship, split-ticket voting, low turnout, the erosion of traditional ties between certain ethnic and interest groups and the major parties, the volatility of opinion and voting decisions, and the use of party-bypassing devices such as referenda and initiatives, all seemed to persist in spite of the 'Reagan Revolution'. (See Dean McSweeney's chapter in this book for a discussion of party dealignment).

Of course, it could be (and has been) pointed out that dealignment is nothing new in American party politics. Evidence of dealignment has been spotted in previous historical party systems. It is a natural feature of the cycle of party history, both because of the difficulties of maintaining enthusiastic party loyalty long after the critical election battles have been fought and won, and because of the confusion of party loyalties in pre-realignment periods. Beck (1979) drew our attention to the fact that previous dealigning periods also included high levels of divided government. Could not the current dealignment simply be setting the stage for a contemporary realignment?

This raises two further and final questions about party realignment in the contemporary period: are political leaders currently exploiting the opportunities for realignment as well as they might? And are there any difficulties in the way of realignment that make such exploitation harder today than for political leaders in the past?

Even many conservative supporters of Reagan have come to doubt that he served their cause and the Republican party as well as he might have. His 1984 campaign, in particular, in spite of (or because of) its leading to a presidential landslide, seemed singularly lacking in any major and timely attempts either to define a set of polarizing issues and gather a presidential mandate or to spread the Republican electoral victory farther down the ballot. Reagan was well adapted to the cool politics of television, but little interested in carrying on hot and divisive political battles of the kind that have been essential to critical realignments in the past. Critical realignments require political leaders who are not afraid of being hated as well as loved. Reagan's personal popularity rarely dipped very low, but the percentage of the electorate with a Republican partisan identification at the end of Reagan's two administrations was about what it was at the beginning (around 35 per cent – still slightly less than Democratic identification). For his electoral victories, he relied more on 'Reagan Democrats' than on massive conversions of voters or mobilizations of new voters as loyal Republicans. Thus, according to the *New York Times – CBS News* exit poll, in November 1988, half of the Democrats who had voted for Reagan in 1984 supported the Democratic nominee, Michael Dukakis, the first-time voters split fairly evenly between the presidential candidates, with George Bush receiving 51 per cent of their votes, to Dukakis' 47 per cent (in contrast to 1984, when Reagan received 61 per cent, to Walter Mondale's 38 per cent).

This is not to deny the fact that Bush may well owe his election to his discovery of the power of the cross-cutting social or cultural issues that appeal to many of those Democrats who have recently voted for Republican presidential candidates. The Bush campaign transformed a 17-percentage-point lead for Dukakis in the polls in the summer to an 8-point lead for Bush in the elections in November, mainly on the strength of what was called 'negative' campaigning. Bush's attacks on Dukakis' record on the punishment of crime (the prison furlough issue) and on dedication to American political principles (the pledge of allegiance issue) may have been distasteful to many observers, both in America and abroad. But the success of these attacks clearly proves that the conventional wisdom of the 1960s and 1970s of television campaign professionals who taught that such 'negative' tactics were too risky now needs to be revised at the presidential level, just as it has already been revised at other levels of American politics. Dukakis and his advisers seriously underestimated the effects of these attacks. Failing to see that many American voters would take these issues seriously, Dukakis unwisely chose to ignore them at first, and as Ben Wattenberg has pointed out (Wattenberg, 1988) when he did respond, he failed to respond to the charge made, which was not that he was (as he now admitted) a New Deal, Roosevelt-Truman-John Kennedy-Johnson liberal, but that he was – on the social issues – a 1960s McGovern-Carter-Ted Kennedy-Jesse Jackson liberal. The Bush 'negative' campaign helped to double between July and October the percentage of the electorate with negative ratings of Dukakis, largely because it succeeded in identifying Dukakis clearly as a liberal on social issues (however much he was a fiscal conservative), in the minds of key groups in the electorate, including many socially conservative Democrats and independents.

However, it seems unlikely that President Bush will prove any more inclined or able than President Reagan was to transform socially conservative support into a partisan realignment. Although he may owe his election to his stand on certain social issues, he clearly felt more uncomfortable than Reagan did in fighting on that ground; it seemed ungentlemanly to him. He may have helped to demonstrate that television can after all be used for heated partisanship, but he seemed more interested in being known for a 'gentler, kinder' politics than for a divisive partisanship. He was not the social conservatives' candidate in the nomination contest, and in spite of his campaign tactics he is still distrusted by many of them. He will be anxious to maintain their support, and will therefore do things that they will applaud (especially things like conservative judicial appointments, which divert the partisan battle between liberals and conservatives into the courts). But he will probably not be trying to reshape the American electoral universe by forcing a public, partisan choice between social liberalism and social conservatism – if only because he has already failed to use this tactic to persuade the electorate to vote for Republicans in general, who did much worse in 1988 than in 1980 and 1984. The Republican Party continues to grow in the traditionally Democratic southern states, but elsewhere the Democrats have stopped losing support to Republicans. So not only did the Democrats in 1988 increase their majorities in the Senate and House of Representatives, they also put a stop to the drift of state legislative seats to the Republican Party. The Republicans, while remaining the majority party in most state legislatures, had nevertheless enjoyed a net gain of more than 300 of these seats in 1980 and 1984, but they lost a net total of twenty-nine of them in 1988 (although gaining twenty-seven in the south).

Of course, one cannot abolish television and the other modern techniques of contemporary American political campaigns, many of which do interfere with any attempt to strengthen candidates' and voters' partisanship. And there are also other institutional difficulties in the way of realignment today that did not exist in the past; the chief example must be the level of incumbency protection that has become established by Congressmen, making any serious bid by the Republicans for control of the House of Representatives seem out of the question. (In 1988, out of all of the Democratic incumbents running for re-election in the House and Senate, only one Representative and one Senator were defeated). It may also simply be the case that no single realigning issue or set of issues of sufficient potency has been available in the last two decades, in spite of the apparently greater importance in party politics since the 1960s of issues and ideologies in general, and of social issues in particular.

In spite of these contemporary barriers to partisan realignment, major party realignment remains a possibility for American politicians to pursue or to avoid.

John Zvesper

References

Adamany, David (1980) 'The Supreme Court's Role in Critical Elections', in Bruce A. Campbell and Richard J. Trilling (eds) *Realignment in American Politics: Towards a Theory*, Austin: University of Texas Press.

Anderson, Kristie (1979) *The Creation of a Democratic Majority: 1928–1936*, Chicago: University of Chicago Press.

Beck, Paul Allen (1979) 'The Electoral Cycle and Patterns of American Politics', *British Journal of Political Science* 9: 129–56.

Brady, David W. (1980) 'Elections, Congress and Public Policy Changes: 1886–1960', in Bruce A. Campbell and Richard J. Trilling (eds) *Realignment in American Politics: Toward a Theory*, Austin, University of Texas Press.

Brady, David with Joseph Stewart (1982) 'Congressional Party Realignment and Transformations of Public Policy in Three Realignment Eras', *American Journal of Political Science* 26: 333–60.

Burnham, Walter Dean (1970) *Critical Elections and the Mainsprings of American Politics*, New York: Norton.

Campbell, Angus, Philip E. Converse, Warren E. Miller, and Donald E. Stokes (1960) *The American Voter*, New York: Wiley.

Chambers, William N., and Walter Dean Burnham (eds) (1967) *The American Party Systems: Stages of Political Development*, New York: Oxford University Press.

Clubb, Jerome, M., William H. Flanigan and Nancy H. Zingale (1980) *Partisan Realignments: Voters, Parties and Government in American History*, Beverly Hills: Sage.

Converse, Philip E., Angus Campbell, Warren E. Miller and Donald E. Stokes (1961) 'Stability and Change in 1960: A Reinstating Election', *American Political Science Review* 55: 269–280.

Erikson, Robert S. and Kent L. Tedin (1981) 'The 1928–1936 Partisan Realignments: The Case for the Conversion Hypothesis', *American Political Science Review* 75: 951–62.

Funston, Richard (1975) 'The Supreme Court and Critical Elections', *American Political Science Review* 69: 795–811.

Ginsberg, Benjamin (1972) 'The Critical Elections and the Substance of Party Conflict: 1844–1968'. *Midwest Journal of Political Science* 16: 603–26.

Hansen, Susan B. (1980) 'Partisan Realignment and Tax Policy: 1789–1976', in Bruce A. Campbell and Richard J. Trilling (eds) *Realignment in American Politics: Toward a Theory*, Austin: University of Texas Press.

Hofstadter, Richard (1969) *The Idea of a Party System: The Rise of Legitimate Opposition in the United States, 1780–1840*, Berkeley: University of California Press.

Jaffa, Harry V. (1965) 'The Nature and Origin of the American Party System', in *Equality and Liberty*, New York: Oxford University Press.

Key, V.O. (1955), 'A Theory of Critical Elections', *Journal of Politics* 17: 3–18.

184

Key, V.O. (1959) 'Secular Realignment and the Party System', *Journal of Politics* 21: 198–210.

Key, V.O. (1966) *The Responsible Electorate: Rationality in Presidential Voting, 1936–1966*, Cambridge, Mass.: Harvard University Press.

Kleppner, Paul *et al.* (1981) *The Evolution of American Electoral Systems*, Westport: Greenwood Press.

Ladd, Everett Carll, Jr. (1970) *American Political Parties: Social Change and Political Response*, New York: Norton.

Ladd, Everett Carll, Jr., with Charles D. Hadley (1975) *Transformations of the American Party System; Political Coalitions from the New Deal to the 1970s*, New York: W.W. Norton & Company.

Ladd, Everett Carll (1981) 'The Brittle Mandate: Electoral Dealignment and the 1980 Presidential Election', *Political Science Quarterly* 96: 1–25.

Lasser, William (1985) 'The Supreme Court in Periods of Critical Realignment', *Journal of Politics* 47: 1174–87.

Lubell, Samuel (1965) *The Future of American Politics*, Third Edition, New York: Harper and Row.

MacMahon, Arthur W. (1948) 'Conflict, Consensus, Confirmed Trends and Open Choices', *American Political Science Review* 42: 1–15.

Meier, Kenneth J. and Kenneth W. Kramer (1980) 'The Impact of Realigning Elections on Public Bureaucracies', in Bruce A. Campbell and Richard J. Trilling (eds) *Realignment in American Politics: Toward a Theory*, Austin: University of Texas Press.

Nexon, David H. (1980) 'Methodological Issues in the Study of Realignment' in Bruce A. Campbell and Richard J. Trilling (eds) *Realignment in American Politics: Towards a Theory*, Austin: University of Texas Press.

Nie, Norman, H., Sidney Verba and John R. Petrocik (1976) *The Changing American Voter*, Cambridge, Mass.: Harvard University Press.

Phillips, Kevin D. (1970) *The Emerging Republican Majority*, Garden City: Doubleday.

Pomper, Gerald M. (1967) 'Classification of Presidential Elections', *Journal of Politics* 29: 535–66.

Schattschneider, E.E. (1956) 'United States: The Functional Approach to Party Government', in Sigmund Neumann (ed.) *Modern Political Parties: Approaches to Comparative Politics*, Chicago: University of Chicago Press.

Schattschneider, E.E. (1960) *The Semi-Sovereign People*, New York: Holt, Rienhart and Winston.

Schneider, William (1981) 'The November 4 Vote for President: What Did It Mean?, in Austin Ranney (ed) *The American Elections of 1980*, Washington, D.C.: American Enterprise Institute.

Seligman, Lester, G. and Michael R. King (1980) 'Political Realignments and Recruitment to the U.S. Congress, 1870–1970', in Bruce A. Campbell and Richard J. Trilling (eds) *Realignment in American Politics: Towards a Theory*, Austin: University of Texas Press.

Sinclair, Barbara Deckard (1977) 'Party Realignment and the Transformation of the Political Agenda: the House of Representatives, 1925–1938', *American Political Science Review* 71: 940–53.

Sinclair, Barbara (1978) 'From Party Voting to Regional Fragmentation: The House of Representatives, 1933–1956', *American Politics Quarterly* 6: 125–46.

Sinclair, Barbara (1982) *Congressional Realignment 1925–1978*, Austin: University of Texas Press.

Stewart, Charles V. (1980) 'The Federal Income Tax and the Realignment of the 1980s', in Bruce A. Campbell and Richard J. Trilling (eds) *Realignment in American Politics: Toward a Theory*, Austin: University of Texas Press.

Sundquist, James L. (1973) *Dynamics of the Party System: Alignment and Realignment of Political Parties in the United States*, Washington D.C.: Brookings Institution.

Sundquist, James L. (1983) *Dynamics of the Party System: Alignment and Realignment of Political Parties in the United States*, revised edition, Washington D.C.: Brookings Institution.

Trilling, Richard J. and Bruce A. Campbell (1980) 'Toward a theory of Realignment: An Introduction', in Campbell and Trilling (eds) *Realignment in American Politics: Toward a Theory*, Austin: University of Texas Press.

Wattenberg, Ben J. (1988) 'The Curse of Jesse' *The New Republic* 5 December: 20–21.

Index